£21.50
AF744543

Handbook of Neuropsychological Assessment

ALEX GILANDAS, B.Sc., M.Sc., Ph.D.(Oregon), Dip. Ed.
Senior Clinical Psychologist, Royal Prince Alfred Hospital, Sydney;
Clinical Lecturer in Psychiatry, The University of Sydney.

STEPHEN TOUYZ, B.Sc.(Cape Town), B.Sc.(Hons)(Wits), Ph.D.(Cape Town)
Senior Clinical Psychologist, Royal Prince Alfred Hospital, Sydney;
Clinical Lecturer in Psychiatry, The University of Sydney.

PIERRE J. V. BEUMONT, M.B.,Ch.B.(Pret.), M.Sc., M.Phil., F.R.A.N.Z.C.Psych.,
Professor and Head, Department of Psychiatry, The University of Sydney;
Head, Department of Psychiatry, Royal Prince Alfred Hospital, Sydney.

H. P. GREENBERG, M.B., B.S., F.R.A.N.Z.C.Psych., F.R.C.Psych., D.P.M.
Honorary Associate, Department of Psychiatry, The University of Sydney;
Senior Visiting Psychiatrist, Royal Prince Alfred Hospital, Sydney.

Handbook of Neuropsychological Assessment

by

Alex Gilandas
Stephen Touyz
Pierre J. V. Beumont
and
H. P. Greenberg

G&S

Grune & Stratton
A Subsidiary of Harcourt Brace Jovanovich, Publishers
Sydney Orlando San Diego San Francisco New York
London Toronto Montreal Tokyo São Paulo
1984

UNIVERSITY LIBRARY
28 MAY 1985
LANCASTER

GRUNE & STRATTON AUSTRALIA
Centrecourt, 25–27 Paul Street North
North Ryde, N.S.W. 2113

United States Edition published by
GRUNE & STRATTON INC.
Orlando, Florida 32887

United Kingdom Edition published by
GRUNE & STRATTON, INC. (LONDON) LTD.
24/28 Oval Road, London NW1 7DX

Copyright © 1984 by
GRUNE & STRATTON AUSTRALIA

Material appearing on pp. 87–89 is copyright © 1984 by Raymond S. Dean. It is reproduced here with the permission of the copyright owner, to whom any questions regarding its use should be directed.

All rights reserved. No part of this publication may be reproduced or transmitted in any form or by any means, electronic or mechanical, including photocopy, recording, or any information storage and retrieval system, without permission in writing from the publisher.

Printed in Australia

The Appendices may be reproduced by clinicians and neuropsychologists who wish to use the forms in the course of their investigations.

These Appendices may be reproduced without written permission of the publisher, provided proper credit is given by including the following notice on the first page of each Appendix reproduced:

Copyright © 1984 by Grune & Stratton Australia
Reproduced from *Handbook of Neuropsychological Assessment*.

Permission to make copies may be revoked at any time.

National Library of Australia Cataloguing-in-Publication Data

---

Handbook of neuropsychological assessment.
Includes index.
ISBN 0 8089 1645 9.

1. Neuropsychology. 2. Brain damage.
3. Psychodiagnostics. I. Gilandas, Alex J.
(Alex John), 1942— .

616.8

Library of Congress Catalog Card Number: 84-70605

84 011037

Contents

Preface

THE EVOLUTION of neuropsychology as one of the fastest growing disciplines within clinical psychology has revitalized interest in psychological testing. Accurate assessment of cognitive functioning is crucial for documenting an organic component in emotional or behavioural disturbance. If patients are thought about quantitatively this may have qualitative implications for them.

Despite growing interest in the study of brain–behaviour relationships, the number of clinical neuropsychology texts remains limited. Those available tend to adopt a theoretical approach, with a corresponding neglect of clinical techniques and guidelines.

This book is designed to serve as a convenient guide to neuropsychological assessment for practicing psychologists and also as an adjunct training device for students. It is a selective guide as it attempts to lead the way towards acceptable cognitive evaluation by means of the easiest available path, even at the risk of oversimplification and undue structuring.

The number of tests available for monitoring cognitive functions is overwhelming. Thus neuropsychological assessment is most efficiently learned as a well defined routine. A comprehensive battery which contains a limited number of appropriate tests tends to monitor a broad spectrum of cognitive functions in a cost-efficient manner. Intact cognitive strengths which are important in rehabilitation need to be documented, as well as residual deficits. This book is designed to encourage such wide range testing.

Efficient clinical problem solving relies more upon coherent structure than intuition. Even the most sophisticated form of neuropsychological examination contains a basic structure designed to monitor brain output, but the emphasis varies according to the needs of the individual patient.

Neuropsychological report writing represents a significant proportion of the work load of many clinical psychologists at some stage in their career. Patients are constantly being referred for assessment of the presence or absence of cognitive deficits, and most psychologists have to consider these problems routinely. Questions regarding the presence or absence of cognitive deficits may be appropriately answered with the recommended battery even when the battery is administered by the majority of psychologists who have never received specialized training in neuropsychology. It is unlikely that most clinical psychologists will, or even wish to, become neuropsychologists, but it is highly probable that the majority will often be expected to assess a patient's cognitive functioning.

Most clinical psychologists will remain generalists because of the heterogeneous nature of the duties they are expected to perform. Being already familiar with the rationale of the psychometric tradition they will find the structured battery approach a logical medium for transition to comprehensive neuropsychological assessment.

Neuropsychological and other forms of psychological evaluations do not differ in kind but only in degree of emphasis placed upon the multitude of behavioural determinants. Similar parameters are encompassed with patient characteristics influencing the focus of assessment. Generalist clinical psychologists focus more upon personality trait and/or environmental determinants of behaviour whereas clinical neuropsychologists deal more specifically with the influence of cerebral dysfunction upon functional integrity. Consequently, the latter rely more upon psychological tests specifically sensitive to cerebral dysfunction. Both types of assessments are holistic in that they estimate the quality of global personality functioning, be it disrupted by cerebral, purely environmental, or other combination of factors.

In fact a "neuropsychological assessment" is only rarely administered in its most strictly specialized sense. Normally, the psychologist is required to provide a comprehensive evaluation of an individual with specific coping resources who is reacting to either psychological or physical dysfunction (or an interaction of both factors) in a uniquely characteristic way. Cerebral dysfunction is a variant of normal behaviour. Brain damaged patients tend to have reduced information processing capacity. Many seemingly bizarre behavioural characteristics of brain damaged persons are similar to the behavioural variations of normal subjects under stress (be it psychological or physiological) as such stress also tends to reduce information processing capacity. Consequently, many of the routine tasks of generalist psychologists and neuropsychologists, as students of behaviour, have considerable overlap.

This handbook will also be useful for school psychologists, psychiatrists, neurologists, neurosurgeons, rehabilitation personnel, lawyers and others who have occasion to understand and to make efficient use of psychological reports. It can also serve as a useful supplementary text in a course on psychological testing. No previous background in neuropsychology is necessary to appreciate the contents.

No attempt is made to describe the myriad of organic brain syndromes in a comprehensive manner. Many excellent and detailed texts on clinical and behavioural neurology are available to meet this need. Nor can a practical guide to testing pretend to serve as an encyclopaedic reference to the field. Discussions of such important academic issues as the methodological problems inherent in neuropsychological research, and theoretical models of lateralization, localization and anterior/posterior concepts of brain functioning are intentionally avoided. Most of the available texts in clinical neuropsychology already emphasize such empirical concerns. These may be referred to in the list of references.

The limitation of this starter's guide to neuropsychological assessment is obvious. Like the Halstead–Reitan battery, it is empirically derived without adequate statistical analyses to validate it. No battery with acceptable standardization and definitive statistical analyses has yet been formulated. Despite this, many clinically useful batteries exist. We have found the one introduced in this text to be particularly comprehensive, yet cost-efficient.

It must be reiterated that no attempt is being made to introduce an experimentally or statistically derived original neuropsychological instrument. Rather, a cost-efficient system administering and interpreting already available widely accepted and well validated tests is explained in detail. Of course, familiarity with such a practical strategy for taking care of the psychologist's routine testing "housework" does not instantly produce an expert neuropsychologist. This expertise is produced from theoretical knowledge integrated with clinical skill and experience and it is impossible to achieve this through the reading of any one book.

Ideally, the specialist clinical neuropsychologist should become formally qualified through a doctoral level competency-based curriculum jointly administered by departments of psychology and the neurosciences. Such a model training scheme would be based upon an integrated scientist–practitioner curriculum. This would develop dual competency in basic research and clinical practice. Such a curriculum would necessarily stress a knowledge of the neurological literature (basic anatomy, physiology and pathology of the nervous system). Applied skills are most efficiently learned under an apprenticeship system. This necessitates learning by doing with intensive supervision to control the errors in such trial and error learning. Unfortunately, the time involved in an ideal training programme spans six or more years of full-time postgraduate study. The time, expense and talent required limits this model curriculum (which as yet only exists in isolated, experimental stages) to a few exceptional students. In reality, most practitioners currently involved in neuropsychological assessment have attained professional competence on an *ad hoc* basis. As this trend will continue for the foreseeable future, this book meets an important need. The references in this volume, together with pertinent professional journals, should be consulted as a necessary, though insufficient, first step in the long journey toward clinical maturity.

Specialist neuropsychologists perform only a small proportion of routine cognitive testing in the same way that only a small proportion of specialist physicians are involved in the general practice of medicine. It is interesting that most forms of cognitive testing are not even carried out by psychologists but rather by teachers, special educators and school counsellors. This is acceptable as long as the allied professions carry out psychological tests only within their areas of competency.

Since the major purpose of this text is to act as an applied workbook of guidelines for neuropsychological assessment and report writing, the authors have provided some contents which may be reproduced for these purposes. Readers may find it of use to reproduce the Appendices where examples of a report title page, neuropsychological report format and profile are to be found.

The contents of this book are as follows: Chapter 1 introduces a selective review of key issues in neuropsychological assessment; Chapter 2 briefly surveys some of the more common clinical presentations of brain disease routinely met during evaluation; Chapter 3 describes the development of test batteries; Chapter 4 provides a sample structured neuropsychological interview integrated with the test battery recommended in this text; Chapter 5 deals with the description and administration of the tests in the battery; Chapter 6 serves as a guide to an interpretation of these tests, together with the derivation of clinical inferences; Chapter 7 contains guidelines for neuropsychological report writing; Chapter 8 discusses the relationship of clinical neuropsychology to the law; Chapter 9 discusses the relationship between clinical neuropsychology and pertinent areas of medicine; Chapter 10 contains some sample clinical reports; and the Appendices contain examples of worksheets, standardized report formats and profiles useful in writing up an actual assessment.

In keeping with the goal of providing a practical guide to neuropsychological assessment, it is hoped that this wide range of topics, although only briefly surveyed, will facilitate clinical report writing. Since this volume reflects well established practices within the mainstream of neuropsychological assessment, most of the issues discussed are elaborated upon in other sources. As these data are scattered rather inaccessibly throughout a voluminous literature, there is value in collecting the more practical aspects of test battery material under one cover.

Acknowledgements

WE WISH to thank the following for their help in the preparation of this manuscript: Grant Walker of Grune & Stratton for his faith in the project; Philip Ley and Don Byrne who kindly reviewed the early drafts and reinforced our belief in the value of producing a practical guide to neuropsychological assessment and report writing; David Ivison and Lorna Channon whose constructive suggestions and critique were incorporated in later drafts; Bob Haynes of the Audio-Visual Department of Royal Prince Alfred Hospital, for his help with the artwork; Jeremy Fisher of Grune & Stratton whose meticulous attention to the fine details has made the book more coherent and easily understood; and finally our typists, particularly Sylvia Murphy, whose efficiency and industriousness was much appreciated.

It is unworthy of excellent men to lose hours like slaves in the labour of calculations.
Leibniz

1
Key Issues in Neuropsychology

NEUROPSYCHOLOGY is concerned with the study of the relation between brain function and behaviour. Hecaen and Albert (1978) state that the discipline is at the interface between the neurosciences (neurology, neuroanatomy, neurophysiology, and neurochemistry) and the behavioural sciences (physiological psychology, developmental psychology, and psycholinguistics). Neuropsychology draws from many disciplines, but its central focus is the development of a science of human behaviour based upon brain function. Clinical neuropsychology attempts to relate brain dysfunction to observable, empirically documented behavioural deficits (Crockett, *et al.,* 1981).

Historically, clinical neuropsychology has had a two-fold nature. Any definition must include both its research and applied aspect. Every neuropsychological assessment of a brain damaged individual involves a scientific attempt to monitor brain output as evidenced by behaviour, thus representing an opportunity for a deeper understanding of brain–behaviour relationships. Luria (1980) states that this not only makes a clinical contribution to coherent treatment but that it also has great importance for the advancement of scientific theory about the very structure of psychological processes (that is, for the founding of a more scientific psychology). The aim of this chapter is to introduce a selective review of current trends in neuropsychological assessment.

IMPORTANCE OF THE FIELD

During the last decade, neuropsychology has emerged as one of the fastest growing areas within clinical psychology. Lipowski's (1980) review of the organic brain syndromes suggests that such interest will continue. Demographic and epidemiological trends show that the organic mental disorders are a major public health, social, and economic problem because of their high prevalence among the aged, the number of whom is steadily increasing. For example, 25 per cent of the total number of psychiatric hospital beds in the United States are occupied by patients with an organic psychosis. Epidemiological studies suggest that there will be a dramatic increase in the number of individuals suffering from organically related disorders resulting from abuse of alcohol and other types of toxic substances. The increase in the number of head injuries caused by motor vehicle accidents is an intrinsic fact of modern life. High velocity transport, mechanization in industry and the increasing prevalence of violent street crimes have increased the incidence of head injuries. As a means of keeping pace, developments in the neurosciences have provided new technical tools for the study and treatment of cerebral dysfunction.

The occurrence of the neurobehavioural syndromes is extremely common in both hospital and community settings. Consequently, all clinical psychologists would find it an advantage to familiarize themselves with the indications of organic brain dysfunction.

Professional Organizations, Publications and Training Programmes

Russell's (1981) historical review of neuropsychology reveals that neuropsychologists have initiated a number of professional organizations. An International Neuropsychological Society was formed in 1966. The growth of interest in brain–behaviour relationships has recently resulted in the establishment of a new Division of Clinical Neuropsychology (Div. 40) within the American Psychological Association.

The vigour for research within this emerging discipline is reflected by the proliferation of such relatively new journals as *Neuropsychologia, Clinical Neuropsychology, Cortex, Brain and Cognition, Brain and Behaviour,* and *Brain and Language.* Unfortunately, the total number of available textbooks is limited. However, it is encouraging that a number of books on clinical neuropsychology has been published since 1978 and readers will find them included in the reference list at the end of this book.

As in other disciplines, there is concern in neuropsychology about formal qualifications for competent functioning in that area. Meier's (1981) recommendations for graduate education in neuropsychology are based on the fact that many practitioners attain professional competence on an informal basis. He admits that a competency-based curriculum and a public process for defining and assessing neuropsychological practice have not yet been developed.

Meier's models for training neuropsychologists

There is a need for the education and training of neuropsychologists in universities, and Meier (1981) discusses four potential models which are outlined below. Various institutions modify aspects of these models according to the staff and facilities available, the ratio of research to service and the needs of their graduate students.

Model I may be described as a subspecialty in a clinical psychology programme requiring the integration of neuropsychological theory and clinical experience into a traditional curriculum. The graduate of such a programme would be a generalist. The subspecialty approach is the cheapest and, administratively, least disruptive means of incorporating neuropsychology into an existing curriculum. A disadvantage is that the traditional curriculum may relegate neuropsychology low priority because of time constraints and commitment to more established clinical areas.

Model II may be termed an interdepartmental programme in clinical neuropsychology and the neurosciences. This programme requires joint sponsorship by a psychology department and a neurosciences department. Clinical research and service skills tend to get higher priority under joint sponsorship arrangements compared with Model I. This approach is only possible in universities with established programmes in both basic and clinical neurosciences. A disadvantage is the possibility of conflict of interests between two faculties sharing the one curriculum.

Model III is best explained as an integrated scientist–practitioner curriculum for a higher degree, and parallels the scientist–practitioner curriculum recommended by the Boulder Conference (as outlined in Korchin, 1976), research and practice in neuropsychology being the nominated field of specialization. This model increases the potential availability of neuropsychology as a field of study for psychology graduate students. Basic research and sophisticated clinical training are guaranteed. Disadvantages are the time and cost involved in developing competence in both clinical practice and research. It is also necessary for a neuroscience department to provide support for the psychology faculty.

Model IV is a co-ordinated graduate curriculum containing separate components for doctorates obtained by either coursework or coursework and thesis. Meier (1981) terms this the ideal fulfilment of the Boulder Conference model as equal attention is given to both research and practice competencies. A major disadvantage of this approach is that the time involved (six or more years of graduate work) may limit the course to a small number of exceptional students. Joint co-operation between a department of psychology and a department of neurosciences is again a prerequisite.

Few data are available concerning education and training in neuropsychology. Models I and II have already been successfully applied, but

Models III and IV are still in the experimental stages. Meier (1981) pleads for competency-based curriculum development to be an important priority if neuropsychology is to advance.

Theoretical Implications

The clinical method in neuropsychology has enormous implications for psychology in general. Accidents of nature (both development and acquired) which cause cognitive, emotional and behavioural deficits in patients in conjunction with known areas of brain damage contribute to further understanding of the relationship between brain function and human behaviour. Neuropsychologists such as Luria (1980) and Teuber (1964), emphasizing an applied approach, have generated widely acceptable theories of the nature of cognitive functioning. Kolb and Whishaw (1980) note a strong trend for psychologists to be more sensitive to the concept that understanding the function of the brain is a prerequisite for understanding human behaviour. There has been a drift away from the traditional philosophical and phenomenological approach.

The goal of any serious neuroscientist is to contribute to answering the most fundamental question in psychology and philosophy: what are the inter-relations between brain and mind? Current study of the operational properties and mechanisms of human consciousness is being accomplished within the context of sophisticated paradigms. Simplistic reductionism, the "straw man" of philosophical criticisms, has long been abandoned. Contemporary neuropsychology makes no attempt to explain all aspects of human behaviour. Nor do neuroscientists ascribe perceptual or cognitive functions solely to the activity of single cells or localized anatomical regions. More global views of the nervous system prevail, with consideration of the spatio-temporal and configurational characteristics of neuronal activity and neuroanatomy. The work of behavioural neuropsychologists provides support for the notion that biologically oriented explanations of human behaviour do not inherently favour somatic treatments, nor do they threaten psychology's status as an independent discipline.

Meier (1981) notes that psychology generally seems to be increasingly more divided, with experimental and applied activities developing in disparate directions, while neuropsychology, in contrast, is experiencing explosive growth on the basis of overlapping rather than diverging experimental and applied interests. The inherent subject matter of brain–behaviour studies encourages harmony between experimental and professional service perspectives. Consequently, clinical neuropsychology serves as a model to the whole field of psychology for co-operation between the scientific and professional approaches.

Manpower Trends

The proliferation of publications, professional societies, and training programmes, and the growing number of skilled practitioners in neuropsychology are making referral sources and the mass media more familiar with the roles in this discipline. Such educational input and the availability of practitioners further generates community awareness of the benefits of neuropsychology.

Meier's (1981) review of manpower trends in psychology identified a movement away from academe towards clinical practice for both economic and social reasons. Academic institutions now have a surfeit of experimental, physiological, cognitive and developmental psychologists. Employment in colleges and universities will be virtually unobtainable over the next two decades. This lack of opportunity for academic careers has resulted in an increased interest in applied programmes which is further reinforced by a social climate encouraging the better provision of clinical services. In these circumstances there has been rapid growth in the influence of clinical neuropsychology.

Social Concerns

The integration of theory, research and practice in clinical neuropsychology takes place within an interdisciplinary context and with an orientation to broad social concerns. Forensic neuropsychology exemplifies these concerns in real life as its major role is to assist courts in both criminal and civil matters. Such a tradition of social involvement ensures that prospects for further development have not ended, but just begun. For example, Russell (1981) notes an exciting opportunity for clinical neuropsychology to contribute to the new area of behavioural toxicology, a science which officially did not exist until 1970. Drastic alterations in the human chemical environment caused by pollution have obvious implications for brain–behaviour functioning.

Exposures to environmental toxins have the potential for causing both structural and functional damage in the central nervous system. Strub and Black (1981) describe the ability of some toxic substances to disrupt the normal metabolic processes of the neurons. With minor levels of exposure the neurons can withstand this threat. High doses or repeated medium level doses may cause the cells to shrink and, eventually, to die. With sufficiently extensive cell death, irreversible cognitive changes and atrophy occur.

Strub and Black (1981) reviewed the cognitive and behavioural sequelae of exposure to toxic substances. Many hydrocarbon substances have been produced since the industrial revolution and all people receive some level of daily exposure. Petrol, paint solvents and cleaning fluids are routinely used in the home. Industry uses vast amounts of lead and mercury. There have been instances of mass cases of poisoning when lead and mercury have inadvertently been introduced into the food chain. For example, organic mercury was used as a fungicide on grain in Iraq in 1972. The waters of Minamata Bay, Japan, were polluted by mercury from factories leading to the poisoning of the surrounding population who lived on a predominantly fish diet, and thus initiating mass scale litigation (Rustam, 1975).

TARGET POPULATIONS

The largest number of referrals for neuropsychological assessment has traditionally come from departments of neurology, neurosurgery and psychiatry. For example, typical referral patterns to the psychology unit at Royal Prince Alfred Hospital (a teaching hospital of the University of Sydney) during the period 1978–1982 are as follows: approximately 70 per cent of patients were referred by the departments of neurology and neurosurgery; 20 per cent came from the department of psychiatry (adult population); five per cent came from the psychiatric adolescent unit; and the remaining five per cent were referred from departments of rehabilitation medicine, general medical and surgical services. These referrals commonly involve the following categories: Alzheimer's disease; Huntington's disease; cerebrovascular disorders; multiple sclerosis; cerebral tumour; Parkinson's disease; epilepsy; closed head injury; senile dementia; and dialysis dementia.

Neurologists often request comprehensive neuropsychological profiles in order to help clarify the diagnostic significance of "soft" neurological signs (for example, patients with attention deficits, borderline electroencephalograms (EEGs), motor deficits, personality changes, and memory lapses). The differentiation of focal and diffuse cognitive deficits, together with an estimate of the nature and extent of intellectual deterioration, is a common concern.

Neurosurgeons are particularly interested in documenting the functional integrity of patients with acute organic brain syndromes. These baselines can then be compared with follow-up monitoring of the integrity of brain output after surgery. Such follow-up monitoring may help define the course of either continued deterioration or the restitution of function.

Psychiatrists commonly refer patients for neuropsychological evaluation in order to obtain assistance in differentiating between the organic and functional aetiology of disturbed behaviour. Practical issues such as estimating the patient's ability to resume work or return to schooling are also regular concerns.

The pattern of referrals discussed above has shown a significa change over time. A current trend is the broadening of tradition of referral to include physicians, paediatricians, special educators, re tion specialists and lawyers involved in medico-legal issues. As the ...ri-butions of neuropsychology become better known service requests inevitably escalate. For example, pulmonary, cardiovascular, renal and hepatic diseases may be associated with cognitive deficits and such cases have generated a rapidly developing literature on medical disorders with neuropsychological sequelae. Developmental concerns (paediatric and geriatric neuropsychology), and rehabilitation placement and retraining are important topics which are considered in the following sections. The evolution of forensic neuropsychology and the contribution of neuropsychological assessment to medico-legal issues will be dealt with in detail in a later chapter. Social concerns have been suggested previously. Thus, target populations of possible clinical interest to neuropsychologists can be seen to be increasingly heterogeneous. There is also the research pool of subjects who are integral to the advancement of any science, although discussion of this more academic aspect is outside the scope of this book.

Geriatric Neuropsychology

A major trend in neuropsychological assessment is an increasing concern with developmental issues. The implications of cerebral dysfunction are given added meaning by considering them within the context of various stages of life. The age of the patient at the onset of brain injury is recognized to be a pertinent factor in interpreting test results and even in selecting the types of tests to be used (developmental issues concerning children are discussed in a separate section in Chapter 9).

The study of the aging brain is an increasingly important sub-discipline in developmental neuropsychology as the proportion of old people in the total population is increasing. This has wide political, socioeconomic and neurobehavioural consequences. In developed countries, demographic trends suggest that, by the end of this century, the number of persons over 65 years of age will increase by approximately two-thirds and the number of those over 75 years will double. The United States is a "greying" nation. The Administration on Aging Document (1978) reports that the number of Americans aged over 60 years in 1977 was 32.9 million (15.2 per cent of the population). The number of people in this age group has increased by 15 per cent since 1970, compared to an increase of only six per cent for the country's population as a whole.

It is not unusual for the neuropsychological performance of healthy individuals over the age of 50 years to fall into the brain dysfunction range when test results are assessed using available norms based on a younger standardized sample. Bak and Greene (1980) treated age as an independent variable and replicated previous findings that various memory functions and other neuropsychological abilities decline in older individuals. However, further studies are needed to generate more accurate norms representing the functioning of older, healthy normal adults. Neugarten (1975) suggests that the aged be categorized into two groups: *young-old* (55-75 years); and *old-old* (over 75 years). The results of many psychological measures tend to be significantly different for the two groups.

A major difficulty exists in validly differentiating "normal" age-related memory changes from "abnormal" forgetting. The prevailing attitude is that the degenerative organic brain syndromes are pathological and thus not classified as a process of normal aging. However, Terry and Wisneiwski (1975) remind us that there is a difference only in degree of the extent of neuronal loss and plaque formation since these processes are found in both healthy aged people and those with senile dementia.

The interaction of supportive social environments with individual personalities inherently obscures the real-life manifestations of brain–behaviour relationships. Despite this, some useful generalizations may be made. The neuropsychological literature about aging may be summarized in terms of the "classic aging pattern". That is, there is a differential decline of verbal and perceptual skills, with the former tending to hold up until the age of 70 or so, whereas the latter show evidence of some deterioration even after the age of 30. Thus, normal aging appears to retard sensory-perceptual skills whilst a decline in verbal skills is more characteristic of abnormal aging.

The evidence for age-related decline in visual information processing has important implications for remediation. For example, popular memory improvement programmes based upon imagery mnemonics may have no valid foundation for the aged.

Contribution of Neuropsychological Assessment to Rehabilitation

Clinical neuropsychology is well established as a diagnostic discipline. Psychological intervention in the rehabilitation of brain damaged patients is a more recent development. However, the treatment of such patients is officially recognized as an important concern. For example, federal law in the United States requires that rehabilitation services are to be made available to the disabled as a right rather than as a privilege. A review of rehabilitation hospitals by Keith *et al.* (1977) emphasizes the significance of this area in terms of numbers and cost. Patients with brain damage make up the single largest group of individuals in medical rehabilitation units. Thirty-one per cent of patients in rehabilitation units are stroke victims. In the United States, the annual expenditure in the rehabilitation of stroke victims is estimated to be US$12.5 billion.

After the medical team has stabilized the condition of brain damaged patients, a large proportion is then referred to rehabilitation units for the treatment and remediation of residual problems. Such rehabilitation is inherently an interdisciplinary enterprise as patients with brain damage tend to have multidimensional problems (for example, medical, cognitive, language, sexual and social impairments). Effective treatment is an active process emphasizing practical interventions which focus on real life situations.

Neuropsychological evaluation and treatment need to be logically integrated as assessment is futile unless some contribution is made to a patient's recovery. A comprehensive evaluation of underlying symptoms of brain dysfunction in terms of neuropsychological strengths and deficits facilitates the formulation of a coherent rehabilitation programme. This encourages an individual treatment plan in which specific interventions may be cross-indexed to the broad spectrum of problems and assets elicited from the results of testing.

Strategy for improving brain-damaged patients' adaptation

A typical strategy for improving the level of adaptation of brain damaged patients is as follows: (i) retrain specific skills where possible; (ii) compensate for any deficits by restructuring the physical, interpersonal and social environment; (iii) capitalize upon the patient's areas of intact functioning; (iv) reinforce new functional activity patterns; and (v) integrate the patient's family into the treatment plan. Neuropsychological assessments are incomplete unless they contain a recommendations section emphasizing a practical rehabilitation strategy logically derived from the test results. Horton (1979) describes a particularly creative strategy of integrating neuropsychological assessment with behaviour therapy.

Perhaps the major lesson clinical neuropsychologists can learn from an involvement with rehabilitation services is not to rely upon an isolated view of discrepant test scores. The philosophy of viewing the patient as a problem list *per se* and myopically confining treatment to isolated deficits may result in the neglect of vast areas of intact functioning. A balanced view of the patient also requires recognition of the patient's strengths.

ASSESSMENT STRATEGIES

Since World War II, neuropsychology has evolved a considerable number of psychological tests sensitive to cerebral dysfunction. Empirical correlations of behaviour change with the site and type of lesion in the higher nervous system have been consistently documented by such eminent investigators as Luria (1980), Benton (1974) and Teuber (1964). Consequently, a broad spectrum of neuropsychological techniques is now available to elicit a comprehensive profile of specific abilities and impairments related to the integrity of the brain. Lezak (1976) provides an encyclopaedic review of available tests.

Two differing approaches are commonly used in neuropsychological assessment. One strategy employs a standardized test battery whereas the other emphasizes an inductive approach in which hypotheses are formulated and tested. The advantages and disadvantages of both these methods may be reviewed by contrasting the quantitatively oriented Halstead–Reitan battery with Luria's qualitative syndrome analysis scheme (Luria and Majovsky, 1977). Attempts at resolving the paradigm clash by integrating quantitative and qualitative strategies are described using the Luria–Nebraska neuropsychological battery as an innovative example (Golden, *et al.*, 1980) The theoretical implications of these attempts for clinical neuropsychology are also discussed.

Test Battery Approach

The Halstead–Reitan neuropsychological test battery (HRNTB) has a distinguished tradition beginning with the early studies of Halstead (1947). Reitan (1969) progressively revised and added to Halstead's contribution over a period of 25 years to establish a battery capable of monitoring a broader range of functions. The success of the battery may be gauged from the fact that it is widely accepted throughout the United States and overseas. Golden and Kuperman (1980) report that the Halstead–Reitan approach is taught in over 50 per cent of clinical psychology programmes. As well, it is frequently utilized in internship settings. Such extensive availability of supervised training is a major advantage to students desiring to learn neuropsychological assessment.

The Halstead–Reitan test battery has generated a prolific literature testifying to its validity. It is based upon empirical standards, giving users acceptable levels of evidence for relationships between test scores and known diagnostic interpretations.

Test batteries may be termed intervening variables as they study brain–behaviour relationships indirectly but in a quantitative way. In the battery approach the same tests are administered to all patients, regardless of their condition. This accumulates a standardized data base providing a comprehensive profile of a person's abilities and deficits. Such documentation of a relatively controlled, standardized sample of behaviour makes it unlikely that significant cerebral functions will remain unmonitored inadvertently. Hence, the probability of a valid diagnosis is increased.

The test battery approach remains the simplest and most cost-efficient method for inexperienced psychologists to use for neuropsychological assessment. Generalist psychologists who are already familiar with the rationale of the psychometric tradition find the battery approach a structured learning experience that serves as a smooth medium for transition to comprehensive cognitive evaluation.

The emphasis upon standardization and normative guidelines means that there is less reliance upon clinical intuition. This reinforces pattern analysis upon which any study of intercorrelations of symptoms may be based. Consequently, test battery results may be easily replicated for comparative purposes.

Test batteries tend to cast a broad net which documents the patient's strengths as well as deficits. This allows a more integrated view of the whole person and serves as a practical basis for rehabilitation programmes.

Finally, a major advantage of test batteries is their amenability to computerization. Standardized data, quantitatively scored, may be viewed as software that can be easily adapted to electronic processing. With data in this form it is possible to utilize all the advantages of computer technology.

A major disadvantage of the test battery approach is that it is atheoretical. In other words, it lacks a guiding theory of cognitive functioning to give satisfactory meaning to its results in terms of how the brain actually works.

A quantitative approach relying upon such global measures as group norms cannot elucidate the direct relationship between structure and function in an individual's nervous system. Consequently, the test battery approach, traditionally applied in the form of percentile scores, does not contribute to an appreciation of the underlying deficits in brain dysfunction.

An inflexible and broad spectrum battery may unselectively focus on time-consuming irrelevant issues. The Halstead–Reitan test battery takes approximately one full working day (six to eight hours) to administer. This magnifies the problem of fatigue when testing brain-damaged patients.

Finally, a laboratory situated test battery requires cumbersome equipment and involves relatively expensive capital investment. The patient must come to the laboratory since the equipment is not readily portable.

Qualitative Syndrome Analysis

Luria's (1980) approach represents the tradition of behavioural neurology. Christensen's (1979) translation of *Luria's Neuropsychological Investigation* is the best available example of the inductive approach. Luria's approach uses a flexible but systematic set of tests chosen for their qualitative significance in assessing a patient. Instead of employing such global measures as the Benton visual retention test (with its cut-off points), Luria uses specific measures designed to reduce the symptomatology of brain damaged patients to basic measures of a patient's deficits, an activity which would be impossible solely using a percentile score on a quantitative test. Thus there is an avoidance of intervening variables in favour of the most direct approach to brain–behaviour relationships that is possible. Neuropsychology is represented as the latest and most complex chapter of neurology.

A major advantage of the inductive approach is that its flexibility allows the clinician to ignore irrelevant issues and focus on testing within the areas most significant for the patient. Such an economical use of time makes it possible for skilled practitioners to complete assessment within two hours. Another advantage of qualitative syndrome analysis is that it elucidates the relationship between the structure and function of the nervous system. This clarifies the underlying nature of cerebral dysfunction and assists in the accurate localization of lesions and the formulation of specific rehabilitation programmes.

Hypothesis testing is a selective exercise of leads and interests. A disadvantage of qualitative syndrome analysis is that it can only be successfully used by experienced neuropsychologists who have mastered an acceptable theory of brain functioning. The absence of standardization of administration and a lack of normative interpretive guidelines puts extreme emphasis on clinical interpretation as no help is available from standard scores. Such an absence of norms rules out the pattern analysis upon which any study of intercorrelations of symptoms is based. The lack of a comprehensive profile of abilities and deficits may omit the documentation of significant cerebral functions. Such a lack of information obviously may have deleterious effects on diagnosis and rehabilitation. Finally, there is a paucity of literature documenting the reliability and validity of the Luria procedures.

Integrated Assessment

One of the most promising current trends in clinical neuropsychology is the attempt at integrating quantitative and qualitative assessment strategies (Golden, *et al.*, 1980). For example, the Luria–Nebraska neuropsychological battery (LNNB) developed by Golden and his associates (1980) is an ambitious attempt to apply the Halstead–Reitan quantitative methodology to Luria's qualitative syndrome analysis scheme. This battery is designed to be a standardized version of Luria's neuropsychological tests, thus capitalizing on both quantitative and qualitative approaches. At the time of writing, the test manual has been marketed for two years by Western Psychological Services (see Appendix V). The LNNB has also been automated for on-line computerized administration, scoring and interpretation by Psychsystems Fasttest Inc. (see Appendix V).

The rationale behind the LNNB is an acceptance of Luria's extensive theoretical and clinical contribution to our understanding of brain functions. At the same time it attempts to compensate for the disadvantages in his qualitative syndrome analysis methodology (discussed above). Consequently, the LNNB relies upon the following three factors: Luria's (1980) studies of brain functioning for its theoretical orientation; Christensen's (1979) translation of *Luria's Neuropsychological Investigation* as the clinical source for test items; and attempts at standardization of such test items to make them compatible with quantitative as well as qualitative strategies. The battery comprises a total of 269 simple test items that can be administered in 2.5 hours.

The items of the LNNB are divided into 11 test sections to represent a comprehensive profile of neuropsychological functional categories as follows: motor skills; rhythmic and pitch skills; tactile skills; expressive language skills; receptive language skills; reading; writing; arithmetic; memory; visuospatial skills; and intellectual skills.

Eleven indices were formulated by summarizing the items in each test section. In addition to indices representing the 11 specific functional categories, three more indices were created from the test items as follows: pathognomonic scale which serves as a measure of overall dysfunction; a right hemisphere scale; and a left hemisphere scale (the last two facilitate a comparison of tactile and motor functions for two sides of the body and hence assist in determining lateralization of brain damage). Each of these 14 sections of the battery can be graphically represented by plotting raw scores on a T-score form profile sheet, thus forming 14 scales. The normative data can make allowance for age and educational level variables.

The clinical, interpretative scheme of the LNNB takes into account both quantitative factors (represented by the T-score form profile sheet) and qualitative data (based on the pattern of test item errors together with observations of the patient's response style on individual test items).

The quantitatively oriented standardized interpretation of the battery is derived from a data base of 700 persons subjected to validity studies by Golden and his associates (1980). T-score cut-off points are provided to enable differentiation between normal and neurologically diseased patients. Patterns of test results that can be associated with lateralization and localization of brain damage are suggested.

The qualitative analysis of the nature of the patient's deficits requires an identification of the specific pattern of the patient's performance on the

LNNB. Such patterns are then interpreted within the context of Luria's (1980) theories of brain functioning. The most important of these is the concept of the functional system. This theory synthesizes the paradox of localization and equipotential tendencies in brain–behaviour relationships. That is, localized cortical areas can mediate specific functions. However, these functions are so specific that even the simplest forms of human behaviour require a variety of basic skills and thus are dependent upon the activity of multiple cortical locations. Consequently, a functional system denotes the patterns of interaction within the brain required for any specific behaviour. An analysis of the neuropsychological skills inherent in dysfunctional systems identifies those skills that are responsible for the patient's specific pattern of test item errors. The identification of specifically determined neuropsychological skills theoretically may then point to syndromes that localize areas of brain dysfunction. Apart from the identification of specific patterns of test item errors leading to syndrome analysis, clinical observation of the patient's response style on individual test items may add further useful qualitative data.

Detailed interpretation of the LNNB requires five steps, each of which allow evaluation of the data from a range of one to three different interpretative schemes discussed above (that is, the quantitative approach, the syndrome analysis and the qualitative analysis of performance on individual test items). These five steps are as follows: *(a)* a profile analysis of the general pattern of the 14 scales comprising the battery; *(b)* the use of localization scales (McKay and Golden, 1979) as a guide to the localization of brain damage; *(c)* the application of 30 factor scales (McKay and Golden, 1981) which break down the original scales into sample clusters of elementary skills, thus facilitating syndrome analysis; *(d)* the analysis of test item patterns as a further step in syndrome analysis; and *(e)* a qualitative analysis of response style on individual test items to add further data (Golden *et al.*, 1982).

Golden and his associates (1982) emphasize that the theory of functional systems precludes the existence of any "pure" test item influenced by only one area of the brain. Thus, the 14 neuropsychological scales in the LNNB are loose clusters of skills with some degree of overlap. Consequently, scales cannot be interpreted as if they represent a specifically "pure" skill. Rather, they represent a flexible category of interrelated abilities. This may serve as a general warning that no psychological test item can directly represent or measure any specific area of brain structure or function. Complex neuropsychological functions such as intelligence and language skills cannot be unitary.

The successful development of a new neuropsychological instrument is a monumental task requiring decades of scholarly labour. This evolutionary process is exemplified by the progressive development of the Halstead–

Reitan test battery over a period of 30 years and also by the maturation of *Luria's Neuropsychological Investigation* over an even longer period. The Luria-Nebraska neuropsychological battery (LNNB) has only been in use for two years and is already in its second revision. Only time will tell whether it is destined to become a major force in neuropsychology, as confidently predicted by Golden (1981).

The ambitious attempt by Golden and his associates to create a new and comprehensive assessment approach inevitably attracted critical reaction (Adams, 1980a,b; Spiers, 1981; Crosson and Warren 1982; Delis and Kaplan, 1982). These criticisms are succinctly reviewed and summarized by Spiers (1982), who accepts that there are two well established traditions in clinical neuropsychology but prefers to categorize them as actuarial and descriptive rather than as quantitative and qualitative. Both methodologies are scientifically respectable as they can be investigated experimentally and may generate data amenable to statistical analysis.

Being a behavioural neurologist, Spiers considers the actuarial approach, as exemplified by test batteries, to be less useful than descriptive methodology. He asserts that the descriptive tradition wherein the actual behaviours produced by the patient in response to specified tasks are the focus of observation has yielded more reliable identification of syndromes. This is allegedly because this approach more easily takes into account the fact of individual differences in brain structure.

Spiers (1982) concedes that Golden and his associates describe valid principles regarding theory and methodology derived from Luria's contributions but goes on to assert that they fail to show how the LNNB is compatible with these principles to effectively provide a test of Luria's approach. Consequently, he denies that the LNNB represents a valid standardized version of Luria's neuropsychological tests. Behavioural neurology is suspicious of quantitative scoring systems inherent in the LNNB and other batteries as the substitution of an abstract number for an actual test behaviour implies loss of valuable information.

In criticizing the prolific literature of Golden, *et al.*, in support of their tests, Spiers (1982) concludes that the LNNB has not met the stringent research standards expected of any new neuropsychological instrument marketed for clinical consumption. He claims that the research literature generated with the LNNB is invalid *a priori* because of significant methodological errors in the control of the neuropsychological status of the subjects used. Consequently, the clinical utility, validity, reliability and theoretical potential of the LNNB have not yet been established and thus are still open to debate.

Despite the trenchant criticisms of behavioural neurologists, Golden must be credited for his creative attempts. Whatever the ultimate fate of his battery, it does have some attractive features—a nominated theoretical base; test items covering a comprehensive range of specific skills; portability; low capital expense; short administration time; amenability to computerization; and access to exploration of its diagnostic validity.

Currently, the most obvious contribution of the LNNB is to affirm the ideal goal of attempting to integrate the equally important strategies of quantitative and qualitative assessment. Actuarial and descriptive methodologies are more complementary than contradictory. Spiers (1981) has admitted that quantitative measurement and qualitative syndrome analysis need not be inherently antithetical. For example, quantitative data have been shown to contribute to the description of certain brain–behaviour relationships. Also, as a matter of routine, competent psychometricians are aware of qualitative signs, take into account premorbid personality and interpret the results of their tests within the context of an individual clinical interview. Russell (1981:214) suggests that what appears to be a complete dichotomy between the clinical and psychometric approach "may well be setting up the proverbial straw man. Discussions with both clinical and neuropsychologists usually leave an impression that clinical and psychometric approaches are better seen as extremes of continuum".

Diament (1981) studied the question whether the same conclusions concerning brain–behaviour relationships could be reached by assessing patients with both the Halstead–Reitan battery and *Luria's Neuropsychological Investigation.* He concludes that both assessment strategies yield equally adequate results in identifying the presence and nature of brain dysfunction and recommends the complementary use of both approaches.

Thus, an "either–or" choice between quantitative and qualitative strategies appears to be more arbitrary than real. The use of a standardized test battery does not necessarily impede the ability of a clinician to observe behaviour qualitatively at the same time. The variety of simple tasks in a comprehensive battery allows ample opportunity to observe response styles. The so-called "organic signs" (with a careful interpretation of both their utility and limitations) may be noted as "behavioural observations" during testing as follows: rotation of sketched figures; neglect of one side of stimulus; perseveration; lateralizing signs on motor, tactile and cognitive tasks; scattering of performance levels; constructional dyspraxia; and behavioural anomalies (such as hyperactivity, distractibility, mixed dominance, motor incoordination, and clumsiness).

After the completion of standard procedures which allow documentation of standard scores there is nothing to stop the experienced clinician from further testing of hypotheses about the patient's errors. Creative adaptation of commonly used "testing-the-limits" procedures (for example, repetition of items, readministration in non-standardized ways, suspending time limits, and so on) may virtually duplicate Luria's qualitative syndrome analysis. Enough simple items exist in a standardized comprehensive test battery to allow the experienced clinician to search for the reason for certain error patterns and, hence, to elucidate the nature of a specific neuropsychological deficit. Consequently, it is possible to accomplish both quantitative and qualitative testing at the same time.

A quantitatively oriented test battery approach does not stop clinicians from making qualitative observations. However, the converse does not easily apply. For example, the use of qualitative assessment strategy without inbuilt standardization and norms effectively rules out the generation of standardized quantitative data. Golden (1980) chose to resolve this problem by applying the Halstead–Reitan methodology to Luria's syndrome analysis scheme. The building-in of a quantitative scoring system to a standardized version of Luria's neuropsychological tests resulted in the creation of a radically new instrument with all the attendant responsibilities of demonstrating adequate standards of validity.

The purpose of the battery approach recommended in this book, and described in Chapter 5, is infinitely less ambitious and more conservative. There is a strict avoidance of the creation of a new neuropsychological instrument. Well established psychometric tradition is the base upon which further refinement of the open-ended Halstead–Reitan model is undertaken. The evolutionary tradition of using some of the well validated and better accepted cost-efficient tests for inclusion in the battery at the expense of less promising, outmoded tests was adhered to. Such upgrading of a tried and tested model, with the inclusion of better subtests as they become available, is a logical and productive enterprise.

In summary, it must be emphasized that no final resolution of assessment strategies is possible or even desirable. The evolution of competing strategies and tests for cerebral dysfunction remains an ongoing process which should be encouraged since it is intimately associated with advances in research on brain–behaviour relationships. Differing neuropsychological strategies reflect different perspectives about the same subject matter (that is, the human brain), and make their own unique contribution to this increasingly important field. Familiarity with variety of such differential perspectives is an obvious advantage for the neuropsychologist.

COMPUTER ASSISTED ASSESSMENT

Perhaps the most revolutionary current trend in neuropsychological assessment is the impact of computer technology. Society is becoming more receptive of computerization and there is now abundant enthusiasm for the changes it is having upon our way of life. Personal computers have become a much sought after commodity and sales figures have increased dramatically over the past few years. A recent survey revealed that nearly 80 per cent of Americans thought that personal computers would be common household items by the turn of the century (*Time*, 1983). It is generally acknowledged that advanced computer technology will free humans from many routine, repetitive tasks and enable them to pursue more creative and rewarding venues and thereby enhance productivity (Williams, 1977). If calculators are useful, then computers are infinitely more so as they calculate in more sophisticated ways. Increasingly, computers are being used in homes, government, commerce and industry, schools, and medicine. They have the potential to alter our lifestyle as much as motor vehicles and television did.

In medicine, computers were employed initially to record patient's demographic data and to send accounts. More recently, the computer has been programmed to assist in diagnosis (Couch, 1976; Croft, 1972; Wardle and Wardle, 1978; Wiener, 1975; Catanzarite, *et al.*, 1981) and diagnostic programs such as 'Caduceus', 'Mycin', and 'Neurologist' have been developed in this regard. Moreover, electronic data bases have been establised which provide invaluable information for both clinical practice and research. Microcomputers have recently been used to control pacemakers surgically implanted in patients with chronic cardiac disease and to regulate the quantity of insulin administered to diabetic patients (*Time*, 1983). Neurology is increasingly relying upon computer technology—for example, computerized tomography.

Computer technology was first employed in mental health care services to streamline administrative procedures by automating patients' data systems (Graetz, 1966; Laska, Logemann and Weinstein, 1971; Glueck, 1974; Johnson, Giannetti and Williams, 1976; Kaplan and Smith, 1974). This was followed by the automation of standard clinical procedures such as the mental status examination (Colby, *et al.*, 1966), social history (Laska, 1974), developmental and psychiatric history (Martin, 1972) and nursing notes (Rosenberg and Glueck, 1969). The most recent application of computer technology in psychiatry has been the introduction of computers in complex decision making tasks (Altman, *et al.*, 1972, 1974; Mirabile, *et al.*, 1971; Hedlund, *et al.*, 1973), including diagnosis (Spitzer and Endicott, 1968, 1969, 1974; Wing, *et al.*, 1974).

The first individually administered test of intellectual functioning was developed by Binet towards the end of the 19th century (Anastasi, 1976). During World War I psychologists were requested to develop appropriate individual and group tests to screen military personnel for selection and placement. This renewed interest in objective psychological assessment formed the foundation for the subsequent development of training courses in clinical psychology at academic institutions (Korchin, 1976).

Psychological assessment has developed into a highly specialized and technical area with tools derived from statistics. There has been a diversification of psychological testing to include personality, diagnostic, neuropsychological, aptitude, education and vocational tests (Anastasi, 1976; Cronbach, 1970; Buros, 1978). Psychological tests are now almost universally used in clinical assessment and their validity, reliability and clinical applications are reported in relevant psychological journals.

It was not until the early 1960s that computers were introduced into clinical psychology to score and interpret psychological tests (Johnson, *et al.*, 1978; Pearson, *et al.*, 1975; Fowler, 1967; Piotrowski, 1964). Patients recorded their responses on optical scanning answer sheets which were then usually mailed to central computer centres for analysis and interpretation as few mental health agencies could afford to install their own computer facilities. One of the major limitations of this approach was the delay between the patients' initial assessment and the availability of the computerized report. This resulted in the development (Cole, *et al.,* 1976; Williams *et al.,* 1975; Johnson, *et al.,* 1976) and subsequent introduction of online microcomputer technology which provided a more rapid, cost-efficient and comprehensive evaluation of psychological, medical and social problems in the form of a narrative report (Johnson, *et al.,* 1975; Johnson, *et al.,* 1977; Johnson and Williams, 1975; Klingler, *et al.,* 1976; Klingler and Miller 1977). This information was made available to primary care clinicians shortly after the patient was admitted to hospital and therefore could be used in planning the future management of patients. However, Klingler and Miller (1977: 111) have cautioned against the routine application of online microcomputer technology in mental health care services until the quality, validity, clinical acceptance and cost-effectiveness of such procedures has been thoroughly investigated: "... an emerging maxim accompanying the introduction of new methods, technologies or strategies in social action programs must be evaluated on the basis of merit before being blindly adopted as superior. It is our contention that we, as behavioural scientists, must hold ourselves increasingly accountable in our expenditure of public monies ... we must strive to justify adequately our growing utilization of costly computer systems".

Several investigators have evaluated computerized assessment systems (Weitzel, *et al.,* 1972; Maultsby and Slock, 1971; Meikle and Gerritse, 1970, Spitzer and Endicott, 1969), but none of these were fully automated online systems. Cole, *et al.* (1976) provided guidelines for the development of online computer systems which could be used with unskilled psychiatric patients. They suggested that terminals should be easy to read and operate and should not be overly distracting to the patient. They also recommended a brief validity questionnaire at the commencement of the assessment which could identify those individuals who were deliberately malingering or who were too psychotic to provide meaningful data.

Online computerized assessments have been reported to reduce treatment workloads and the interpretations made compared favourably with those of experienced consultants (Russell, *et al.,* 1970; Klingler, *et al.,* 1976; Klingler and Miller, 1977). Computer generated test reports are now well received by physicians and psychiatrists and a preference for computerized reports has been reported (Mathews, 1981). Goldstein (quoted in Mathews, 1981:660) believes that: "... a well thought-out computer generated report can provide the referring physician or other professionals with all they really want to know and that we as psychologists too often write for ourselves rather than for those requesting our services, some of whom are too busy to read our overly lengthy prose".

The acceptance of computerized assessment and reports by consumers has resulted in the development of commercially available hardware and software to assist in the administration, scoring and interpretation of psychological tests. They vary from the basic to the more sophisticated systems which enable the clinician to administer tests in any location using a portable assessment terminal and then relay the data by means of a telephone to a central computer system for analysis, interpretation and report writing. It is now possible to have a large number of portable assessment terminals connected to a single computer system. Psychsystems (see Appendix V) have introduced the Fasttest System which is based upon the pioneering work of Johnson and his fellow workers at the Veterans Administration Hospital and University of Utah Medical Centre, Salt Lake City (Johnson, *et al.*, 1975, 1976, 1977, 1978a,b, 1979; Johnson and Williams, 1975, 1978; Klingler, *et al.*, 1976; Klingler and Miller, 1977; Gianetti, *et al.*, 1977). This comprehensive system includes social, medical and psychological assessment which is presented to the patients by means of a cathode ray tube (CRT) terminal. The system presently comprises 17 tests and/or questionnaires. Compu-Psych Inc. has developed the Psychomotor 3000 systems with portable assessment terminals. This system currently has 15 tests. Compu-Psych Inc. intends to add additional tests in the near future (see Appendix V).

Software programs such as the Wechsler intelligence scale for children–revised (WISC–R), Wechsler adult intelligence scale–revised (WAIS–R) and Minnesota multiphasic personality inventory (MMPI) are now commercially available and can be used with personal computers such as Apple II Plus, and TRS-80 Model I or Model III computers. These software programs are relatively inexpensive and provide adequate interpretations of the above tests as well as a narrative report. Further details of software and software suppliers are contained in Appendix V.

The application of computer technology in psychological assessment has flourished over the past decade and innovations such as the online administration of the WISC–R and WAIS–R should become available to psychologists in the not too distant future. The most recent computerized version of a neuropsychological instrument is that of the Luria–Nebraska neuropsychological battery. Software for the Wechsler memory scale and the

Halstead–Reitan neuropsychological test battery is also being advertised, but the quality of such material still needs to be evaluated. Three dimensional colour graphics may be created as aids for visualizing neuropsychological deficits.

All innovations arouse anxiety when they promise to challenge well established practices. The telescope, the telephone and radar were all initially rejected. Today, we sit in judgement on computers in psychology. Children growing up with personal home computers tend to have more positive attitudes towards such technology. These future psychologists will have less attachment to laborious paper and pencil routines than do those of us trained intensively in the use of hand scoring techniques. Learning to be literate with computers, like learning any new language, requires flexibility. Most computer diskettes caution in their automated narratives that they are not designed to be the sole basis of a final report. Rather, such data serve as objectively derived hypotheses which need to be further clarified from other clinical sources. Ultimately it is clinicians who must use their skills in order to interpret any standardized electronically derived data base to meet the needs of the individual patient.

The names and addresses of some of the companies manufacturing hardware and software for clinical psychologists are listed in Appendix V.

A dagger of the mind, a false creation
Proceeding from the heat-oppressed brain.

Shakespeare, *Macbeth*, II, i, 38–39

2
Clinical Presentation of Brain Disease

ILLNESS implies the presence of subjective complaints (symptoms) and objective evidence of disturbance (signs). Once recognized, illnesses are grouped together either because of similarities in their symptoms and signs, or because they share a common cause. The first is called the syndromal approach; the second is called the aetiological (Scadding, 1967).

In physical medicine nowadays, diagnostic terms usually refer to aetiological concepts. This is not yet true for psychiatry. The cause of most psychiatric illnesses remains obscure and diagnoses such as schizophrenia or obsessional neurosis refer simply to clusters of symptoms and signs which are commonly associated with each other and which point to a common outcome. They do not necessarily imply knowledge of causation. The organic mental disorders are exceptions to this general rule. Their aetiology is known: they are the direct result of disordered brain functioning.

There are four major ways in which disordered brain function may manifest itself through psychiatric disturbance. These are delirium, dementia, non-specific presentations and epilepsy. The various features of these conditions have been described with great clarity by Lishman (1978).

DELIRIUM OR THE ACUTE ORGANIC REACTION

Clinical Presentation

Delirium is the clinical presentation when the disturbance of brain function has occurred recently and rapidly. It is usually reversible. Its outstanding feature is an impairment of consciousness, commonly called clouding (Lishman, 1978).

Consciousness may be defined as awareness of oneself and one's environment. It is that state of mind that allows normal cognitive processes to occur. Consciousness is not synonymous with wakefulness (alertness) or arousal (activation), and disturbances of consciousness are qualitatively different from physiological variations that affect these latter functions. Sleep for instance is a normal variation of alertness and is in fact an active process encompassing a number of different physiological states, each associated with specific electroencephalographic and neuroendocrine changes. Characteristic of sleep is the observation that the subject can easily be awakened and restored to full alertness. In contrast, it is difficult to get through to patients whose consciousness is grossly disturbed and, even when this has been achieved, they rapidly regress once stimulation is withdrawn. However, clouding of consciousness does not necessarily imply lessened activity and it may be associated with varying levels of arousal—from lethargy and torpor through to excitement and agitation.

The most extreme disorder of consciousness is coma, a life-threatening condition of more concern to neurologists and physicians than to psychiatrists or psychologists. In coma, patients are insensible to most external stimuli or inner needs, show little spontaneous movement except respiration and give no evidence of continued mental activity. They respond only to the grossest of stimuli, such as a pin-prick, and then merely by grunts and ineffectual movements.

The term stupor is often used to describe the state of semi-coma, a similar condition but less severe than that of coma. However, stupor is sometimes used in reference to a completely different phenomenon, one which is perhaps best termed akinetic mutism. Patients with this latter condition are aware of their environment and what is happening but are unable to respond. They will not answer questions or obey instructions but may appear alert and are likely to follow the examiner with their eyes. Unlike the amnesia reported by patients recovering from coma, recall of events after recovery from akinetic mutism is often vivid. The disorder is sometimes caused by lesions in the vicinity of the third ventricle of the brain. More commonly, it is associated with functional psychiatric illnesses such as catatonic schizophrenia and retarded depression. In at least some instances akinetic mutism appears to be under volitional control (Joyston-Bechal, 1966).

Disturbances of consciousness in psychiatric practice stop short of coma. Nevertheless, they vary markedly in severity and may be followed along a continuum. The mildest degree of impairment is manifested chiefly by difficulty in sustaining attention and a tendency to distractibility. Patients complain vaguely of discomfort and uncertainty. They are unable to judge the passage of time accurately and realise that their thinking is less coherent than usual.

With increasing impairment, there is neglect of appearance and of physical needs and incontinence may occur. Patients have difficulty in thinking, attending, perceiving and remembering, so that they are muddled, bewildered and disorientated for time, place and person. It becomes increasingly difficult to gain their full attention, they respond slowly and inadequately to requests, and appear not to understand or to be unwilling to co-operate. Attention is sustained for only a few minutes at a time and they soon lose the thread of conversation. They are drowsy and lethargic and spends much of the day sleeping.

In the stage of semi-coma, patients are clearly out of contact with their environment. They can be aroused by vigorous stimulation, but are then confused and irritable. Speech is reduced to incoherent mumbling. There is an excessive tendency to startle reactions and the patient's usual torpor may at times be replaced by episodes of violent hyperactivity and noisy shouting, usually in response to hallucinatory experiences. In others, overactivity takes the form of ceaseless restless movements such as groping and picking at the bedclothes (Lishman, 1978).

Characteristic of the milder stages of clouding of consciousness is the tendency to fluctuate. During the day when patients are being constantly stimulated no abnormality is noted. At night with increasing tiredness and decreased stimulation patients become confused. This phenomenon is important from a number of points of view. First, it is helpful in distinguishing clouding of consciousness from the more constant impairment associated with dementing processes or functional psychiatric illness. Second, it suggests that acute organic reactions often present first to the most junior members of the therapeutic team, namely the nurses who look after the ward at night when the medical and senior nursing staff are off duty. Hence it is important that all staff members are encouraged to report any peculiarities they may observe in respect to their patients' behaviour.

The impairment of consciousness or clouding is but part of a more global disorder in which all aspects of brain function may be involved. Changes in perception, emotion and memory are particularly prominent.

Although perceptual abnormalities are not always present in delirium, when they do occur they are often florid. Not infrequently they are the first features of the illness to be noted. Initially the disturbance is subjective. Patients become aware of inaccuracies in their perception, particularly in regard to sight. Distortions such as micropsia and macropsia may occur. Disordered awareness of internal sensations proceeds to a dissolution of boundaries between inner experience and the environment, and derealization and depersonalization are common, albeit poorly formulated (Lishman, 1978).

Perceptual disturbances most frequently occur in the visual modality, but auditory, tactile, gustatory and olfactory sensations may also be affected.

Faulty perception couples with reduced clarity of thinking to produce misinterpretations and illusions which often have a frightening and persecutory flavour. Hallucinations are associated with further progression of the condition, and probably arise partly from inability to distinguish inner images from outer reality and partly from the confused recall of dreams.

Changes in mood are likely to be evident in delirium. In the early phases, anxiety, irritability and fluctuating depression are common. As the condition progresses, some patients become apathetic and indifferent to their situation. Others become suspicious, hostile and excited, and delusional ideas of a persecutory kind are common. Perplexity and fearfulness are elicited by frightening perceptual experiences which patients are not able to understand. Patients may go on to become frankly terrified, with rapid pulse, trembling limbs and other evidence of high arousal.

These affective reactions are usually transient and abrupt changes of mood occur, particularly excitation and fearfulness. Episodes of increased disturbance are probably elicited by misinterpretations and hallucinatory experiences.

Thinking is characteristically affected in states of impaired consciousness. Initially, patients are aware of difficulty in focusing their thoughts and fatigue easily. Later, thinking becomes less coherent and eventually the train of thought is fragmented. Their ability to distinguish between the internal world of the mind and the external world of the environment is weakened so that reality testing becomes defective. Ideas of reference and persecutory delusions may develop, but are poorly elaborated and usually transient, in marked contrast to the systemized delusions of paranoid schizophrenia. Patients' insight into their condition is variable, fluctuating markedly in association with changes in the level of consciousness.

Memory is disturbed. For clinical purposes, memory is most easily thought of as embracing three functions: registration; retention; and recall. Registration may be tested simply by asking patients to repeat a series of digits, retention by requesting that they remember a name and address for a period of about 20 minutes, and recall by careful attention to the details given during history taking. In states of impaired consciousness registration of current experience is defective because of patients' inability to sustain attention and their problems with comprehension. Retention is also affected and inability to learn new material is a sensitive indicator in the early stages of the disorder. On the other hand, long term recall may be well preserved.

Results of electroencephalography (EEG) are almost always abnormal in delirium. Disorganization of normal cerebral rhythms and slowing are the most consistently reported changes, but low voltage fast wave predominance also occurs particularly in patients in whom drugs have been involved in the causation of the condition (Engel and Romano, 1959).

In summary, delirious patients show an impaired level of consciousness of varying degrees of severity. They are usually awake and capable of responding verbally. They show evidence of defective attention, perception and memory and have difficulty in thinking and comprehension. Disorientation for time, space and relationships with other persons is present, but patients are often aware of their cognitive dysfunction and use the defences of denial, projection and withdrawal. The EEG record is usually abnormal.

Delirium is a common complication of severe medical illness and of surgical operations, and the condition is sometimes missed until patients' behaviour becomes grossly disturbed. A high index of suspicion on the part of staff members and attention to details such as episodes of strange behaviour at night, sudden changes in the level of anxiety and disturbed relationships with staff and other patients, may prevent such crises from arising.

Causation

The cause of delirium is most frequently systemic, that is, a disorder of general bodily function which brings about changes in blood chemistry or oxygenation and ultimately affects brain metabolism. As the internal structure of the brain is not disrupted in such instances, the condition is potentially reversible. The major systemic causes may be grouped into nine clusters.

Intoxication

Intoxication may occur with alcohol and with illicit drugs such as cannabis, opiates, amphetamines and hallucinogens. Substances which are used as medicaments need also be included under this heading. They may cause delirium because they are taken in excessive quantities, for example, in cases of deliberate abuse, or because the patient is unduly sensitive to normal therapeutic dosages. Common offenders include the psychotropic drugs, particularly barbiturates and benzodiazepine tranquillisers such as diazepam (Valium); anaesthetics and analgesics; antiparkinsonian agents such as levodopa and amantadine and the anticholinergics atropine and benztropine; digitalis; appetite suppressants; and many others. Patients who use several different drugs concurrently are at an increased risk because of the danger of summation of adverse effects.

Withdrawal states

Abrupt cessation of a drug on which a patient has become dependent may lead to a withdrawal reaction which includes delirium. Alcohol is the most important agent to consider in this regard and the alcohol withdrawal syndrome, delirium tremens, is justifiably notorious.

It is not only skid-row alcoholics who develop delirium tremens. So-called social drinkers who do not show evidence of addictive drinking may also have become physically dependent on the drug and when alcohol intake is terminated abruptly, for instance when the patient is admitted to hospital for elective surgery, a withdrawal reaction is provoked. It is important to remember that up to 30% of patients admitted to general hospital have an alcohol problem, at least in some communities (Williams, *et al.*, 1978). Continued use of other drugs, notably the barbiturates and probably also the benzodiazepines, may also lead to withdrawal reactions.

High fevers

High fevers, particularly in children and almost always due to infectious diseases, are frequently associated with delirium. In some instances a local element (encephalitis, meningitis) may be involved, but the most common infectious cause of delirium is the indirect effect of generalized sepsis on the brain. It is of interest to reflect that the illnesses typhus and typhoid, each caused by very different microbiological agents, are named after the Greek word indicating a confused mental state.

Metabolic disturbances

The decompensations that result from organ failures are important causes of delirium. The condition brought about by renal failure is known as uraemia because of its association with raised blood levels of urea, a protein breakdown product. Although mental changes become more frequent as urea levels rise, there is no simple relationship between the two, and a raised urea level does not actually cause the brain disorder. It merely reflects the severity of the renal failure. Electrolyte imbalance appears to be the most important factor, with changes in the levels of sodium, potassium, chloride, and phosphate, the acid/base ratio and osmolality all being relevant. Other causes of electrolyte imbalance need also to be considered in the differential diagnosis of delirium.

Hepatic failure causes mental disturbance because of the liver's inability to metabolize intoxicating substances absorbed from the intestinal contents. The precise toxins involved remain uncertain, but they are of a nitrogenous nature. It follows that the severity of the mental disorder is influenced by the amount of protein in the diet. A large amount of dietary protein may lead from delirium to hepatic coma, while a rigid restriction of protein intake can cause considerable amelioration in the clinical picture.

Many metabolic diseases may cause delirium. Examples include intermittent porphyria and porphyria variegata, conditions which are due to inborn errors in the biosynthesis of the blood's pigmented substances and which are frequently associated with transient delirious states and even with episodes of coma. Attacks are often precipitated by acute infections, alcohol or the use of drugs such as the barbiturates, sulphonamides and the contraceptive pill.

Endocrine diseases

Delirium is common during the course of diabetes mellitus. It may be associated with hyperglycemia, with or without acidosis (the nonketotic hyperosmolar state), or with hypoglycemia which is often the result of too large a dose of insulin. Hypothyroidism is another important cause, the clinical picture resulting being known as myxoedema madness. Both hyperactivity and hypoactivity of the adrenal and parathyroid glands need also be considered in the differential diagnosis of the delirious patient (Beumont, 1979).

Vitamin deficiencies

Chronic and severe malnutrition is an important cause of psychiatric symptoms in impoverished countries. In more affluent communities there are categories of people prone to similar disorders because of imbalanced nutrition, particularly vitamin deficiency. At risk groups include the mentally retarded, persons suffering chronic psychotic illness, patients with malabsorption due to gastrointestinal disease, and aged people living in isolated circumstances, especially when depressed and withdrawn. Alcoholics are even more vulnerable as their poor eating habits are compounded by increased demands for vitamins resulting from their high alcohol intake.

The vitamins of which deficiency leads to mental changes are those belonging to the B complex. When it develops insidiously, thiamine deficiency leads to the classical picture of beriberi with mainly physical symptoms. Acute and fulminating depletion, such as that found in alcoholics, leads instead to Wernicke's encephalopathy, a delirious state associated with specific neurological signs. Nicotinic acid depletion similarly leads to a systemic illness called pellagra when it develops gradually. Following acute and total deprivation, a severe delirium develops. Deficiencies of vitamin B_{12} and folic acid usually present with anaemia. They frequently cause psychotic symptoms, but these are more commonly those of a dementia rather than of a delirium.

Anoxia

Cerebral anoxia may arise in a number of ways. Congestive heart failure and cardiac arrythmias effectively reduce blood flow, pulmonary diseases such as chronic bronchitis and emphysema impede oxygenation in the lungs, and anaemia from whatever cause decreases the oxygen carrying capacity of blood. The brain is exquisitely sensitive to these changes. Anoxia during surgical operations, usually due to a combination of hypertension and inadequate ventilation during anaesthesia, is an important cause of confusion in the immediate post-operative period.

In addition to systemic causes, delirium may also result from local disturbances within the cranium. Some of the conditions that need to be considered are fairly obvious and easily diagnosed. Others are more obscure and are frequently missed.

Trauma

The most constant effect of head injury is an impairment of consciousness. It may vary in severity from a short period of clouding to profound and prolonged coma. Concussion is the term used to indicate an immediate and transient defect of neural function, including disturbances of consciousness, equilibrium and vision, that follows on a closed head injury. It is less common after penetrating injuries (Caveness and Walker, 1966).

The course of coma following severe head injury is characteristic. Recovery is slow and the condition fades gradually into a phase of confusion. The patient usually has amnesia for almost the whole period of disturbance, and the duration of this post-traumatic amnesia is directly proportional to the severity of the head injury.

Vascular conditions

There are a number of vascular conditions that can produce delirium and clouding of consciousness. A variable period of clouding follows a "stroke" or cerebral infarct. The acute picture is gradually replaced by chronic neurological deficits such as hemiplegia and aphasia, but in some instances the delirium may be prolonged. Subdural haematomata are caused by the gradual accumulation of blood from venous leakage, often following relatively trivial injury. The condition develops insidiously, sometimes days or even weeks after the original trauma, and the characteristically fluctuating impairment of consciousness may not be recognized until the patient is in a life-threatening situation. Cerebral vasculitis such as that associated with systemic lupus erythematosus and hypertensive encephalopathy are additional causes that need to be considered.

Neurological Diseases

Delirium is a manifestation of a number of neurological diseases. The mechanism involved is often an increase in intracranial pressure, secondary to tumour, infection, obstruction to the cerebrospinal fluid or to the condition known as benign intracranial hypertension. Seizure disorders (epilepsy) are also important causes of various types of acute organic brain syndromes and they will be considered later.

Predisposition

Susceptibility to developing delirium varies markedly between individuals. Although it is difficult to predict precisely who will develop the condition, there are some factors that clearly play a role in predisposition.

In general, the very young and the old are at increased risk. A phase of delirium is common during infectious illnesses in preschool children. Similarly, persons aged over 60 years are more likely to become confused following operations or during physical illness than are younger adults or adolescents. Previous brain damage of whatever cause, and even if of very long duration, is also important. The middle-aged man who sustained a serious head injury in early life is more likely to develop a state of clouding following surgery than are other adults who do not have a similar history. Excessive use of alcohol or other drugs plays a major predisposing role as such abuse contributes to brain damage.

Certain types of psychological stress seem particularly important. Delirium frequently occurs when patients' ability to initiate action is severely curtailed. Enforced immobilization in an intensive care unit is a good example of this kind of situation. Variation in the quality and pattern of sensory input is also highly relevant. The danger of sensory deprivation in patients who have undergone eye surgery is well recognized, but it is not often realized that an elderly patient in the unfamiliar and frightening environment of a medical or surgical ward, neglected by the busy nursing and medical staff, may be subjected to almost as intense an isolation.

Sleep deprivation increases the chance of developing a delirium. Many intensive care settings in hospitals contribute to this risk because patients are subject to multiple awakenings during the night. Persons who are chronically anxious and who regularly use hypnotic drugs tend to sleep badly in hospital and their insomnia may be a prodromal symptom of delirium.

High levels of anxiety also appear to predispose to delirium. Many factors conspire to make patients anxious: innate constitution; worry about their physical illness; domestic difficulties; and poor relationships with the medical team concerned in their treatment. Reassurance, explanation and the offer of support confer great benefit to the majority, but individuals who try to repress or deny their anxiety, who have a great fear of losing control and a need to please and placate authority figures by pretending all is well, tend to cope badly. It is often they who develop delirium.

Course

Characteristically, the onset of a delirium is abrupt. The course of the illness usually lasts for no more than 10 days but may be very much shorter.

Occasionally the illness persists for months. There are three possible outcomes.

First, and fortunately most frequently, the patient may recover completely. The subject usually has only patchy recollection of what happened during the illness and likens the experience to a bad dream.

Second, some patients progress on to an irreversible focal syndrome or dementia. The classical example of this progression is the case of Wernicke's encephalopathy, a delirious condition with associated neurological deficits caused by thiamine deficiency and usually occurring in alcoholics. Unless the patient is correctly treated, and in particular is given high doses of thiamine parenterally, the picture changes to that of the amnestic syndrome, Korsakoff's psychosis.

Third, many patients progress to irreversible coma and eventually die. The cause of death is usually the underlying illness that has provoked the delirium. However, in some unfortunate cases, death results from complications arising during coma, such as hypostatic pneumonia or electrolyte disturbance, which could have been prevented by optimal medical treatment.

Treatment

The treatment of delirium is medical. Perhaps no other area of clinical practice is so demanding of psychiatrists' medical skills, as opposed to their expertise in personal relationship and psychotherapy. The account given here derives largely from the practice of our colleague, Dr R. Vickery, of the Royal Prince Alfred Hospital. Treatment is based on the following principles:

1. Treat the underlying cause (or causes) adequately. Correction of even a mild anaemia or treatment of an infection may bring about a dramatic improvement.
2. Check all drugs being prescribed. The elderly in particular are very susceptible to anticholinergics. Digitalis, levodopa, steroids and of course sedative and psychotropic drugs may be involved. Even therapeutic doses of common drugs such as acetylsalicylic acid may precipitate delirium on the basis of individual idiosyncrasy.
3. Remember that the patient may be suffering from a withdrawal state. Withdrawal symptoms relating to alcohol are not confined to skid-row alcoholics and patients may of course have abused other drugs such as barbiturates.
4. Ensure electrolytes are balanced, hydration is adequate and nutrition and vitamins are properly maintained. Large parenteral doses of thiamine are necessary in patients with Wernicke's encephalopathy.

5. Nursing care should provide orientation and increased familiarity and physical restraint should be avoided if at all possible, as should excessive excitement and sensory deprivation. Nurses should be encouraged to communicate frequently with patients, but make sure that they are not over stimulated. There should be only one stimulus at a time.

Sedation is needed when the patient is agitated, violent or extremely anxious. Haloperidol is a good drug to use for this purpose. It can be given orally or parentally and has little effect on blood pressure, pulmonary artery pressure, heart rate or respiration. In severe cases a loading regime is recommended: 2-10 mg haloperidol should be given every half hour until adequate sedation is achieved. Paradoxical responses to haloperidol may occur so 60 mg should be considered a maximum dose. The total amount of drug used to bring about sedation is then calculated, and half as much is given again when agitation recurs, or up to 12 hours later, as long as the patient remains calm. The dosage is gradually reduced while the agitation remains under control. Benzodiazepines are probably best avoided in delirium as they may worsen the clouding of consciousness.

In patients who do not respond to haloperidol the physician should suspect that the condition may be due to anitcholinergic drugs. If so, an immediate response will be brought about by administration of 1 mg physostigmine intravenously.

Delirium tremens demands its own special therapy. It is a medical emergency. Fluid replacement is essential, and the patient will need about five litres of fluid a day of which 1.5 litres should be given as normal saline. Potassium replacement and the correction of magnesium deficiency may be indicated. Thiamine 100 mg should be given by intravenous injection immediately to prevent the development of Wernicke's encephalopathy. The drug of choice to use for sedation is chlormethiazole which is prescribed according to a reducing schedule over the course of six days.

Involvement of a psychiatrist in the management of the patient should be arranged sooner rather than later. Psychiatrists working in medical consultation and liaison services are experienced in the early diagnosis and management of delirium. They should be consulted at the earliest sign of clouding of consciousness, especially in patients with previous brain damage, elderly patients, and patients who are highly anxious or who have a history of heavy drug usage or previous psychiatric illness.

DEMENTIA OR THE CHRONIC ORGANIC REACTION

Conditions which interrupt the normal development of intelligence lead to amentia (mental subnormality). When the disturbance occurs later in life it leads to a deterioration of intellectual performance and is then called dementia. Like delirium, the term dementia refers to a distinctive clinical picture which may result from a variety of pathological causes. The pathology is usually within the cranium so that brain architecture is destroyed. For this reason dementia is often irreversible. However, this is not inherent in the definition, nor is it always true in practice (Lishman, 1978).

Clinical Presentation

The outstanding feature of dementia is diminished intellectual function. Patients become less able to deal with new ideas. Their own capacity to produce anything new is decreased; thought is impoverished; they have particular difficulty in handling abstract ideas; they are better able to cope with details than with concepts of a more general nature; judgement and insight are impaired; and there is a loss of flexibility of thinking and of the capacity to respond appropriately to changes in the environment, leading to a tendency to perseverate. In advanced cases, thinking is restricted to circumscribed themes and eventually becomes completely disorganised.

The disorder in thinking is reflected in speech, with excessive use of cliches, poorly constructed sentences, paraphasic errors and sometimes aphasia. Memory is disturbed and the functions of registration, retention and recall may all be affected. There is a faulty appreciation of time sequences leading to temporal disorientation, and of topographic memory leading to spatial disorientation.

Affective changes accompany and often precede the intellectual disturbance, the most characteristic of which is lability of affect. The patient reacts excessively to minor frustrations and disappointments, but the reaction is evanescent. In advanced cases, patients' incapacity to control the expression of their emotions may show in pathological laughing or crying. A tendency to paranoid suspiciousness is common. Lasting mood changes may also occur, the most important of which are depression or a persistent fatuous and euphoric equanimity.

Dementia often first manifests itself with behavioural changes. Typically there is loss of interest and initiative, inability to perform to the usual standard, inappropriate or disinhibited actions and episodes of muddle and confusion.

An important aspect of the behaviour of the dementing patient is the so-called catastrophic reaction. Dementing persons unconsciously attempt to re-adjust their lives so as to be able to meet all the demands made on them by the environment. If these demands are excessive, they react by showing signs of extreme anxiety and agitation. That this response is not simply due to an awareness that they have failed in the task is evident from the observation that the response develops simultaneously with their performance, not after it, and that the patients are unable to explain the cause of their distress. In order to avoid these "catastrophic reactions" patients severely restrict their environment to protect themselves from situations with which they cannot cope. An example of this form of restriction can be seen in "organic orderliness" (Goldstein, 1936).

Consciousness is preserved in dementia unless there is a superimposed delirium. Of course patients with dementia, reflecting chronic brain damage, are highly susceptible to the development of an acute brain reaction.

Focal Lesions

It is important to realize that the picture described above is the result of a combination of a general loss of neurones throughout the cortex together with features arising from particular focal lesions. Where focal pathology occurs with minimal general neuronal loss, specific deficit syndromes occur. Careful mental state testing can define the precise position of focal lesions because of the high degree of localization of certain mental functions (Piercy, 1964). As the two sides of the brain are not identical, it is necessary to decide the side of cerebral dominance in these cases. Remember that all right handed persons have left hemisphere dominance, and so do many left handed persons (Benton, *et al.*, 1962).

Neurological

Most of the effects of localized brain pathology are most conveniently considered as neurological conditions. For instance, this is true of the hemiplegia that results from damage to the internal capsule (a bundle of fibres passing down from the motor areas of the cortex) which is within the vascular territory of the middle cerebral artery.

Syndromes in which there is a disruption of the brain's ability to deal with symbols have a stronger psychiatric flavour. Aphasia refers to a condition in which the ability to use language is impaired although the motor elements of speech production are intact. The underlying lesion involves damage in or near the cerebral cortex of the dominant hemisphere and its site determines the precise nature of the defect. There are two main categories of aphasia. In motor or expressive aphasia, patients are able to formulate their ideas but cannot choose the correct words or sentence construction. Speech, as a result, is slow, hesitant and staccato. The lesion in motor aphasia is in Broca's area of the premotor cortex. In sensory or receptive aphasia the primary problem is a lack of comprehension of speech. The ability to express oneself is also impaired because auditory association is defective. Words are wrongly used or inverted and sentences are poorly constructed with many errors. However, the flow of speech is preserved, unlike motor aphasia. The lesion is in the auditory association area of the first temporal convolution of the dominant hemisphere (Wernicke's area). Other forms of aphasia include pure word deafness (subcorticol auditory aphasia) and nominal aphasia, in which the principal difficulty lies in calling up names at will.

Apraxia refers to an inability to carry out purposive voluntary actions in the absence of paresis, incoordination, sensory loss or involuntary movement disorders (Ajuriagnerra and Tissot, 1969). In the great majority of cases it is associated with aphasia. In ideomotor apraxia patients cannot perform simple movements when requested to do so, although they fully understand the instructions. The lesion is usually in the parietal lobe of the dominant hemisphere, but in some instances the temporal lobe is involved. In ideational apraxia patients are unable to carry out a sequence of actions, such as striking a match, although they are capable of performing simple movements on request. Again, the pathology is usually in the parietal or temporal lobes of the dominant hemisphere. Dressing apraxia is the term used when patients cannot relate the spatial form of their garments to that of their bodies. It probably is not a distinct entity. Constructional apraxia, manifested by the inability to copy patterns, is broadly synonymous with visuospatial agnosia.

Agnosia is an impaired recognition of an object which is sensorially presented that is not due to sensory defects, mental deterioration, disorder of consciousness and attention, or to non-familiarity (Frederiks, 1969). The concept has been criticized recently as lesions producing restrictive defects of this type are indeed rare. However, agnosias do occur frequently in conjunction with other symptoms and may be grouped in respect to the sensory modality involved, namely, visual, auditory and tactile.

The Gerstmann syndrome results from a lesion in the parietal lobe in the dominant hemisphere. It is said to consist of finger agnosia, right–left disorientation, dyscalculia and dysgraphia. Although the essential clustering of these features to form a syndrome is questionable, the concept has proved useful in pointing to some of the subtle defects that may be found with lesions in the dominant hemisphere.

Psychiatric

The chronic amnestic syndrome or Korsakoff's psychosis is a condition of severe short term memory loss occurring with little other evidence of dementia. It is frequently associated with chronic alcohol abuse, causative of thiamine depletion, and may emerge when an acute delirium of the Wernicke type gradually resolves. The rehabilitation of patients with Korsakoff's psychosis is a major load on psychiatric services.

There are two areas of the brain which are specially important in relation to the amnestic syndrome, namely the hypothalamic–diencephalic region, which is the area predominantly affected by thiamine deficiency, and the hippocampal apparatus. Damage to either has a devastating but selective effect on "the capacity to form durable records of experience" (Lishman, 1978). However, remote memories are largely intact, which suggests that the regions described are not repositories of memory, but serve rather in the process of encoding.

Lesions of the frontal lobe may bring about marked alterations in temperament and behaviour. Disinhibition, fatuous euphoria, lack of spontaneity and initiative and complete lack of concern for others are characteristic features of this type of personality change. Although concentration and the ability to plan are grossly undermined, intellectual function as tested by intelligence test is often surprisingly well preserved. The frontal lobe syndrome is important diagnostically, as the area is relatively "silent" in respect to hard neurological signs. This means that extensive areas of pathology may exist in the frontal regions and present only with insidiously developing changes of personality. Incontinence is the one exception. It is frequently found in the absence of other evidence of neurological disturbance.

Causation

Localized lesions

Focal syndromes are usually caused by localized pathological processes such as vascular lesions, primary or secondary tumours, abscesses or traumatic haematomata. Many of these lesions can be treated surgically, so it is very important that the correct diagnosis is made. The association of the chronic amnestic syndrome with alcohol abuse has already been mentioned. It must be emphasized that in many cases this condition could have been prevented by prescribing high doses of thiamine, administered parenterally, in the presence of Wernicke's encephalopathy.

Reversible dementia

With respect to more generalized dementia, the important task facing the physician is the diagnosis of cases due to reversible causes. Neuronal damage rather than neuronal death accounts for the symptomatology in this group. The following account, aimed at providing a practical guide rather than an exhaustive list, derives largely from notes prepared by our colleague Dr J. Phillips of the Northside Clinic, Sydney.

Psychiatric symptoms are usually present in hypothyroidism and are often the presenting feature of the illness. Lack of initiative and spontaneity, inability to concentrate and a defect in cognition can be demonstrated even in mild cases by appropriate psychological tests. Irritability and excitement may also occur. The classical signs of myxoedema may be minimal, but the condition rapidly responds to appropriate treatment (Beumont, 1979).

Normal pressure hydrocephalus is characterized by progressive dementia, ataxic gait and incontinence. However, this classic triad of symptoms need not always be present. Pathological changes include enlargement of the cerebral ventricles with free communication into the subarachnoid space, but obstruction of cerebrospinal fluid flow into the venous sinuses. It is sometimes related to previous subarachnoid haemorrhage, head trauma or meningitis. The surgical insertion of a ventriculoatrial shunt usually relieves symptoms (Adams, *et al.*, 1965).

Partial occlusion in the extracranial course of the internal carotid artery can have both physical and mental sequelae. As well as neurological symptoms, such as transient hemiparesis or temporary monocular loss of vision, there may be episodes of confusion and a stepwise deterioration in intellectual functioning. Improvement may follow surgical intervention.

A subdural haematoma occasionally presents as dementia. It may result from a minor head injury especially when the patient is elderly. Localizing signs may be minimal and angiography is desirable if there is reason to suspect its presence. Where the haematoma is of recent origin, surgical evacuation can lead to a remission of symptoms. The situation is less hopeful with a chronic haematoma, and in the aged.

Cerebral tumours, including meningioma, may present as dementia. Not uncommonly the surgical removal of a meningioma will bring about a marked improvement in the mental state.

Vitamin B12 deficiency, with or without clinical evidence of megaloblastic anaemia and neurological signs, may be accompanied by deteriorating mental functioning (Shulman, 1967). Characteristically there is memory impairment, increasing difficulty in coping with intellectually demanding tasks and a general disinterest in everyday activities. In a person who has undergone gastric surgery or who has a family history of pernicious anaemia, vitamin B12 deficiency should always be considered.

Pellagra, although rare in this community, does occur among the socially underprivileged, in alcoholics and in people consuming unusual diets. It is caused by a deficiency of niacin or its precursor tryptophan. The characteristic diarrhoea, and dermatitis involving exposed areas, is usually accompanied by apathy and intellectual impairment. The disorder is corrected by a balanced diet.

Cerebral syphilis is a cause of dementia. About 5% of untreated syphilitics develop general paralysis which may become evident years after the initial infection. There is progressive deterioration of mental functions. Typical physical signs include Argyll Robertson pupils, dysarthria, gait disturbance and epileptic seizures. Prompt chemotherapy can lead to recovery.

Other forms of chronic meningitis, meningoencephalitis and brain abscess may masquerade as dementia. Herpes simplex encephalitis occurs sporadically as does tuberculous meningitis.

A syndrome suggestive of dementia occurs in chronic renal failure. Symptoms include deterioration in intellectual functioning, apparent defects of memory and changes in personality, particularly in the direction of excessive fatigability, decreasing concentration and loss of interest and drive. Correction of the renal failure generally leads to improvement.

Psychiatric disorders can present with a dementia-like picture, pseudo-dementia (Kiloh, 1961). Not uncommonly, a patient with severe depression presents in a state of physical and mental dilapidation with apparent evidence of intellectual deterioration. A past history of affective illness, or a fairly rapid onset of symptoms, point towards depression which usually remits with antidepressant medication or electrotherapy.

The Ganser syndrome is a pseudo-dementia characterized by the giving of absurd or approximate answers to simple questions. There is some concomitant clouding of consciousness. It may be associated with head injury, or functional psychiatric illness (Whitlock, 1967).

The conscious feigning of dementia is uncommon, but worth keeping in mind, especially if there is a question of compensation.

Irreversible dementias in middle age

In irreversible dementias neuronal death has occurred. Consequently there is a disruption of brain anatomy, if only at a histological level.

Carbon monoxide poisoning, sometimes the result of a failed suicide attempt, may result in dementia.

Dementia accompanying parkinsonism is often recorded. There is a positive correlation between the prevalence of mental defects and the duration and severity of the illness. Cerebral atrophy probably underlies the mental changes (Mindham, 1974).

Intellectual deterioration ranging from mild to severe is found in up to two-thirds of all people suffering from multiple sclerosis. The degree of mental incapacity correlates with the extent of physical impediment (Surridge, 1969).

Degenerative diseases are important causes of presenile dementia. Alzheimer's disease is the most common. Although the onset of the disease is insidious, once established the course is rapidly progressive. Paranoid ideation and speech difficulties may be the first features noted. Neurological signs and seizures may occur. Dementia is soon apparent and increases until the patient leads a vegetative existence. The pathology is characteristic with neurofibrillary tangles, generalized fall-out of cortical neurones and the development of plaques. The condition is familial and women are affected more commonly than men.

Pick's disease is rarer than Alzheimer's disease. It is said to be characterized by so-called 'frontal lobe' signs–general coarsening of personality with breakthrough of uninhibited and inappropriate behaviour. It is a familial disorder with more women affected than men.

Jakob-Creutzfeldt disease is a rare, rapidly expanding dementia accompanied by numerous neurological abnormalities. Of diagnostic significance are myoclonic jerks, but there may be wide-ranging problems including blindness, deafness and hemiplegia. The illness is rapidly progressive and the patient is soon bedridden and decerebrate. There is evidence to suggest that a slow virus is the cause.

Huntington's chorea is characterized by a combination of advancing dementia and episodic involuntary choreiform movements. It is inherited as an autosomal dominant gene and therefore approximately half the members of an affected family will eventually manifest the illness. Prodromal signs of importance are an unusual 'peppery' personality and the development of paranoid symptoms.

Dementia in the elderly

The usual age of onset of arteriosclerotic dementia (multi-infarct dementia) is in the sixties, but it may occur earlier. In a large proportion of cases, there is a history of hypertension, and symptoms of giddiness, headache, palpitations and momentary 'blackouts' are frequently noted. A number of strokes may precede the dementia. Neurological signs such as transient hemiparesis, aphasia or visual field defects are pointers of importance. The dementia follows a fluctuating course and is commonly accompanied by periods of delirium and intermittent epileptic seizures. Emotional lability is sometimes a striking feature. Retention of insight if often marked, leading to periods of pessimism and depression.

It is estimated that over 4% of people over the age of 65 suffer from senile dementia (Kay, *et al.*, 1962). The pathology appears to be identical to that of Alzheimer's disease in middle age. Senile dementia is characterized by a gradual and steady deterioration of memory, intellect and personality. Its course may be punctuated by episodes of acute delirium, especially if the patient suffers an infection or fracture. The incidence of the illness increases steadily with age and commonly affects more than one member of a family. The advance of the disorder is inexorable and patients finally retain few features of their previous personality. They will eventually become incontinent and bedridden and the usual cause of death is intercurrent infection.

Treatment

In irreversible dementias, much can still be done to minimize the discomfort of patients and their families. Supportive psychotherapy is important. Both patient and family need the opportunity to talk about the problem. Gradually, they may accept advice as to how patients' day-to-day activities need to be altered so as to cause them the minimum distress. Encouragement of a fairly strict daily routine enables many patients to stay at home or with relatives until relatively late in the course of the illness. Overstimulation should be avoided. Anxiety and guilt on the part of the family will inevitably arise, and need sympathetic handling. When patients become bed-ridden or incontinent, or when serious medical or psychiatric complications arise, they should be admitted to hospital.

Concomitant depression, agitation and nocturnal wandering are common problems. Administration of drugs is best avoided, but if necessary a small dose of a major tranquillizer such as chlorpromazine may be used. Occasionally disinhibited behaviour may cause serious embarrassment and the therapist is called upon to intervene tactfully so as to prevent an over-reaction on the part of the family.

NON-SPECIFIC PRESENTATIONS

Although delirium and dementia are the characteristic clinical pictures resulting from organic brain disease, other types of presentation may occur. This fact has long been recognized, but the recent *Diagnostic and Statistical Manual of Mental Disorders* (DSM III) of the American Psychiatric Association (1980) has emphasized the point by offering diagnostic criteria for a number of additional "organic" syndromes.

In the organic delusional syndrome, the essential feature is the presence of delusions in a state of clear consciousness and associated with known brain disease. Organic hallucinosis is characterized by persistent or recurrent hallucinations, in any modality of sensation, again in clear consciousness but in the absence of predominant delusions. Evidence of associated brain damage should be present. In the organic affective syndrome, the predominant disturbance is one of mood, in the absence of clouding of consciousness, dementia, delusions or hallucinations, together with evidence of a specific organic factor considered to be causative of the disorder.

The organic personality syndrome involves similar restrictions. The characteristic personality change may be of various types, for example, emotional lability, impairment in impulse control, apathy and indifference or suspiciousness and paranoid ideation.

Whether it is really necessary to define these types of organic syndromes with operational criteria remains in dispute. Nevertheless, it serves to remind the clinician that symptoms of this kind can in fact result from organic brain diseases. The complacent acceptance of a functional aetiology in illnesses presenting with symptoms of personality change, mood disturbance, delusions or hallucinations has led too frequently in the past to inadequate physical investigation and inappropriate management, with tragic consequences.

EPILEPSY

Epilepsy may be defined as "a paroxysmal and transitory disturbance of brain function which develops suddenly, ceases spontaneously, and exhibits a conspicuous tendency to recurrence" (Brain, 1955). It is associated with neuronal hypersynchronous overactivity in electrophysiological terms.

There are two major forms of epilepsy.

Generalized Epilepsy

Generalized epilepsy derives from a disturbance in the subcortical structures of the brain, from whence the discharge spreads rapidly to all areas of the cortex. It is essentially a benign albeit persistent illness of unknown aetiology with an onset usually in the first or second decade of life. The episodic attacks take the form of either grand mal or petit mal.

In a grand mal convulsion there is, at best, a very brief period of warning. Patients then lose consciousness and fall to the ground. Their muscles go into a phase of tonic or constant contraction followed by a phase of clonic contractions (powerful jerk-like movements). During the fall they frequently sustain some injury, may bite their tongue or be incontinent. The fit passes over in a few minutes and a stage of confusion ensues which generally goes on to a deep sleep.

Petit mal usually occurs in children, is always of subcortical origin, and is associated with a typical electroencephalographic pattern of bilateral synchronous spike and wave complexes. The actual fit consists of three different types of phenomena, alone or in combination. The commonest is an "absence" or momentary loss of consciousness. The second is an akinetic seizure, in which there is profound and generalized muscular relaxation so that the patient drops to the ground. The third is the occurrence of generalized myoclonic jerks, sudden shock-like movements lasting only a fraction of a second. These three are referred to as the petit mal triad.

Most cases of petit mal cease in adolescence. In some patients, the condition persists into adult life, or may change form to that of grand mal.

Although most patients with generalized epilepsy have no psychiatric illness, the prevalence of psychiatric disturbance is higher in an epileptic population than in an equivalent non-epileptic group. There are both psychological and organic reasons why this should be so. Unfortunately epilepsy remains a condition of considerable social stigma. Furthermore, it is an unpredictable illness necessitating some restriction of the patient's activities. These features lead to a lowering of self-esteem and psychogenic reactions. The recurrence of fits, and perhaps even more the constant use of anticonvulsant medication, may have an adverse effect of cognitive functioning. Neurotic disorders, personality disturbance, and mild cognitive impairment may result from a combination of these adverse influences.

Focal Epilepsy

Focal epilepsy is due to discharges from an area of damaged cortex with onset usually in middle or late life. Focal epilepsies are characterized by aural phenomena, which may or may not proceed to a grand mal convulsion. The ultimate prognosis is that of the underlying pathology.

Aural phenomena are the symptoms and signs which result from disturbed brain function at the site of the focus. Their nature is determined by its precise location. The phenomena may be elementary or complex. An example of elementary aural phenomena is the Jacksonian "march", a progression of muscular contractions that, for example, starts with the fingers and then spreads to the hand, wrist, forearm and eventually the whole quarter, and which results from a lesion in the motor cortex. A grand mal convulsion may or may not ensue.

Limbic Epilepsy

Complex aural phenomena result from foci within the limbic region. Temporal lobe epilepsy is in fact the most common variety of focal epileptic disorder, and is usually due to sclerosis in the area of Ammons horn consequent upon a hypoxic episode during infancy (Falconer, 1974). Such foci are demonstrable with elaborate and careful electroencephalographic investigation, which is extremely fortunate as the symptomatology is at times difficult to distinguish from that of functional psychiatric illnesses.

In addition to the increased susceptibility to psychiatric disturbance noted in epileptic patients in general, those with temporal lobe or limbic epilepsy often present other mental symptoms that are more directly related to their actual disorder.

The aural symptoms of limbic epilepsy often take the form of a disturbance of mental functioning. With foci on the medial aspect of the temporal lobe there may be: alterations in mood (anxiety, irritability, depression or even elation); visceral, olfactory and gustatory hallucinations; distortions of memory known as *déjà vu* and *déjà vécu* experiences; depersonalization; and various perceptual abnormalities such as micropsia and macropsia. In cases where the focus is on the lateral aspect of the temporal lobe, auditory and visual hallucinations of a complex but stereotyped nature are found. Patients sometimes report that the hallucinatory experience is clearly familiar, but that they are unable to recall what it is. These various anomalies, due to a disruption of brain function at the site of the focus, may progress to a grand mal convulsion as the electrical disturbance spreads over the cortex. On the other hand, the fit may be aborted and no convulsion occurs. In the latter case, the symptoms may be confused with those of a functional psychiatric illness such as schizophrenia unless the examiner pays careful attention to the repetitive and stereotyped nature of the phenomena.

Aural symptoms are part of the epileptic process and are associated with electroencephalographic changes. They must be distinguished from the prodromal phase of epilepsy, namely, the vague feeling of anxiety and malaise that may be present for some days before an attack and which is terminated once a convulsion occurs. The pathogenesis of the prodromata is not understood and they are not accompanied by changes in the electroencephalogram.

Alterations in consciousness, short of a grand mal convulsion, also occur in limbic epilepsy, with or without preceding aural symptoms. A psychomotor attack or "complex partial seizure" is a period of impaired awareness, lasting for seconds or minutes, during which patients do not know where they are or what they are doing. Strange and even violent behaviour, for which there is no subsequent recall, may occur during these states of so-called "epileptic equivalence". Longer periods of clouding of consciousness or delirium, often associated with disturbances of mood (anger, excitement or apathy), hallucinations and impulsive, reckless behaviour, are known as twilight states or epileptic fugues and appear to be due to a persistent epileptic discharge, similar to status epilepticus.

Personality disturbance is common in patients with temporal lobe epilepsy. Blunting of emotion, intellectual slowing, circumstantiality, hypocritical religiosity, querulousness, intolerance of frustration and outbursts of violent and aggressive behaviour have all been noted (Bingley, 1958). It is not clear whether these features are causally related to the epilepsy itself or whether other factors such as the use of drugs and chronic institutionalization are involved.

Schizophrenia occurs in a high proportion of patients with temporal lobe epilepsy and there appears to be some causal relationship between the two conditions in these cases. The usual familial loading is not present, the psychotic symptoms occur about 15 years after the onset of epilepsy, the clinical picture is that of a paranoid schizophrenia with little affective disturbance and no evidence of intellectual deterioration, and the prognosis tends to be better—all these features suggest that the schizophrenic illness associated with temporal lobe epilepsy is a distinct entity, probably a direct result of the brain lesion (Slater, *et al.*, 1963).

During twilight states and fugues, some patients engage in antisocial, violent or criminal activities. However, the association is far less common than was previously believed as surveys from Scandinavian countries have shown (Lishman, 1978). Unfortunately these surveys were largely confined to patients attending hospitals or clinics, and epileptic subjects who were not being treated were inevitably omitted. Gunn (1969) approached the problem from a different perspective. He surveyed the inmates of prisons and borstals in England and Wales and found that the proportion of epileptic subjects in this population was disproportionately high. Therefore it does seem that epilepsy does have some relationship to criminal behaviour—or at least to conviction—though the reason why this should be is by no means clear.

CONCLUSION

The psychiatric manifestation of organic brain disease are many and varied. They constitute a major part of psychiatric and indeed of general medical practice. Knowledge of their symptomatology and expertise in their management are necessary accomplishments for all medical practitioners and for all clinical psychologists.

There are four major conditions which account for most cases of serious organic brain disease in our communities. In young adults, the long term effects of head injury are most important. Motor vehicle accidents, which are the most common cause of death in the 15–40 years age group in countries such as Australia and the United States, are also the most frequent cause of severe and irreversible brain damage in this age group.

In middle age, the effects of alcohol abuse are predominant. Thirty per cent of all patients in a general hospital have a problem with alcohol according to a recent survey undertaken in Sydney (Williams, *et al.*, 1978). A proportion of these will eventually develop the dysmnesic syndrome or Korsakoff's psychosis.

Multi-infarct dementia is associated with other evidence of vascular disease and occurs particularly in late middle age and the senium. Even more common is senile dementia, Alzheimer's type, which affects an increasing proportion of people aged over 65 years. As the number of elderly people in our community increases so do the number of cases of senile dementia, placing an increasing load on geriatric services. The health professional of the future will need to be equipped to deal with this problem.

It is you who has got to do the running. Some people are always wanting to buy from the chemist, or seller of dreams, a little gadget for making talent or genius. Poor fools! Nothing exists except what is deep within us, and the modulor only does the housework—no more. Which is a great deal!

Le Corbusier

3 Development of Test Batteries

THIS CHAPTER surveys the evolution of the test battery approach in neuropsychological assessment and reviews the recent plethora of validity studies concerning this technique. The inherent difficulties in researching complex brain–behaviour variables are also briefly acknowledged. Within this broad historical review of half a century of clinical research, a contemporary perspective is taken by specifically describing current test battery revision at Royal Prince Alfred Hospital, Sydney. The specific battery described in this volume is one of the outcomes of this revision.

Although Halstead's specific tests are fated to be eventually replaced and/or modified by advances in psychology, his conceptual framework and descriptive tradition remain a viable core entity for the forseeable future. The specific battery described in this volume exemplifies a particularly cost-effective multimodal approach to a psychologist's routine "housework" and remains within the well validated conceptual framework of the Halstead–Reitan tradition. This well documented tradition is the focus of concern in this chapter.

Further studies on the validity of the psychological and neuropsychological procedures which make up the test battery approach are reported in separate chapters dealing with guides to the assessment and description of neuropsychological behavioural patterns within specific patient populations (children, medico-legal, psychiatric and neurological). It is worthwhile to discuss the implications of batteries in detail at the risk of reiteration because of the entrenched stereotypes that abound in this area.

EVOLUTION OF TEST BATTERIES

Basic research and clinical research in human neuropsychology have evolved in a remarkably parallel manner, perhaps because both areas of inquiry potentiate each other. For example, in the 1930s Hebb (1945) began collaborating with Penfield at the Montreal Neurological Institute and laid the foundations of Milner's (1975) flourishing basic research programmes. Halstead opened his own neuropsychology laboratory at the University of Chicago in 1935 and inspired almost half a century of applied research on the test battery approach by Reitan (1966) and others, research which is vigorously continuing.

Halstead was interested in documenting the effects of cerebral dysfunction on a broad range of human behaviour. He undertook both naturalistic observations and experimental measures in the search for tests that were sensitive to the psychological effects of brain lesions. Hundreds of tests were developed and discarded during exhaustive field trials. Factor analytic methods developed by both Spearman and Thurstone were applied to the data generated from such tests in order to identify the best available procedures for neuropsychological testing (Halstead, 1947).

Halstead recognized that the vast range of psychological abilities controlled by cerebral functions could not be monitored by a single test. Consequently, he developed a broad spectrum of measures designed to sample a comprehensive range of brain functions. These tests were also sensitive to a variety of more specific cerebral lesions. Halstead published some of these tests in his seminal work, *Brain and Intelligence: A Quantitative Study of the Frontal Lobes* (1947).

Halstead's student, Reitan, began his neuropsychological research in his teacher's laboratory, later leaving to establish his own at the Indiana University Medical Centre in 1951. Reitan (1955) was the first person to validate a comprehensive neuropsychological battery for the identification of cerebral dysfunction. The results of all tests in his battery (except the critical flicker–fusion test) provided a means of distinguishing brain damaged subjects from non-brain damaged subjects. During the following 30 years Reitan revised, modified and expanded Halstead's original battery, validated two batteries for children, and made a great contribution to research on the differential effects of brain lesions. The Halstead–Reitan neuropsychological test battery (HRNTB) is dealt with in detail in the text published by Reitan and Davison (1974).

The seminal contributions of Halstead and Reitan have resulted in the acceptance of the test battery approach as the most widely used neuropsychological assessment technique throughout the United States and the world, including the People's Republic of China (Doerr and Storrie, 1982). Its impact is exemplified by the enormous amount of research that it has generated, documented in prestigious medical and psychological journals. More than half of the clinical psychology programmes in United States universities have courses for students on how to use the HRNTB. Also, the test battery approach is commonly used in the teaching of interns in clinical psychology.

A selective review of the more established United States clinical neuropsychology laboratories by Mathews (1981) shows that most use the HRNTB as a core approach together with allied procedures. Each laboratory surveyed adapts the battery to meet the unique patterns of its own referral sources in a remarkable variety of ways. Such flexibility of application rejects the common stereotype that "laboratories making some use of Halstead-Reitan procedures necessarily operate in an orthodox, rigid manner, applying a single, fixed battery and a set of interpretative principles handed down once and forever (on tablets of stone) from a mountain top in Central Indiana *circa* the year of our Lord, 1955. Such a stereotype is a serious disservice to Reitan and to those who make use of some of the tests he developed and validated" (Mathews, 1981: 647). In fact, the Halstead-Reitan methodology is heterogeneous, as noted by Reitan and Davison (1974), with 12 test batteries and 15 other allied procedures being commonly employed within the clinical setting.

VALIDITY STUDIES

A vast number of studies assessing the value of the Halstead-Reitan neuropsychological test battery (HRNTB) and the allied psychological and neuropsychological procedures has been amassed during almost 30 years of validation research. Validity studies performed before 1974, and supporting the HRNTB specifically, are summarized by Reitan and Davison (1974). Hevern (1980) provides the best available recent commentary on the Halstead-Reitan literature in a review which assessed a comprehensive and representative sample of 50 studies of the core HRNTB with its allied procedures (either partly or fully administered in a loosely organized way to either adults or children) spanning the period 1974 to 1979. Hevern (1980) also elaborated upon the implications of the methodological recommendations of Parsons and Prigatano (1978) when doing neuropsychological research. Some of the more significant studies of the voluminous literature reviewed by Reitan and Davison (1974) and Hevern (1980) are listed below.

Subject-Examiner Variables

The Halstead-Reitan studies share similar complex methodological challenges with most of the published neuropsychological literature. Parsons and

Prigatano (1978) emphasized the importance of the five commonly neglected variables in validation research: (i) age; (ii) education; (iii) sex; (iv) socioeconomic status, including race; and (v) examiner characteristics. These factors must also be taken into account when interpreting test results during clinical practice.

The age of subjects is a variable which significantly influences neuropsychological test performance, yet 22 per cent of Halstead–Reitan studies display a disregard for this factor. Also, there is a bias towards the 25- to 55-year-old age group with a particular neglect of younger and older subjects. For example, 74 per cent of Halstead–Reitan studies dealt with this age range and only four per cent assessed older adults. Consequently, valid norms are suspect or non-existent for young children and geriatric patients. The differentiation between organic and mental disorders continues to be a major problem partly because of a lack of age-related norms for perceptual and cognitive performance. This is particularly important as a high proportion of referrals for the screening of dementia tend to be in the older age ranges.

Many neuropsychological studies including the Halstead–Reitan investigations tend not to report the educational level of selected subjects. There is no doubt that cognitive test performance is related to educational level in normal subjects, but the literature is equivocal regarding the effect of years of schooling in brain damaged patients. For example, Prigatano and Parsons (1976) found that educational achievement was not significantly related to the test performance of brain damaged persons. This study was cross-validated by Finlayson, Johnson and Reitan (1977). Thus neuropsychological techniques may be better able to identify cerebral dysfunction independent of educational level than is commonly thought.

The potential impact of sex as a subject variable has been largely ignored in the neuropsychological literature. Sex differences are most evident on the gross strength monitors of neuropsychological functioning. Unfortunately, valid norms are lacking for females as they are for the other relatively neglected populations of young children and geriatric patients.

The close relationship between socioeconomic and educational status suggests that these variables should be taken into account when assessing their possible effect upon the performance. The impact of vocational level, and ethnic and racial differences is usually ignored in neuropsychological research. Perhaps, as for educational level, the racial factor may be a relatively independent variable in the identification of brain damage, but this hypothesis has never been explored.

Examiner variables can be important in that, obviously, incompetent examiners may fail to elicit a maximal performance in patients with a resultant lack of valid test results. Consequently, researchers should document both the extent of training of their test administrators and the degree of co-operation of the subjects concerned. These variables are rarely cited in the literature.

The five validation issues reported above appear to be more of a problem where academic researchers (who perhaps have limited clinical experience) are concerned and have less effect upon the results obtained by experienced clinicians working daily with patients. During clinical work, premorbid factors such as education, intelligence, sex, socioeconomic status and other baseline data are routinely taken into account before the clinician attempts to interpret test scores. Also, as with computers, "garbage in means garbage out" is the first consideration of supervisors when assessing the validity of neuropsychological test scores obtained by trainees working with potentially unmotivated patients. More importantly, the concerns of Parsons and Prigatano (1978) are limited to the level of performance inferential technique. However, this is the least powerful of the four methods of inference typically used in test interpretation. For example, a lack of group norms (for age, education, sex, socioeconomic status and race) is irrelevant in such inferential methods as comparison of the performance of two sides of the body wherein the individual serves as their own control. Reitan (1964) dramatizes the significance of multiple inferential methods in successfully yielding remarkably specific neurological diagnostic validity in contrast to the lack of clinical utility resulting from group statistical procedures based upon level of performance alone.

The validity of the test battery approach when used in clinical practice tends to be greater than when used in academic research. Most research studies still rely solely upon the level of performance as the sole mode of inference. In contrast, during clinical practice premorbid factors are routinely taken into account and the four modes of multiple inference (to be described later) are applied. Also, test scores are not interpreted "blind" during clinical practice. Rather, the rest of the patient's data base gives meaning to quantitative measures. Moreover, the clinician has the opportunity to continue to treat the patient after assessment and this fosters "growing recognition of the unique dynamics of discrete evolving and resolving neuropathologic[al] processes" (Smith, 1979:237). Such feedback serves as a corrective to the initial interpretation of test scores and is perhaps the most important, but least acknowledged, available research procedure. Consequently, the academic literature documenting the validity of the Halstead–Reitan approach is all the more remarkable in the absence of long-term clinical feedback and contextual data that provide more meaning to test scores.

Differential Diagnostic Validity

As mentioned previously, Reitan (1955) was the first to validate the neuropsychological test battery approach. Wheeler, Burke and Reitan (1963) demonstrated that a composite score derived from weighted test scores was able to differentiate control subjects from all other categories of brain damage with a high degree of accuracy.

Such results have been repeatedly cross-validated. Wheeler and Reitan (1963) showed that the cross-validation accuracy rate approximated 80 per cent between control subjects and subjects in all other brain damaged subgroups. An additional cross-validation study by Vega and Parsons (1967) reported a 73 per cent accuracy rate in assigning patients correctly to their diagnostic groups. Kiernan and Mathews (1976) showed that the results of neuropsychological tests were able to be used to differentiate between patients with cerebral lesions and those with signs of brain damage, but without neurological evidence of cerebral dysfunction (84 per cent correct classification rate).

Spreen and Benton (1965) showed that the proportion of accurate identification of severity and laterality of brain lesions derived from the results of neuropsychological tests ranged from 71 per cent to 90 per cent and these statistics compared favourably with those reported by other neurological diagnostic techniques. These results were cross-validated by Filskov and Goldstein (1974). They demonstrated the actuarial ability of neuropsychological test results to identify the presence, lateralization and process of cerebral dysfunction in a manner congruent with the results of other neurodiagnostic procedures (X-ray examination, angiography, etc.). Mean hit rates for accurate diagnosis of lateralization and process by the HRNTB fell at the 0.80 level. Goldstein, *et al.* (1973) showed that even inexperienced testers using the HRNTB were more successful in identifying the presence of cerebral dysfunction than more experienced colleagues using less specific tools from traditional clinical psychology.

Golden (1976) reported accuracy hit rates of more than 0.90 for presence of brain damage, 0.97 for left laterality and less than 0.60 for right laterality when patients with such neurological disorders were compared with non-brain damaged control subjects. Golden (1977) also applied a discriminant function analysis to differentiate brain damaged patients from psychiatric (mainly schizophrenic) patients using the HRNTB and the Wechsler adult intelligence scale (WAIS) in combination. He documented a hit rate of 1.0 for psychiatric patients and of 0.94 for brain damaged patients, and a lateralization of impairment rate ranging from 0.91 to 1.0.

Independent studies in various "neuropsychological laboratories in Wisconsin (Mathews, *et al.*, 1966), British Columbia (Klonoff, *et al.*, 1970), Oregon (Goldstein, *et al.*, 1973), and St Louis (Schreiver, *et al.*, 1976) have confirmed the statistical and clinical validity and utility of these procedures in the hands of well trained neuropsychologists" (Boll, 1981: 598).

Adequate validity implies the probability of reliability. Matarazzo and his associates (1976) have investigated the reliability of neuropsychological test batteries within the context of changes in the disease process of patients and practice effects. Their findings documented impressive reliability for neuropsychological techniques, even when used with heterogeneous groups of patients.

Subgroup Behavioural Patterns

Specific subgroups of brain damaged patients demonstrate differential behaviour patterns on the HRNTB. For example, those with Huntington's disease display impaired motor and psychomotor skills together with some deterioration of higher cognitive functions (Hevern, 1980).

Selz and Reitan (1979) note that learning disabled children resemble normal children in their adequate performance for motor tests, but they resemble brain damaged children when they are tested for cognitive and attentional tasks. Selz and Reitan (1979) hypothesize that learning disability may suggest a degree of cerebral dysfunction which can be monitored by neuropsychological tests, but which often cannot be elicited from clinical neurological examination. Because of the heterogeneous aspects of learning disability and its undocumented aetiology no firm conclusions can be made about the alleged nature of the cerebral dysfunction involved.

The behavioural patterns of various types of alcohol abusers on the HRNTB are equivocal and require further research. However, chronic alcohol abuse is associated with diffuse cognitive deterioration. As regards other drugs, Fields and Fullerton (1975) were unable to isolate a drug effect upon schizophrenic HRNTB performance with the administration of either chlorpromazine or perphenazine.

Patients with multiple sclerosis demonstrate characteristic performance patterns on the HRNTB which differentiate them from persons with other types of brain damage and psychiatric syndromes. They will show unstable sensory-motor symptoms, deficits in performance IQ and will have abnormal results for finger-tapping and other sensory-motor tests.

It is encouraging that a quantitatively oriented test battery can yield meaningful descriptions of independently well documented syndromes. The obtaining of detailed descriptions of neuropsychological test performance from different categories of patients appears to be a productive area of research within the test battery approach.

CONCEPTUAL FRAMEWORK

Paradoxically, the most productive mode of introducing a conceptual framework for the test battery approach is a negative one—that is, to define what it is not! This dispels some archaic concepts still appearing in the literature of the 1980s. For example, Rathbun and Smith (1982) were moved to reiterate warnings against the use of any single test in screening for brain damage: "Any single test for 'brain damage' reflects a widespread inherent assumption not only that 'brain damage' is a unitary disorder but that once brain damaged, always brain damaged" (Rathbun and Smith, 1982:281).

Modern medicine never relies upon any single diagnostic tool to the exclusion of others. For example, the physical neurodiagnostic strategy is an integrated step-by-step broad spectrum approach able to cast a wide net of specific and sometimes overlapping techniques in order to obtain a comprehensive understanding of both structural and functional problems. Indirect psychological tools which monitor complex cerebral functions require at least as comprehensive an approach as that utilized by the more direct interventions of diagnostic neurology.

The naïve concept of brain damage as a unitary disorder which can be assessed in an all-or-none fashion by a unidimensional test is moribund. The uselessness of the unitary scheme is a very good reason for the popularity of the test battery approach. Human behaviour, especially cognitive functioning, involves the interaction of multiple modalities or functional categories. Consequently, comprehensive assessment and treatment in clinical psychology requires a multimodal perspective (Lazarus, 1981).

The movement away from discrete "either–or" diagnostic labels for brain damage in favour of detailed descriptions of varied behavioural patterns and profiles possibly related to cerebral dysfunction has brought about the eclipse of the formerly influential concept of an "impairment index". The impairment index is computed from test scores and symbolizes the degree of general neuropsychological impairment. Such a gross summary score masks and averages out the very differential brain–behaviour patterns that are of most interest to clinicians.

The advances of technology ensure that a static battery permanently programmed with unchangeable tests cannot be crystallized. Any particular battery is an experiment in progress. As recently as 10 years ago, Reitan and Davison (1974) noted the use of 12 test batteries and 15 other allied procedures by their associates. Mathews (1981) notes that most neuropsychological laboratories use test batteries in a fluid and dynamic way rather than in a stereotyped, mechanical manner.

Despite the open-ended, creative, clinical application of this loosely organized, albeit well validated, set of allied test procedures, a coherent conceptual framework exists. The following core orienting concepts have their genesis in the contributions of Halstead (1947) and Reitan (1955):

A. A neuropsychological test battery must be comprehensive.
B. It should also yield differential descriptive patterns and profiles of brain–behaviour relationships.
C. It needs to be amenable to valid neuropsychological inferences and interpretations.
D. A seemingly paradoxical balance needs to be struck between standardization and open-endedness.
E. An atheoretical stance with a reliance upon technical eclecticism continues to be an advantage.

A useful clinical analogy may be drawn between the neuropsychological test battery approach and the widely used multimodal therapy of Lazarus (1981) in clinical psychology in order to help generalist psychologists more appreciate the five core concepts above.

Lazarus (1981) emphasizes the advantages of flexibility and maintenance of an atheoretical stance toward both therapeutic techniques and personality theories. His system of intervention monitors the full range of human functioning. He divides such functions into seven convenient modalities represented by the acronym BASIC ID which stands for: *b*ehaviour; *a*ffect; *s*ensation; *i*magery; *c*ognition; *i*nterpersonal relations; and *d*rugs and somatic functioning. Because human beings function holistically, most patients tend to have overlapping problems. A clinical assessment which does not survey the full range of modalities may omit crucial problem areas.

Lazarus (1981) is also committed to technical eclecticism. Although he is primarily a behavioural therapist, he finds no conflict in applying any other techniques (psychoanalysis, etc.) which might help the patient. Comprehensive behavioural assessment yields a modality profile. Specific problems are indexed to the pertinent modality, with specific treatments cross-indexed to such problems.

After a standardized general assessment of the seven modalities of functioning, Lazarus (1981) makes a further, more focused, investigation of any modality where there is a problem. Lazarus refers to this as a second order analysis. The focus is microscopic in contrast to the basic analysis in which there is a macroscopic assessment of human behaviour. The depth and detail of such specific analyses can be extended to an infinite degree and are only limited by the level of the clinician's training and experience.

The initial focus of concern for the neuropsychologist is Lazarus' seventh (somatic) modality under which brain functions are conveniently categorized. The clinical neuropsychologist studies the way in which cerebral dysfunction relates to the other six remaining modalities. As an executive organ, the brain influences sensory-motor, visuo-spatial, language, memory and higher cognitive functions as well as the other psychological modalities. In Lazarus' terms, the comprehensive test battery technique may be interpreted as a multimodal assessment of brain damage.

Multimodal assessment implies multimodal treatment. The test battery approach is uniquely compatible with this applied emphasis as it yields a neuropsychological profile of strengths and deficits to which specific treatments may be logically cross-indexed. Thinking in terms of functional categories provides an artificial, although clinically heuristic, schema for ordering complex data. The same concern for integrating information into a logically continuous entity is the basis of the problem-oriented medical record approach (Gilandas, 1972).

Cerebral dysfunction can cause a wide range of behavioural disruption. Thus, comprehensive neuropsychological assessment involves an evaluation of the complete range of brain-related functional categories. A narrowed approach may omit vital areas associated with cerebral deficit. Reitan (1966) suggests that our techniques ideally should be as complicated and sophisticated as the brain itself.

Comprehensive assessment not only facilitates the detailed description of deficits but also documents residual strengths. Intact areas of functioning provide a meaningful context for estimating the real life significance of identified deficits. For example, to focus solely upon reported instances of specific learning disability in such eminent men as Leonardo da Vinci and Albert Einstein whilst ignoring their genius would be an absurd approach to understanding the whole person. To borrow Smith's (1979: 233) phrase, this would be "focusing on the hole rather than the doughnut". Clinicians are prone to what Kaplan (1967) called "a trained incapacity". Trained to recognize deficits, there is a difficulty in recognizing adaptive behaviour.

Although the prime goal of both Halstead and Reitan was descriptive rather than diagnostic *per se,* their batteries have validated, differential, diagnostic validity. This is due to the inclusion of tests that are highly sensitive to specific as well as general deficits. Such a combination of tests tends to yield differential profiles of brain–behaviour relationships.

Brain damaged individuals are not a homogeneous group. Thus, neuropsychological profiles need to be formed from a pattern of scores differentially obtained from characteristic clinical subgroups. This approach not only implies study of the levels of performance but also emphasizes a description of differential pattern of strengths and deficits. It is necessary to realize that a battery which is sensitive to developmental problems such as learning disabilities at one time may need to be modified at a later stage of a child's development. This results from changes in cognitive function associated with the plasticity of the maturing brain.

Specific tests can only be usefully included in a test battery if they are amenable to valid neuropsychological inferences and interpretations. Tests that can be evaluated by multiple inferential techniques contribute validity and cost-efficiency to a battery. Reitan's four inferential methods (level of performance; pattern of performance; specific behavioural deficits or pathognomonic signs; and comparison of performance of the two sides of the body) have been described by Boll (1978) and are discussed in Chapter 6.

Though standardized test batteries facilitate valid and reliable assessment, the procedures are used in an open-ended, dynamic manner. For example, Halstead and Reitan developed, then discarded, hundreds of tests during their careers. This exhaustive process continues to characterize the diverse work of most neuropsychology laboratories. All tests have a limited lifespan. They are ultimately replaced or modified by advances in technology. Thus, it is unlikely that the specific tests described in this volume, in contrast to the conceptual framework of the test battery approach, will have a lifespan of more than one decade. Revision of content and norms is inevitable.

A computer analogy illustrates the relationship between the relatively permanent conceptual (albeit atheoretical) structure of the test battery approach and the interchangeable tests which compose it. The *Oxford English Dictionary* defines a computer as "one who computes", and to compute as the process of reckoning. Thus, computing implies structured thinking in the human. A mechanical computer is an apparatus for performing computations electronically according to stored instructions called a program. The comprehensive test battery approach, as a conceptual framework for data processing, is a strategy for structuring and improving the quality of human thinking. The specific tests that are chosen to program a particular battery allow this conceptual structure to function. They can be symbolized as software, and should be immediately replaced as better test programs become available. Advances in technology promise fully automated computer-compatible electronic test batteries which can be tailored to respond immediately to clinical presentations.

The conceptual framework of the test battery approach relies upon technological strategies rather than theories. Such an atheoretical stance, with reliance upon technical eclecticism, has many advantages. There is danger inherent in total dependence upon one school of thought, even one as promising as Luria's, as such dependence may prove to be the means to a dead end.

The empirical orientation of the test battery approach allows the incorporation of any technique which proves to be useful, whatever its theoretical origin. Lazarus (1971) has suggested that a methodology is often effective for reasons which are at variance with the beliefs of its originators. Technical electicism does not suggest a random collection of techniques. Instead it facilitates experimentation with empirically useful methods rather than relying upon certain theoretical pedigrees: "However interesting, plausible, and appealing a theory it may be, it is techniques, not theories, that are actually used on people" (London, 1964: 33).

During the administration of a standard battery there is nothing to stop an experienced clinician pausing and examining any aspect of the patient's functioning according to the qualitative syndrome analysis of Luria if this may be useful. Most batteries contain enough specific test items to incorporate, with adaptation, an infinite variety of hypotheses suggested by the clinician's theoretical orientation. However, less experienced and more conservative examiners gain greater advantage from standardized administration.

The atheoretical approach has a productive history in many areas of both the physical and the social sciences. For example, behaviour therapy (which is, perhaps, more correctly described as antitheoretical than atheoretical) has been a dominant influence in clinical psychology. Its many practical applications, ranging from the precision teaching approach in remediating learning disabilities to biofeedback technologies facilitating voluntary control of the autonomic nervous system, have been widely used. Another example is the most recent (American Psychiatric Association, 1980) edition of the *Diagnostic and Statistical Manual of Mental Disorders* (DSM-III), an atheoretical system for describing and classifying psychiatric syndromes. A third example is the microcomputer, a purely technical atheoretical apparatus used by virtually all disciplines. Of course, philosophers may pedantically attribute an implied theory to all atheoretical systems, but the important point is that hypothesizing is not the main concern of technical eclecticism.

TEST BATTERY REVISION: AN "INSIDE" VIEW

The number of requests for a more personal description of the actual context within which research occurs, and of the day-to-day ebb and flow of the research projects together with subject-examiner variables, has increased (Parsons and Prigatano, 1978; Mathews, 1981). These requests indicate that research technology is not an abstract entity, but is shaped by the needs of the individuals involved and the demands of the clinical environment in which work is performed.

As a demonstration of this we illustrate the vicissitudes involved in refining a cost-efficient neuropsychological test battery, and the context in which such activities occur. Our example, involving the battery described in this volume, is the result of a four year project (1979–1983). Our inquiry may encourage others to construct their own batteries or to revise the one presented in this volume. To encourage further revisions, the following typical steps in refining a battery are outlined—(i) describe the context in which clinical research occurs; (ii) structure a conceptual framework with explicit functional categories; (iii) decide upon test criteria; (iv) arrange a strategy for test selection (literature reviews); and (v) assess tests in combination (with clinical field trials, diagnostic neurological criteria, single blind studies and other statistical treatments).

Royal Prince Alfred Hospital

The Royal Prince Alfred Hospital was opened on September 25, 1882. It was named after Queen Victoria's son, His Royal Highness, Prince Alfred (later Duke of Edinburgh). Prince Alfred was visiting Australia in 1868 and was the victim of an attempted assassination while attending a picnic at Clontarf. A public subscription fund was commenced when the Prince recovered to show the relief of Sydney's citizens. The money gathered went towards the building of the Royal Prince Alfred Hospital.

As the principal teaching hospital for the University of Sydney, the Royal Prince Alfred has continued to grow. The complex now consists of the Royal Prince Alfred Hospital, the King George V Memorial Hospital for Mothers and Babies, the Page Chest Pavilion, the Neurosurgery and Psychiatry Block, the Dame Eadith Walker Convalescent Hospital and the Rivendell Adolescent Unit. The total number of beds exceeds 1500, while the hospital provides a comprehensive diagnostic and treatment service for the Sydney metropolitan area. Specialist services also attract patients from all over Australia and the surrounding Pacific region (New Caledonia, Papua New Guinea, South-east Asia, and the South Pacific islands). The hospital serves a cosmopolitan community. Interpreter services in Italian, Greek, Arabic, Vietnamese, Kampuchean, Laotian, Spanish, Portuguese, Romanian, Armenian, Croatian, Macedonian, Serbian, Slovene and Russian are available daily.

Neuropsychology at Royal Prince Alfred Hospital

The Psychology Unit, in which the Halstead–Reitan approach and allied neuropsychological procedures are dominant interests, is physically housed in the Neurosurgery and Psychiatry Block, but serves the whole hospital.

Suitably qualified hospital psychologists have a joint appointment with the Faculty of Medicine of the University of Sydney as clinical lecturers (part-time). The Faculty of Medicine of the University of Sydney is the biggest medical school in Australasia and among the largest in the English-speaking world.

The Royal Prince Alfred Hospital and the Medical School of the University of Sydney are large, closely integrated units which generate neuropsychological referrals spanning virtually every possible clinical syndrome. Currently, the institutions manifest strong interest in the assessment and remediation of learning disabilities and the application of computer technology. As well, there is a general commitment to refining neuropsychological assessment techniques.

Almost 70 per cent of patients referred for neuropsychological testing come from the departments of neurology and neurosurgery. Approximately 25 per cent are referred from the department of psychiatry, with a growing proportion from the adolescent unit. Five per cent of patients come from departments of rehabilitation medicine, general medicine and surgical services.

Functional Categories

The first step for anyone interested in refining a comprehensive neuropsychological test battery is to attempt to come to terms (either explicitly or implicitly) with the overwhelming range of brain-related behaviours that may be disrupted by cerebral dysfunction. A purely test-centred approach would be confusing from the outset because of the plethora of monitoring instruments and the fact that they do not always specifically monitor what they purportedly describe. An analogy may be drawn with the parable of the six blind men describing an elephant. Conception of brain functioning cannot easily be derived from the disparate descriptions resulting from a disorganized host of heterogeneous tests.

Obviously, if disparate test data are to become meaningfully integrated, a filing system (or a conceptual framework mapping the boundaries of the "elephant") of brain-related human abilities must be established. An issues-centred approach like this has the advantage of providing a point of orientation by first suggesting empirically related categories of brain output. Thinking in terms of functional categories helps define what needs to be measured and provides an artificial (but clinically convenient) schema for classifying complex variables. Tests sensitive to these variables may then be sought at a later stage of battery construction.

A century ago, Hughlings Jackson (1873) noted the clinical implications of the organization of the brain into functional hierarchies integrated so that each level influenced a large number of behaviours. The usefulness of his application of hierarchical principles to the analysis of brain function was reaffirmed by Luria's (1973) model of the working brain. This concept of a hierarchically organized nervous system is particularly useful to developmental psychology as many facets of the systematic development of sequential behaviour patterns appear to reflect the maturation of progressively higher levels of the nervous system.

Functional categories related to the nervous system reflect principles underlying cerebral functions and are as applicable to brain damaged individuals as to normal individuals at all stages of human development (Smith, 1979). These categories suggest logical, albeit hypothetical, constructions for the hierarchical ordering of test battery data.

Scientific method is based upon the search for more efficient classification systems. Lazarus (1981) provides a succinct multimodal classification of human behaviour suitable for generalist psychologists. Adams *et al.* (1975) use an ability approach to structure neuropsychological batteries amenable to computerized interpretation. Lezak (1976) also formulates neuropsychological ability categories for systematic testing. Christensen (1979) provides a particularly lucid translation of the arrangement of the functional categories in Luria's neuropsychological investigation. Golden's (1981) quantification of Luria's investigation describes a profile of essentially similar skills (motor, rhythm, tactile, receptive and expressive speech, writing, reading, arithmetic, memory, and intellectual processes). Rourke (1981) observes that the Halstead–Reitan approach, including its allied procedures (children's batteries, etc.), considers a hierarchy of adaptive abilities (sensory-perceptual, motor, psychomotor, linguistic, and cognitive skills) sensitive to cerebral dysfunction.

Swiercinsky (1978) has noted 10 functional categories of test behaviour (lateral dominance, motor functioning, auditory perceptual organization, tactile perceptual organization, spatial perceptual organization, language skills, general information processing, memory processes, attention and concentration, and education and experience). These derive from revisions of an already modified Halstead–Reitan battery successfully used at the Veterans Administration Hospital, Topeka, Kansas, for more than a decade. During factor analytic investigations of the structure of HRNTB data, Swiercinsky (1979) isolated eight factors from among 36 variables which accounted for 68 per cent of the total variance. He concluded that the original Halstead–Reitan battery, although highly valid and clinically useful, could be further refined with the addition of updated measures of linguistic performance, auditory function, memory, concentration, and symbolic or abstract information processing functions. Hevern (1980) suggests that such findings point to the need for additional research on improving test batteries. Contemporary instruments, even though they remain clinically adequate, are always capable of improvement.

Reviews of the work of leading authorities reveal a remarkable consensus in defining functional categories of test behaviour, even though the writers come from disparate theoretical (or avowed atheoretical) persuasions. Systematic comparisons of the relatively homogeneous functional category schemes available, followed by an integration of the degree of overlap, suggest that the most commonly accepted areas of neuropsychological functioning are as follows: (1) motor; (2) auditory perceptual; (3) tactile perceptual; (4) visuo-spatial; (5) language ability; (6) memory processes; (7) higher cognitive processes (comprehension, intelligence, abstract thinking, problem solving, planning functions, etc.); and (8) personality organization (Gilandas and Touyz, 1981).

These categories can be used to order test battery contents in a loose, relatively hierarchical manner from the simple to the more complex measures of neuropsychological functioning. These processes are inevitably described in a variety of terms by individual authors (for example, Lazarus, 1981). However, if semantics are set aside the above list of eight categories tends to cover the essential functions consistently designated as being of interest during neuropsychological assessment.

Test Criteria

A decision on the functional categories of a test battery (based upon clinically and statistically derived reviews of literature) will make the choice of tests easier. Cross-indexing selected tests to hierarchically organized functional categories guards against accumulating unduly redundant measures.

Although, like all psychologists, we have an interest in experimenting with a variety of tests, our study studiously avoided creating a new neuropsychological instrument. It is presumptuous to discard the efforts of almost half a century of research on the Halstead–Reitan approach. It is more realistic to use well validated foundations and then make modest cost-efficient refinements. Consequently, criteria for test selection were based upon compatibility with the core-orienting principles of the Halstead–Reitan approach in order to capitalize upon its well validated conceptual framework. The following five general principles for test battery construction were strictly adhered to.

Five principles for test battery construction

1. A comprehensive and heterogeneous range of wide band tests which are sensitive across a wide range of general cerebral dysfunctions should be included (for example, power as well as speed measures; novel problem solving as well as maintaining a particular set). With the results of such tests it is possible to differentiate between the gross categories of brain damaged and non-brain damaged individuals.

2. A combination of specific narrow band tests which are sensitive to more focal deficits and which, together with the above heterogeneous procedures, contribute to differential profiles of brain–behaviour relationships should be included. An arrangement of specific tests sensitive to different neuroanatomical units which are cross-indexed under the same functional category but which do not overlap facilitates identification of discrete types of cerebral dysfunction.
3. All tests under consideration need to be psychometrically valid and reliable *per se*. They should be standardized with adequate norms. This prerequisite makes them more amenable to valid multiple neuropsychological inferences and interpretations as described by Boll (1978).
4. The conceptual framework with its system of multiple inferences takes precedence over any specific test. The battery should not be overly dependent upon any one test or combination, thus allowing instant replacement of measures when they have outlived their usefulness.
5. Tests should be chosen on atheoretical criteria for their technical usefulness rather than for alleged theoretical compatibility with some exclusive system of brain functioning. Such an operational approach is essentially pragmatic and empirical and favours technical eclecticism at the expense of theoretical eclecticism (Lazarus, 1981).

Once these general conceptual principles were met, the following more specific criteria were applied:

1. As recommended by Kazdin (1980) cost-effective tests which did not require excessive time were given high priority.
2. Economical instruments that do not require storage in a special setting bring neuropsychological testing within the reach of developing countries which may not be able to budget for a laboratory environment.
3. Portability was a high priority. It was hoped that the tests selected could easily fit within a briefcase thus allowing the clinician to go to the disabled patient's bedside, make house calls, or test at various maximum security institutions.
4. Tests which were potentially computer-compatible were given priority in anticipation of technological advances.
5. Widely used and available tests, in English, were highly favoured.

Test Selection Strategy

After clarifying the implications of the conceptual framework, coming to terms with functional categories and deciding upon test criteria, the next step in test battery revision is to arrange a strategy for test selection and revision. For our purposes, a strategy was designed to meet test criteria compatible with the Halstead–Reitan neuropsychological test battery (HRNTB) validation studies previously discussed as no attempt was being made to construct and standardize a new neuropsychological instrument.

Our philosophy was to look to the new technology (for example, computers) whilst not lightly discarding tried and tested procedures (the Halstead–Reitan approach). A conservative "fail-safe" approach was maintained by remaining strictly within the mainstream of contemporary neuropsychological assessment. The Halstead–Reitan battery was accepted as a valid foundation. Two of its most time consuming tests (the Halstead category test and the tactual performance test) were considered for replacement as more promising, cost-efficient procedures had been validated in other studies. Also, we attempted to give consideration to functional categories relatively neglected by the Halstead–Reitan battery. These reinforced models were finally tested in a variety of ways to evaluate their clinical performance.

Golden (1981b) describes the HRNTB as consisting of a loosely organized group of independent tests, the number of which varies according to the predilection of the clinician. However, most users of the battery include the following 10 tests: laterality preference schedule; finger tapping test; speech-sounds perception test; seashore rhythm test; tactual performance test; Reitan–Kløve sensory-perceptual examination; trail making test; Reitan–Indiana aphasia examination; Wechsler adult intelligence scale; and the Halstead category test.

The *Halstead category test* is a highly complex monitor of abstract thinking. A normal subject may finish it within an hour, but a brain damaged patient may take more than two hours. Its extreme length fatigues patients and slows down completion of the rest of the battery. This excessive time factor, together with the cumbersome equipment required (a projection box, and slides), makes many clinicians reluctant to administer it. Swiercinsky's (1978) factor analytic studies show that it fails to correlate highly with any factor on his principle component analysis. Deletion of it from a battery does not represent any loss of useful information. Obrzut (1981), like others, has noted its impracticality (the prohibitive expense, the awkward nature of the projection apparatus, and the lack of portability).

The *tactual performance test* is generally an adequate instrument, but it has some unfortunate drawbacks. Its equipment certainly is not portable (formboard mounted on a base). It requires three trials (dominant, non-dominant and both hands) which some patients find confusing and it can take up to 45 minutes to complete. Subjects need to be blindfolded, which is disturbing to some psychiatric patients. Others get dizzy when working blindfolded over a lengthy period of time. This test monitors complex skills overlapping with many functional categories (motor, tactile, spatial, and kinaesthetic) which can be adequately evaluated by simpler allied procedures.

With regard to cost-efficiency, the Halstead category test and the tactual performance test may be considered to be the most awkward aspects of the HRNTB. They were not used by us. The remaining eight tests were acceptable as the foundation for a battery. Thus, approximately 80 per cent of the original HRNTB items were suitable for our purposes with minor modifications.

Many authors have noted room for improvement in the Halstead–Reitan neuropsychological test battery (HRNTB). Golden (1979) states that it tends to be overly concerned with assessment of basic motor skills and neglects the assessment of some more complex neuropsychological functions. Consequently, many clinicians compensate for such a vacuum by adding well established tests. Most often, these include tests for expressive speech, memory processes, educational achievement and personality functioning. Such tests have become integral to neuropsychological assessment and are referred to by Boll (1981) as "allied procedures".

The above strategy eliminates weaknesses (the Halstead category test and the tactual performance test), retains strengths (the remaining HRNTB) and searches for additional improvements (especially for tests covering the areas of expressive speech, memory processes, educational achievement and personality functioning). The search for improvements was basically confined to analyses of the Halstead–Reitan approach which considered items meeting both our general and specific test criteria.

Items with which to reinforce the battery were drawn from a pool of techniques consistently cross-validated when used in combination in the following Halstead–Reitan validation studies: Reitan (1955); Wheeler and Reitan (1963); Wheeler, *et al.* (1963); Reitan (1964); Spreen and Benton (1965); Mathews, *et al.* (1966); Vega and Parsons (1967); Klonoff, *et al.* (1970); Goldstein, *et al.* (1973); Filskov and Goldstein (1974); Golden (1976); Schreiver, *et al.* (1976); Matarazzo, *et al.* (1976); Kiernan and Mathews (1976); Swiercinsky (1978); and Hevern (1980). Boll (1978) succinctly summarizes the voluminous validation literature on these allied procedures when used both alone and within the context of broader batteries.

Confining test selection basically to the HRNTB pool of validation studies raises the probability that items considered for inclusion were compatible with the conceptual framework of the original HRNTB. Tests within this pool which could be logically cross-indexed to the most commonly accepted areas of neuropsychological functioning and which had the most impressive validity and reliability citings naturally received special consideration.

Clinical field trials

Combinations of tests considered for selection created a number of promising batteries. Over a four year period, these combinations were then subjected to a continual trial-and-error, clinical and statistical analysis designed to develop a cost-efficient battery. These steps and trials were carried out repeatedly and simultaneously as part of a continuing investigative process as follows: (1) field trials; (2) comparisons of neuropsychological test results with diagnostic neurological criteria; (3) single blind studies; and (4) additional statistical procedures. A systematic continuing education process such as this provides feedback which gives coherent direction to routine clinical practice (Gilandas, 1972).

The field trial approach had the same rationale used in the development of the American Psychiatric Association's (1980) *Diagnostic and Statistical Manual of Mental Disorders* (DSM-III). This trial and error method relies upon continual feedback from referral sources and subsequent revision of test batteries as problems are encountered. In our situation, the two senior writers evaluated a large number of patients from a busy general hospital and refined the provisional battery whenever any new information on validity and cost-efficiency was acquired. Testing occurred within the context of routine daily referrals from departments of neurology, neurosurgery, psychiatry, rehabilitation medicine and general medical and surgical services.

Routine neuropsychological assessments in large general hospitals provide excellent research material, as long as good clinical records are kept, as there are independent criteria available (for example, diagnostic neurological data) which serve as points of comparative feedback. Corrective feedback was also obtained at the normative and empirical levels.

Normative criteria were based upon the opinions of the professional staff administering the tests and included consultations with colleagues and peer review conferences wherein the merits and disadvantages of provisional test batteries were discussed in detail to facilitate further test battery modification.

The actual quality of adaptation in the natural environment must be taken into account when developing empirical criteria. The function of patients in real life revealed through regular follow-up investigations may show processes that are described poorly by the results of highly regarded tests or even missed entirely (the frontal lobe syndrome is an obvious example). The senior authors are involved in rehabilitation as much as in assessment (since assessment implies treatment). The opportunity to work individually with patients over an extended period provides excellent feedback concerning the strengths and deficits in the clinician's own test battery. One of the writers is involved on an almost daily basis with an adolescent specific learning disabilities remediation programme where this is especially so. Such intensive contact provides a stringent review of assessment procedures in terms of the quality of realistic cognitive processing information they are revealing. The patient's level of functioning outside the neuropsychological laboratory then provides additional criteria for evaluating the differential profiles elicited during neuropsychological assessment.

The field trial approach is a particularly arduous process. However, in the sense that they are the "proof of the pudding", such accumulations of neuropsychological profiles have no substitute for providing comprehensive data in a systematic manner. This exhaustive path is involved in the evolution of most test batteries. For example, Halstead undertook both naturalistic and empirical observations over an extended period of time in the search for tests sensitive to cerebral dysfunction. Similarly, Reitan has spent his whole career testing patients and then refining the results of such tests.

Diagnostic Neurological Criteria

Profiles accumulated from provisional test batteries during field trials were compared with diagnostic neurological and laboratory criteria whenever possible during the four years of the study. Comparisons of functional and structural evidence from the same patient are a particularly valuable mode of research strategy as both levels of information add meaning to each other.

Patients referred for routine neuropsychological evaluation because of suspected brain damage were followed up after testing in order to compare the descriptive profiles including the initial neuropsychological diagnostic impression with subsequent neurological diagnosis. Typical referrals included the following entities which are highly representative of any large metropolitan general hospital: closed head injury; Alzheimer's disease; Huntington's disease; cerebrovascular disorders; differential diagnosis of neuropathological dementia from functionally induced dementia; multiple sclerosis; cerebral tumour; Parkinson's disease; and epilepsy.

The 1982/83 neuropsychological test battery is an example of a comparative study (Table 1) and is adequate for the teaching purposes of this volume. This study used blind interpretation of neuropsychological test results which were subsequently compared to independently confirmed diagnoses of neurological disorders.

Table 1
Adult Neuropsychological Test Battery (1982/83)

Function Tested	Test Used
Motor functioning	Laterality preference schedule
	Grooved pegboard
	Finger tapping test
	Hand dynamometer
Auditory perceptual functioning	Speech-sounds perception test
	Seashore rhythm test
Tactile perceptual functioning	Face hand test
	Finger agnosia
	Graphaesthesia
	Tactile form recognition test
Visuo-spatial functioning	Trail making test (Part B)
	Benton visual retention test
	Rey-Osterrieth complex figure test (copy)
Language ability	Aphasia language performance scales
	Controlled word association test
Memory processes	Modified Wechsler memory scale
	Rey-Osterrieth complex figure test (recall)
	Walton-Black modified new word learning test
Higher cognitive processes	Wechsler adult intelligence scale–revised
	Wide range achievement test
	Stroop colour-word test
Personality organization	Minnesota multiphasic personality inventory
	Neuropsychological structured interview

To begin the study, the first 100 patients for whom the neuropsychological evaluation (using the 1982/83 battery) was completed were selected initially without knowledge of the subsequent final neurological diagnosis. This lack of neurological data was a common phenomenon and did not have to be contrived artificially as most referral sources (especially psychiatrists) requested neuropsychological assessment before obtaining the results of other diagnostic neurological laboratory procedures. In fact, neuropsychological test results often determined the character of the further investigations required.

The final neurological diagnosis was judged to be a conclusive independent criterion for either the presence or absence of brain damage. Patients in whom diagnosis was not confidently confirmed by neurological reports citing computerized tomographic (CT) scans were eliminated from the study. A 92 per cent hit rate for differentiating the presence or absence of brain damage in this heterogeneous group of brain damaged and psychiatric patients was obtained with the neuropsychological battery. Patients with chronic or process schizophrenia (defined as those with a diagnosis of schizophrenia for more than 12 months) were eliminated from the study as there is no evidence that any available battery can discriminate between such subjects and those with brain damage (Golden, 1979).

The results compared favourably with Golden's (1977) report of diagnostic accuracy using the HRNTB. Such findings are quite unremarkable in any comprehensive battery and have been repeatedly replicated during the 27 years since Reitan's (1955) original effort. Of greater value to us was the way subgroup behavioural patterns, described in quantitative neuropsychological profile form, related to diagnostic neurological and other psychiatric criteria. For example, a common difficulty resulted from patients with pseudodementia who proved to be suffering from affective disorders on follow-up. As Lishman (1978) observed, pseudodementia due to affective disorders is the syndrome which most easily results in diagnostic errors.

Single Blind Studies

As part of the Psychology Unit's continuing education, a series of single blind studies was performed on provisional batteries. For example, the differential diagnosis of 25 randomly selected cases from the 100 case comparison study described above proved interesting.

Appendices containing test result data for 13 cases were given to one coauthor and data for 12 cases were given to the other coauthor. Neither coauthor had any familiarity with the case he was given to evaluate. He did not meet the patient concerned nor was he supplied with the case history. Diagnosis for the presence or absence of brain damage was made purely on quantitative terms (that is, from test scores in the battery). Diagnostic accuracy obtained was 88 per cent (22 out of 25 correct), the previously mentioned neurological diagnoses being used as independent criteria.

As noted previously, gross categorical studies of brain damage compared with non-brain damage are of peripheral interest in contemporary neuropsychology relative to the more important task of compiling comprehensively descriptive subgroup profiles. If the aim of neuropsychology was solely to differentiate between the normal and brain damaged populations, a battery would not be required. For example, Gordon (1978) reports a hit rate of 87 per cent with the trail making test: part B which requires less than two minutes to administer. However, such gross information is clinically useless where effective rehabilitation is concerned. Consequently, the hit rates reported in the neurological criteria study and the single blind study reported above, together with the additional statistical procedures noted below, remain of secondary concern. These statistics, although providing added reassurance concerning the sensitivity of the battery to cerebral dysfunction, merely duplicate the familiar history of validation studies involving variants of the HRNTB and its allied procedures.

Additional Statistical Procedures

While methods for the quantification and ultimate computerization of the test battery were being worked out, additional statistical procedures concerning the sensitivity of the tests to various neurological sub-populations were carried out. The advantage of sub-populations research is that it generates quantitative test profiles which make neuropsychological sense and help to relate certain cerebral dysfunctions to specific test battery signs (Golden, 1981b).

Actuarial procedures ranging from studies of developmental learning disabilities in adolescents to the effects of chronic alcoholism in geriatric patients have been carried out on data assembled at the Royal Prince Alfred Hospital, with encouraging results. Our simplest available study discriminating between the presence and absence of brain damage is described below in order to exemplify the rationale of actuarial procedures.

The sub-population consisted of adults with acute closed head injuries sustained in motor vehicle accidents. The presence or absence of structural brain damage was determined independently using the results of computerized tomographic (CT) scanning as a criterion. Twenty consecutive patients referred for neuropsychological assessment, who were later proved to have unequivocal structural damage on CT scanning, were neuropsychologically compared with 20 consecutive patients without structural CT scan abnormalities. Histories of the patients were reviewed in order to exclude those with any neuropsychiatric complications not directly related to their motor vehicle accident. The following complicating factors were a basis for exclusion from the study: neurological or psychiatric disorders existing before the accident; evidence of developmental anomalies such as mental retardation and specific learning disability; estimated premorbid intelligence below average; educational level below the ninth grade; non-English speaking; and age below 20 years or above 55 years. The sample consisted of 16 females and 24 males ($n = 40$) with a mean age of 38.1 years and a mean 10.3 years of education. Stricter matching on age, education, sex and socioeconomic variables was unnecessary in this neuropsychiatrically uncomplicated (before the accident, that is) groups since the monitoring of subtle group differences was not of interest. Rather, the sole focus of concern was to examine the ability of statistical procedures in correctly assigning patients to their respective categories of brain damage.

The patients completed all the tests in the recommended battery. This test battery, illustrated in Table 1, contains the following three strands:

A. Tests that are based upon stored information and well ingrained skills which are relatively resistant to brain damage and hence serve as descriptors of premorbid functioning (Goodglass and Kaplan, 1979);

B. General cognitive tests of new learning and problem solving which commonly show a characteristic deterioration pattern, following brain damage (Walsh, 1978);
C. More specific sensory-motor, language and visuo-spatial tests which may have lateralizing significance and are not necessarily affected by most types of brain damage (Swiercinsky, 1978).

An examination of the literature (discussed in Chapters 5 and 6) on the cognitive tasks of new learning and problem solving which form part of our battery identified the ten tests most generally sensitive to brain damage. They were as follows:

1. Digit symbol subtest of the WAIS.
2. Block design subtest of the WAIS.
3. Picture arrangement subtest of the WAIS.
4. Delayed recall of the logical memory subtest of the WMS (Russell's 1975 modification).
5. Delayed recall of the visual reproduction subtest of the WMS (Russell's 1975 modification).
6. Associate learning subtest of the WMS.
7. Seashore rhythm test.
8. Trail making test: Part B.
9. Walton–Black modified new word learning test.
10. Stroop colour–word test.

When used alone, each of the above tests has impressive hit rates (frequently exceeding 80 per cent) in identifying patients with cerebral dysfunction (Zimmerman and Woo-Sam, 1973; Russell, 1975; Lishman, 1978; Golden, 1978, 1979, 1981b). It is probable that these independently validated and widely used tests which comprise one strand of the test battery will prove to be even more useful when used in combination.

The ten tests comprising the generally sensitive strand served as an index of impairment. An impairment index functions as a summary of the level of performance on tests most sensitive to cerebral dysfunction in a particular battery. It is calculated as the proportion of the number of tests which fall into the brain damaged category.

The test performances of the patients were coded at three levels for actuarial analysis. Moderate impairment was defined as a score at 10th percentile or below. Mild impairment was defined as a score between the 11th and the 25th percentile. If results scored above the 25th percentile, the patients were regarded as normal. These are commonly used normative conventions in the clinical setting (Lezak, 1976). However, it must be remembered that a score above the 25th percentile does not necessarily signify intact functioning in usual instances of patients with superior premorbid intelligence.

Discriminant function analysis is a popular statistical procedure for neuropsychological classification (Wheeler, *et al.*, 1963). In our study, the discriminant analysis procedure used was the econometric linear forecasting (ELF) package, for the Apple II computer (Winchendon Group, 1982). Moderate, mild and normal categories of test performance were coded as 2, 1 and 0 respectively for the purposes of analysis. Two of the tests (Walton–Black and the associate learning subtest of the WMS) had to be excluded since there was no internal variation within a group; that is, the performances of all of the group with abnormal CT scanning results were severely impaired on both these tests. No attempt was made to reduce the test battery although the analysis showed that some tests made only a small independent contribution. The final discriminant function based on the eight test scores currently classified all but one patient into the correct group. Thus all 20 (100 per cent) of the brain damaged patients were correctly classified. Nineteen of the non-brain damaged patients were correctly classified (hit rate of 95 per cent). One patient returned a false positive result by being included in the brain damaged group on the basis of severely impaired neuropsychological test scores, despite computerized tomography showing a normal scan.

It is clinically disadvantageous to exclude two tests (the Walton–Black and the associate learning subtest of the WMS) which discriminate well between the brain damaged and non-brain damaged groups because they fail to satisfy the limitations of a particular statistical procedure. It was found to be possible to include all the 10 selected tests by carrying out a factor analysis of the overall correlation matrix and using factor scores (for example, principal components) in the discriminant analysis procedure. When this was done the first five principal components correctly classified 95 per cent of patients. There were two false positive results. One proved to be the same individual as in the previous analysis. Both of the patients with false positive results had abnormal scores on the Walton–Black and the associate learning subtest. This raises the possibility that these patients may in fact be brain damaged and that their "normal" computerized tomography (CT) scans are diagnostic laboratory errors (false negatives).

A correct classification rate of 95 per cent in the second discriminant analysis procedure supports the logic that the efficacy of highly sensitive individual tests is maximized when they are used in combination. Wedding found that "clinicians are unable to approximate the level of accuracy obtained by the statistical actuarial methods" (1983: 20). This echoes Meehl's (1954) prophetic statement that the actuarial approach is at least as accurate as clinical diagnosis.

Despite the overlap in subjective symptomatology demonstrated in many of both the brain damaged and non-brain damaged patients, neuropsychological test batteries can be used with little difficulty to assign them correctly to their respective categories. (Absence of psychiatric patients contributed to the high hit rate.) Patients with head injuries have been reviewed by Golden (1981b) who notes that most of the generally sensitive tests tend to fall into the brain damaged range when administered to this group (deterioration pattern). However, the effects of head injuries can be quite varied. Moreover, pseudoneurological signs (post-traumatic syndrome) have been commonly observed after trauma which has not involved the head at all (Wells and Duncan, 1980).

A continuing concern in neuropsychological research is the relative inadequacy of independent criteria for brain damage. Although computerized tomography has made a revolutionary contribution, no diagnostic neurological laboratory technique can yet claim to be foolproof. It is a common result, as in this study, to find patients with false positive results on neuropsychological assessment when the CT scanning is used to demonstrate cerebral dysfunction. Lishman (1978) interprets such findings as the tendency for psychometric tests to overdiagnose organicity. An alternative possibility is that such "false positive" results on neuropsychological investigation may in fact be false negative results associated with faulty CT scanning. When neuropsychological assessment is compared with CT scanning, the former may be a more sensitive measure than the latter. For example, Veneklasen and Long (1983) had a 92 per cent accuracy rate in predicting tumour recurrence as against non-recurrence using neuropsychological assessment, compared to a 69 per cent accuracy rate for CT scanning.

In this study, an impairment index of 0.4 or more was associated with abnormal results on CT scanning. This approximates the HRNTB pattern where impairment indices of 0 to 0.4 are regarded as being within the normal range and indices of 0.5 to 1.0 are generally regarded as indicative of brain damage (Golden, 1981b).

In conclusion, discriminant function analysis was a statistically convenient method of discriminating between the presence or absence of brain damage. Such actuarial techniques must not be interpreted as supportive of the outmoded assumption of cerebral dysfunction as a unitary disorder. Rather, it is emphasized that the descriptive role of clinical neuropsychology provides a greater contribution than do solely diagnostic concerns. Consequently, the other two strands contained in the battery shown in Table 1 (tests monitoring premorbidly stored information/well ingrained skills, and the more specific sensory-motor, language and visuo-spatial tests) are necessary complements to the general cognitive tests of new learning and problem solving used as an impairment index in this study. Only such a comprehensive triadic test battery can hope to generate the fine clinical descriptions required to meet the rehabilitation needs of individual patients.

COMMENTS

Using a specific example of a typical approach to test battery revision illustrates some basic issues in neuropsychological assessment. The history of the Halstead–Reitan neuropsychological test battery (HRNTB) shows that no battery is a finished product. Even the most widely established batteries are amenable to improvement. The "perfect" battery is an impossible goal as no clinical techniques are immune from change.

As often occurs in clinical research we have empirically verified commonsense. That is, most clinicians, on the basis of intuition and experience already appear to use the HRNTB in a manner parallel to our empirical recommendations. The Halstead category test and the tactual performance test tend to be omitted because of the great investment of time for relatively marginal returns. Also, neuropsychological assessments routinely include allied procedures which are not part of the original Halstead–Reitan battery to compensate for that battery's deficient coverage of important functional categories (expressive language, memory processes, higher cognitive processes, and personality organization). The tests which met our criteria for operationally defining the most commonly accepted functional categories favourably are cross-indexed to such categories in Table 1. They are described in detail in the chapters on test administration and interpretation.

The HRNTB provides an adequate examination of sensory-motor functioning. However, the addition of the grooved pegboard (Trites, 1977) and the hand dynamometer (Dodrill, 1978) aids differentiation of right and left hemisphere involvement during the assessment of motor functioning.

Auditory perceptual functioning is sufficiently screened with the speech–sounds perception test and the seashore rhythm test in the HRNTB.

Tactile perceptual functioning is also well covered with the Reitan–Kløve sensory–perceptual examination. Its contents are drawn from routine procedures during the physical neurological examination (examining for tactile imperception, suppressions, finger agnosia, graphaesthesia, and stereognosis/tactile form recognition). A particularly cost-efficient approach to the screening of tactile functions (the face hand test, finger agnosia, graphaesthesia, and the tactile form recognition test) is described in Chapter 5.

Visuo-spatial functioning is relatively well covered by the HRNTB. The relationship between parts A and B of the trail making test has not been shown to be clinically useful for differentiating the side of damage. Consequently no benefit is gained by administering part A, especially as part B is considerably more sensitive to cerebral dysfunction (Lezak, 1976). The addition of the Benton visual retention test (Benton, 1974) and the copy version of the Rey–Osterrieth complex figure test (Visser, 1980) contribute to a more thorough visuo-spatial assessment with little additional time.

Language ability is assessed relatively well by the Reitan–Indiana aphasia examination. However, many clinicians may prefer the more cost-efficient aphasia language performance scales (Keenan and Brassell, 1975) which also has the advantage of being specifically oriented towards rehabilitation. These scales were developed from studies of brain injured individuals with similar characteristics to those upon which the rest of the HRNTB tests are based. The addition of the controlled word association test (Benton, 1973) also provides a quick method for monitoring expressive speech with scoring in percentile ranks.

Memory processes are not assessed well by the HRNTB. A modified Wechsler memory scale (Russell, 1975) is an extremely useful general indicator. More specifically, the addition of the Walton–Black modified new word learning test (Walton and Black, 1957) and the recall version of the Rey–Osterrieth complex figure test (Visser, 1980) provide excellent and contrasting measures of verbal and visual learning. These two additions have been well validated and used productively in Europe for the past two decades. They are the only two tests not drawn specifically from the pool of Halstead–Reitan literature in our recommended battery. However, this reflects the latter's limitations regarding specialized learning tests.

Many users of the HRNTB include the wide range achievement test (Jastak and Jastak, 1978) in addition to the Wechsler adult intelligence scale when monitoring higher cognitive functions. The latter provides a meaningful baseline for interpreting the significance of the former. The inclusion of the Stroop colour–word test (Golden, 1979) provides an additional measure of cognitive flexibility when monitoring the higher intellectual processes.

Virtually all clinicians administering neuropsychological assessments are interested in including measures of personality. The most widely used test of personality throughout the world remains the Minnesota multiphasic personality inventory (MMPI).

Finally, neuropsychological assessment is best complemented by a structured form of neuropsychological interview as history taking is the most important diagnostic skill in both medicine and clinical psychology.

In summary, of the 10 tests commonly included in the HRNTB, six cannot currently be easily improved upon (laterality preference schedule; finger tapping test; speech–sounds perception test; seashore rhythm test; trail making test; and the Wechsler adult intelligence scale). Two tests may be administered more cost-efficiently (Reitan–Kløve sensory–perceptual examination;

and the Reitan–Indiana aphasia examination). Two tests are cumbersome, yield marginal information relative to the extreme length of time needed for administration and hence are often omitted by many clinicians (Halstead category test; and the tactual performance test).

In fact, the total time for clinical administration of the 14 additional extremely cost-efficient procedures (grooved pegboard; hand dynamometer; face hand test; finger agnosia; graphaesthesia; tactile form recognition test; Benton visual retention test; complex figure test; asphasia language performance scales; controlled word association test; Wechsler memory scale; Walton–Black modified new word learning test; wide range achievement test; and the Stroop colour–word test) recommended in fortifying the original HRNTB is less than for the administration of the Halstead category test alone and still makes this expanded battery less time consuming than the traditional HRNTB. (The Minnesota multiphasic personality inventory is self-administered by a patient and does not impinge on the clinician's time.) Thus, this battery is reduced in terms of time yet greatly expands the amount of information elicited. As the most significant tests from the original HRNTB are incorporated in the battery described in this volume, the major issue between the former and the latter is not one of validity but rather that of comprehensive cost-efficiency.

The recommended test battery is compatible with the core-orienting principles of the Halstead–Reitan approach as previously described. It contains a comprehensive and heterogeneous range of tests sensitive to a wide range of cerebral dysfunctions, in combination with specific tests sensitive to relatively more focal deficits. This combination generates differential profiles of brain–behaviour relationships. The data so assembled go some way to achieving Smith's (1975) four major goals for a neuropsychological battery (differential diagnosis; descriptive baseline studies; prognostic statements; and facilitation of rehabilitation).

The tests are within the mainstream of clinical neuropsychology and have a record of at least five years' repeated cross-validation, mostly in the Halstead–Reitan literature. Some have a record of over 20 years of such cross-validation. As they are psychometrically valid and reliable, they are eminently amenable to valid multiple neuropsychological inferences. Consequently, it is not surprising that these tests serve as adequate operational representations of adaptive abilities.

The test battery is empirically derived. Such an atheoretical stance capitalizes fully upon technical eclecticism. Consequently, no specific test has any theoretical importance for the valid use of the battery. Thus, tests can be readily discarded as improved versions are inevitably developed.

Together with the above general conceptual principles, our more specific criteria were also adequately attained.

The test battery takes approximately four hours to administer face-to-face once the clinician becomes familiar with such short-form versions of the tests as recommended by Golden (1979). This contrasts with the six to eight hours required for administration of the HRNTB.

The equipment required is portable (with a weight of less than 5 kg) and does not require laboratory facilities. Capital investment would be nominal in reasonably equipped clinical psychology departments in the English-speaking world, as most of the equipment would already be in wide use (for example, the Wechsler adult intelligence scale (WAIS), the Benton visual retention test, etc.). The only capital investment would be a relatively small outlay for some of the sensory-motor equipment (for example, the grooved pegboard, the finger tapping test, etc.) in order to complete the test battery equipment.

The majority of the tests are quantitative in nature and hence potentially computer-compatible. The battery is already partially computer administered, scored and interpreted (for example, MMPI, and scoring and interpretation of the WAIS). A completely computerized neuropsychological test battery package to aid hypothesis testing is anticipated in the near future.

The battery was revised through testing of a group aged from 17-to-84 years. As in the Halstead–Reitan literature there is a bias towards the group aged from 25-to-55 years, reflecting hospital referral patterns. Consequently, age-related norms in the literature remain suspect for children and geriatric patients.

In this chapter, the adult population was used to describe test battery revision as a general example of wide applicability. A twin project administered by the senior author (who has a joint appointment with the Rivendell Adolescent Unit) was also undertaken, however. This studied the extent to which adolescent and adult neuropsychological test batteries may overlap. The adolescent study had some major advantages over the adult study, with better funding, superior facilities and greater staffing. For example, a residential school is incorporated within the adolescent hospital staffed by remedial education teachers. This provided longitudinal, remediationally oriented independent cognitive profiles which could be compared with initial neuropsychological assessments. A focus upon the 12-to-16 year old age group facilitated more detailed descriptive subgroup profiles, and a degree of regular follow-up that was not possible with the adult population.

In general, the adult battery described in Table 1 has significant applicability to adolescents. Sensory-motor, visuo-spatial, language and higher cognitive functions can be monitored by administration of the same types of tests, as children's versions are available. Examples are the Wechsler intelligence scale for children and the children's trail making test. Memory processes pose a minor problem as most of the literature deals with adult norms for the Wechsler memory scale (WMS). However, in our experience, adolescents perform as well as or better than adults on this test, so there is adequate clinical utility. We favoured a behavioural check list yielding a profile for monitoring personality organization in children as described by Achenbach and Edelbrock (1979). The assessment of children is dealt with in more detail in a separate chapter on neuropsychology and medicine.

It must be pointed out that the cross-indexing of tests to functional categories is a clinically convenient artefact and does not imply the existence of "pure" non-overlapping test items. Luria's (1980) concept of functional systems suggests that all forms of behaviour are dependent upon the integration of a variety of basic skills, mediated by different brain areas. Thus, any specific test cannot be directly indicative of a localized brain lesion. For example, the trail making test, which allegedly has significance for the frontal lobe, is also relatively sensitive in assessing a variety of other cerebral dysfunctions. Such diverse functional categories as motor, visuo-spatial and higher cognitive processes are covered. The speech–sounds perception test is classified by some authors under auditory-perceptual functioning, yet can be just as correctly catalogued under language ability as it is central to receptive language skills. Examples are endless and reflect the complexity of brain functions. Unequivocal categorization does not exist in clinical neuropsychology.

The rationale of using functional categories to artificially order tests in a loose, yet relatively hierarchical, manner from the simple to the more complex is meant to serve as a clinical thinking aid. This reinforces the profile concept of adaptive abilities, which has practical implications for deciding upon the treatments, as well as which tests can be cross-indexed to functional categories. It also provides a logical framework for interpreting test results and rehabilitation priorities.

Paradoxically, a multimodal test battery approach is not test-centred but rather issues-centred. Lazarus (1981) clearly indicated that the conceptual structure of well defined modalities is a more important issue than any specific test or treatment cross-indexed to such modalities. An unproductive test can always be discarded without unduly influencing the validity of the whole structure. The significance of any particular test is further reduced in clinical practice as multiple inference methods are used instead of relying solely upon a particular level of performance.

A multimodal approach to neuropsychological assessment ensures a comprehensive coverage of a wide range of functions, yet provides the flexibility for a more specialized assessment of any one of these functional categories. This transcends the paradigm clash between the traditional standardized test battery approach and the more qualitative strategies of hypothesis testing without the difficulties of creating a new neuropsychological instrument such as Golden's (1981) Luria–Nebraska test battery.

For example, when a frontal lobe syndrome is suspected, but not detected on the basic standardized battery, a second order analysis can be made with a specialized frontal lobe battery (Wisconsin card-sorting test; Semmes body placing; Thurstone word fluency; sequencing; and token test) as recommended by Kolb and Whishaw (1980). Mathews (1981) also finds no incompatibility between the deployment of standardized test batteries in conjunction with abbreviated batteries which meet the special needs of a particular patient. He has developed a series of brief test "packages" that can be used with various subgroups of patients (for example, patients with spinal cord injury only; patients with severe brain damage, etc.). Consequently, those who mechanically use test batteries have not fully explored their potential clinical creativity.

The development of sophisticated research methodologies and the invention of computerized diagnostic neurological laboratory techniques (for example CT scanning) for localizing lesions have contributed to remarkable advances in understanding brain–behaviour relationships. However, the most productive mode of describing brain output remains the humble yet arduous clinical task of routine, comprehensive and systematic neuropsychological assessment.

This involves monitoring a broad range of abilities with neuropsychological tests and then interpreting these test findings with multiple inference methods. The accumulation of such routine material via longitudinal face-to-face field studies was the most useful method we could find for generating hard data and testing out the actual performance of potential test batteries. These instruments are designed to go beyond the gross "presence *v.* absence" category and yield information regarding the implications of cerebral dysfunction.

This tedious, albeit invaluable, trial and error clinical methodology parallels the strategy of Ward Halstead, Ralph Reitan and their associates in refining their test batteries. It is also reminiscent of Husserl (1973), the founder of phenomenology, whose quest for the essences of things ("proof of the pudding") was guided by going "back to the things themselves".

The accumulation of retrospective descriptive data from the years of field trials and follow-up studies of various tests permits the application of several basic principles of learning. Knowledge of results about what is happening to patients generates corrective feedback concerning the value of what different tests are describing. Thus, longitudinal studies of neuropathological processes refine the tools used in the study of such processes. The use of instruments in the field is the basis for the evolution of all technology, to which such things as the progressive refinements of surgical instruments and the improved performance of motor vehicles testify.

There are no substitutes for baseline studies and longitudinal follow-up studies in attempting to understand patients with progressive or resolving lesions. Cerebral dysfunction varies with the specific site and magnitude of lesions, the nature, momentum and dynamics of the particular disease, and also the age, time, diaschisis and condition of the whole brain (Smith, 1979). Wilson emphasizes the importance of taking diaschisis into account when he warns us that the "vagaries, surprises and disappointments of surgical neurological practice remind us that the signs and symptoms we discern in our patients depend less upon the lesion than upon the altered function of the whole brain in which that lesion is situated" (1973: 161).

Smith further attests to the importance of longitudinal studies, explaining "although the different findings in neuropsychological studies at different stages in the course of specific evolving or resolving neuropathologic[al] processes have prompted apparently irreconcilable conclusions, the changes in later examinations afford additional facts that contribute to definitions of the significance of the different facts provided by the initial findings" (1981: 219).

Goody also emphasizes the importance of monitoring whole disease processes by noting "that in the end those illuminating and inspiring syntheses and insights which the great figures in philosophy and science have derived from the unwieldy and often contradictory collections of facts can only be achieved by those few who are prepared to study their subject in its completeness, and not in its analytic fragments" (1977: 10).

In conclusion, it is accepted that the test battery described in this volume, like all other Halstead–Reitan procedures, is empirically derived and lacks incontrovertible statistical analyses to explore its full implications. However, no battery with totally acceptable standardization and support from definitive statistical analyses exists as yet. Despite this, many clinically useful procedures are validly in daily use. Such utilitarian criteria also inspired the task force responsible for such a heuristic diagnostic manual as DSM-III to accept that "the ultimate issue in judging any proposed definition and criteria for medical and mental disorder is simply that it is useful" (Spitzer and Endicott, 1978: 37).

Tact, sympathy and understanding are expected of the physician, for the patient is no mere collection of symptoms, signs, disordered functions, damaged organs, and disturbed emotions. He is human, fearful and hopeful, seeking relief, help and reassurance. To the physician, as to the anthropologist, nothing human is strange or repulsive. The misanthrope may become a smart diagnostician of organic disease, but he can scarcely hope to succeed as a physician. The true physician has a Shakespearean breadth of interest in the wise and the foolish, the proud and the humble, the stoic hero and the whining rogue. He cares for people.

Harrison's Principles of Internal Medicine

4 The Structured Neuropsychological Interview

THE PRACTICE of both clinical psychology and medicine is caring for people. Although the bulk of this book deals with technical testing issues, it must be remembered that this whole methodological enterprise is solely to serve the patient's interests. Thus, the approach to the patient should be holistic, not a myopic view of the potentially dysfunctional brain.

It requires emotional maturity to achieve objectivity during testing and still care for and maintain rapport with the patient. The ability to empathize with patients and to meet their emotional needs so that testing is experienced as a supportive, therapeutic experience is a basic requirement of professional practice. In this respect, testing has a treatment component as well as a diagnostic theme.

Since the patient is being tested for maximal cognitive performance, where possible, a mood of active co-operation is essential. In fact, the quality of the clinician–patient relationship significantly influences the validity of the elicited quantitative test performance.

Besides emphasizing the personal context of assessment, the aim of this chapter is to provide guidelines for conducting a structured neuropsychological interview. In line with the practical nature of this workbook, readers are invited to reproduce the sample form guide (Appendix IV) for use in their own assessments.

Meaningful neuropsychological testing needs to be preceded by a structured neuropsychological interview. The patient interview remains the most important diagnostic procedure in medicine and this is also true for clinical neuropsychology. It is on the basis of the history obtained and the data derived during the interview that all subsequent diagnostic and treatment decisions are made. Inadequate data elicited from the interview would over-emphasize reliance upon the psychometric test scores. Since the results of no single test can differentiate brain damaged patients from others without some amount of overlap, test results should be interpreted only within the context of other pertinent information. Lishman (1978) warns practitioners not to rely on test scores in isolation but rather to retain a general clinical impression as a back-up to the detailed psychometric findings. Testing "blind" may be justified for experimental purposes, but this form of testing provides insufficient data for clinical practice.

Persons referring patients for neuropsychological assessment should be strongly encouraged to formulate specific referral questions. This ensures an economical and cost-efficient assessment. Precise questions help to focus on the significant aspects of the problem and avoid directionless wide range testing. A close liaison with the sources of referral allows the psychologist to identify what clinical information or tests can best answer the questions posed.

In some cases, formal neuropsychological testing may not even be necessary. Demographic data, clinical observations, or an interview can elicit the required information. Also it is not unusual to discover, especially with children, that intellectual assessments have been carried out previously by other agencies and are available upon request. One of the unfortunate traditions in psychology is the duplication of services–filing cabinets are filled with psychometric data replicating the same tests on the same individuals with virtually identical results.

AIMS OF NEUROPSYCHOLOGICAL INTERVIEWING

The initial aim of the neuropsychological interview is to integrate patients' available medical, psychological and social history. Thus, they may be asked about the sources and results of any previous investigations. However, it is unwise to rely upon patients' memories. Information from relatives and medical records may be reviewed to help identify any conditions that may have led to cerebral dysfunction. Medications and their prescribed dose at the time of assessment need to be noted since these may influence test scores. Care must be taked to critically evaluate previous assessments. They should not be taken at face value.

Second, it is essential to establish patients' general level of premorbid functioning. This may be inferred from a knowledge of their educational and occupational achievements together with details of their reading and recreational habits. School records are particularly helpful. Knowledge of the premorbid levels provides a baseline for interpreting test results. For example, an individual who had worked at an occupation implying a superior intellectual level (for example, as a university lecturer), but who now can only obtain merely average scores on cognitive tests, cannot be said to be scoring within their normal limits.

Third, patients' state of consciousness needs to be routinely monitored. Orientation for person, place and time becomes quickly apparent when gathering the essentials of personal and family data. The extent of patients' ability to sustain attention also manifests itself during the course of the interview. Inability to pay attention and concentrate for up to a period of 30 seconds needs to be noted since this impairs the normal ability to assimilate information. In some cases, patients may be so distractable and disoriented that attempts at formal quantitative testing will have to be abandoned. The psychologist need not feel a sense of personal failure in such cases. Consultation with the referral source may be useful in reducing the frequency of such referrals.

Fourth, the patient needs to be carefully observed and interviewed to assess the following major areas of neuropsychological functioning: motor; auditory; tactile; visuo-spatial; language; memory; higher cognitive processes; and personality organization. A qualitative review serves to generate further hypotheses which may be quantitatively assessed during psychological testing.

The goal is to integrate the clinical and experimental approaches. Lishman (1978) found that the integration of clinical and psychometric approaches results in the most discriminating assessment since the former tends to "under-diagnose" organicity when used alone, whereas the latter is prone to "over-diagnose" it. The experienced investigator also looks for qualitative signs of cerebral dysfunction such as perseveration, pressure of speech and emotional tone during psychological testing.

A review of neuropsychological functioning may be most naturally initiated by listing patients' subjective complaints. If they are asked to describe their problems in their own words there is less likelihood of the clinician suggesting symptomatology by asking direct questions which tend to be answered with a "yes" or "no". A distinction needs to be made between patients' perceptions of their problems and the investigator's clinical impressions. When more objective probing is undertaken with questions designed to elicit neurobehavioural signs, patients can be asked to give detailed examples concerning their problems.

Finally, the validity of the accumulated data needs to be estimated. For example, the accuracy of patients as historians, and their degree of motivation to perform maximally, significantly influence test results. The possibility of malingering, especially during medicolegal assessments, is being increasingly studied and will be discussed in another chapter.

Cerebral dysfunction is commonly associated with certain qualitative changes in behaviour. It must be reiterated that the accuracy with which such organic signs are identified together with the usefulness of the history elicited is a function of the clinician's skill, knowledge and experience. There is an artistic component in following significant threads from a mass of conflicting data. Symptoms need to be assessed according to their nature and context. The validity of historical sources needs to be estimated. The line of questioning must have a coherent focus which can only evolve with accumulated experience concerning the organic brain syndromes.

Readers should consult Appendix IV which contains the specific contents which may be used as a guideline for a structured neuropsychological interview. Such a guideline qualitatively delineates problem areas and provides a focus for a quantitative analysis of the extent of the patient's deficits through the use of objective tests.

Both clinical interviewing and psychological testing can be logically cross-indexed in terms of both a qualitative and quantitative review of human functioning. In order to facilitate the integration of qualitative and quanitative data, it will be noted that the order of the areas of neuropsychological functioning listed in the sample interview form (Appendix IV) correspond identically with the order of the functional categories in the test battery described in this text. Such an integration of neuropsychological functioning may contribute to the resolution of the paradigm clash between the clinical–intuitive hypothesis testing approach and the psychometric tradition.

It is by testing that we discern fine gold.
Leonardo da Vinci

5
Description and Administration of Tests

THE AIM of this chapter is to introduce recommended neuropsychological tests from both the adult and adolescent batteries. There is a brief description of each test, with an address of a supplier of the equipment required. The method of administration is also outlined with an explanation of scoring procedures. Clinical interpretation is discussed in Chapter 6.

Norms are provided after a description of each test. They are an integration of norms from other literature and the Royal Prince Alfred Hospital neuropsychological data base. Useful normative guidelines may be found in Reitan and Davison (1974), Lezak (1976), Trites (1977) and Swiercinsky (1978). Spreen and Gaddes (1969) and Knights and Norwood (1979) are particularly good sources for norms for young children.

Norms that can be expressed as percentile scores are favoured because of ready compatibility with much of the contemporary normative literature. A useful convention is to perceive the 25th percentile as a cut-off point mildly suggestive of brain damage in people with an average or above average premorbid intelligence. It has been hypothesized that the 10th percentile is moderately suggestive of brain damage. In order to avoid false positives, the use of the 10th percentile as a cut-off point may be of greater value. A *Codebook For Report Writing* is available for those people interested in detailed statistical and comprehensive neuropsychological probability statements from Codebook Inc., 110 Main, Suite 111, Evanston, Wyoming 82930 U.S.A. This book contains a digest of neuropsychological test descriptors and lays out a series of interpretive steps that are computer compatible.

GENERAL TESTING CONSIDERATIONS

Before beginning to administer any tests, certain general routine considerations need to be taken into account when assessing the brain damaged patient. Despite their importance, such process variables tend to be neglected. Interpersonal issues have pertinence even in automated testing. The rationale for computerized evaluation is to liberate clinicians from clerical routine so that they can spend more creative time with their patients.

Flexibility and commonsense are intrinsic to valid test administration. For example, brain damaged patients tend to tire easily. If a patient becomes unduly fatigued, rest breaks must be scheduled if maximal performance is to be documented. Such simple details as the need for persons who wear glasses to bring them along obviously contribute to valid evaluation.

The ideal enviroment in which testing should take place is well lit, adequately ventilated, free from distractions and contains comfortable furniture. However, clinical skills can compensate for environmental inadequacies. For example, much useful testing may still be accomplished in maximum security institutions, nursing one's own equipment on one's lap with the subject separated from the examiner by prison bars, and visiting hours cutting testing time down to half that one normally wishes for.

The most important requirements during test administration are the establishment of rapport and the creation of a supportive environment to facilitate maximal performance. The ability to empathize with patients and to meet their needs is a basic requirement of professional practice. Since the publications of Orne's (1962) classic article, "The social psychology of the psychology experiment", it has been accepted that examiner characteristics significantly influence results of tests. Skills in test administration, interpretation, and the ability to establish therapeutic interpersonal relationships with patients vary with each examiner. Maximal test performance requires motivated patients who feel that their needs are being met by the clinician. For example, Parsons and Stewart (1966) report that brain damaged patients show less improvement on a perceptual-motor test when assessed by a "detached" examiner compared with the results of tests conducted by an examiner who was "supportive".

Rapport is enhanced by orienting the patient to the purposes of testing and describing some of the activities this will entail. Such knowledge alleviates fear of the unknown and is reassuring to many patients.

It is the responsibility of the clinician to compensate for any extraneous emotional and physical variables that may be disruptive to maximal performance, even if this means administering a test in a non-standardized manner. Thus, if patients are not prepared for an item or appear to be unaware of what is expected of them, they should be appropriately oriented if possible. Fear of failure may also be controlled by an empathetic attitude. Neuropsychological tests attempt to measure the cognitive "ceiling" (maximal performance) rather than monitor the disruptive "noise" of intruding non-cognitive factors.

There is a widespread belief that neuropsychological assessment must inherently remain an inordinately time-consuming burden. This may be so for a beginner or a technician, but it does not necessarily apply to an experienced clinician. To use a medical analogy, "most physicians have learned that although a 'complete' survey of the heart, lungs, abdomen and other structures can take hours, intimate knowledge of the examination and repeated practice enable them to obtain essential information in a very brief time". (Geschwind, 1979: vi). Similarly, those who have mastered neuropsychological assessment and are intimately familiar with their test battery can obtain more cost-efficient data than rank beginners fumbling pedantically through their manuals. Their counter-productive labours are hardly a criterion for estimating how long testing potentially takes. The maxim in most neuropsychological laboratories is that "good testing is fast testing" (Boll, 1981).

Although the phrasing in some test manuals suggests disagreement (for the protection of beginners), the purpose of assessment is to obtain useful information and not to indulge in a mindless stereotyped ritual. Administering a test battery not only assesses the patient's performance but also provides evidence of the examiner's skill and experience. The patient's neurological and psychiatric condition will also influence the time necessary for the administration of the test. Consequently, an arbitrary average time will not be given for each test described below.

It is not normally necessary to administer every item for each modality in a test battery to obtain valid results. Experienced examiners are more concerned with meeting the needs of their patients than in being totally preoccupied with a strictly mechanical presentation of tests. If ludicrously easy items are presented (such as counting 1 to 10 for a professor of mathematics) or if impossible questions are asked (authorship of Faust to illiterate patients), rapport is destroyed. Empathetic clinicians avoid embarrassing patients by administering test items that are too easy or too difficult.

After interviewing patients, reviewing their history and eliciting some sample responses on a few test items, experienced clinicians have formulated a working hypothesis concerning patients' degree of cognitive sophistication. During testing, a zone of response becomes apparent, with a characteristic "floor" and "ceiling" which may vary between the functional categories. Concentrating testing time on the range of items where the patient's "ceiling" may lie reduces redundancy. The process of testing supplies continual corrective feedback. Thus one can move up or down the scales of difficulty if there is under or over estimation of patients' performance levels until the critical level of maximal performance is approached.

Not all tests are constructed with a response scale calibrated according to degrees of difficulty. Also, some patients have islands of uneven or "splinter" skills which allow them to complete some difficult items while failing to perform easier tasks. Consequently, caution must be used when attempting advanced methods of cost-effective test administration. Such departures from orthodoxy are not recommended for neophytes.

Trites (1977) suggests that, whenever tests are administered in a modified manner, it is helpful to identify this fact by making an appropriate comment in parentheses (for example: incomplete; unreliable score; disability related to actual condition; non-standardized administration; prorated scores; short form version, etc.). Not all patients yield valid and reliable test results, and in fact a small minority of persons is unable to be tested. Noting the probability of valid scores during administration is a prerequisite for meaningful test interpretation.

The test battery described in this chapter takes approximately three to four hours of clinical time for the experienced examiner, dependent upon the patient's condition. Consequently, most patients can comfortably complete assessment at one sitting without having to schedule additional appointments. Such cost-efficiency is obtained by deleting the two most time-consuming of the Halstead–Reitan procedures, shortening the tests within the Halstead–Reitan (as successfully demonstrated by Golden (1979) and others), substituting short forms and well validated alternate tests, and testing within the critical zone of maximal performance.

There is an infinite number of clinical adaptations that may be made to meet the needs of individual patients during test administration. However, for the sake of brevity, only standardized methods of administration will be described.

LATERALITY PREFERENCE SCHEDULE

The HRNTB lateral dominance examination is an adequate clinical tool which was used during our research and may still be safely recommended. However, the recently developed laterality preference schedule appears to be a more promising and sophisticated contribution (Dean, 1982).

Description

The laterality preference schedule (LPS) is a self-report measure of lateral preference. For the standardization of the measure, its 49 items were organized by eye, ear, foot, arm, and hand into a final laterality preference schedule. From a psychometric viewpoint, the LPS is a multifactorial measure of lateral preference patterns.

Equipment Supplier

Raymond S. Dean, Washington University School of Medicine, Department of Psychiatry, The Jewish Hospital of St Louis, 212 South Kingshighway, St Louis, Missouri 63110, U.S.A.

Administration and Scoring

The LPS is administered and scored as described in the schedule provided by the author listed above, who has kindly allowed reproduction of the schedule below (and Tables 2 and 3). Copyright for the schedule remains with Dr Dean to whom any requests regarding its use should be directed.

Name: *Age:*
Date: *Sex:* Male ☐ Female ☐

People have different ways of doing the same task. For example, I may hit a drum with my left hand while someone else may use their right; and still others use both hands equally as much.

For each of the following statements about which eye, ear, foot, arm and hand you use, imagine that you are performing the task and decide whether you use your:

LA–Left always
LM–Left mostly
E–Left and right equally
RM–Right mostly
RA–Right always

After deciding, draw a ring around your choice after each statement. Be sure to answer each statement. Do not skip or miss any. Please begin.

With which eye do you or would you:					
1. Look into a microscope	LA	LM	E	RM	RA
2. Use to look through a small hole	LA	LM	E	RM	RA
3. Look into a telescope	LA	LM	E	RM	RA
4. Keep open when threading a needle	LA	LM	E	RM	RA
5. Use to aim a camera	LA	LM	E	RM	RA
With which ear do you or would you:					
6. Listen on the telephone	LA	LM	E	RM	RA
7. Turn toward a soft sound far away	LA	LM	E	RM	RA
8. Wear a radio earphone	LA	LM	E	RM	RA
9. Put near a wall to hear a strange sound	LA	LM	E	RM	RA
10. Listen to a secret	LA	LM	E	RM	RA

With which foot do you or would you:	
11. Hop	LA LM E RM RA
12. Kick a ball	LA LM E RM RA
13. Put a shoe on first	LA LM E RM RA
14. Step on a bug	LA LM E RM RA
15. Stand the longest	LA LM E RM RA
Which arm do you or would you:	
16. Raise to be called on in school	LA LM E RM RA
17. Wipe a table with a sponge	LA LM E RM RA
18. Pull a waggon with	LA LM E RM RA
19. Clean a blackboard with	LA LM E RM RA
20. Touch your chest with when crossing your arms	LA LM E RM RA
With which hand do you or would you:	
21. Turn on a water faucet	LA LM E RM RA
22. Pet a dog	LA LM E RM RA
23. Hold a glass when drinking	LA LM E RM RA
24. Put a coin in a piggy bank	LA LM E RM RA
25. Rub out a pencil mark	LA LM E RM RA
26. Hold a brush when painting	LA LM E RM RA
27. Pick up a penny	LA LM E RM RA
28. Draw a circle	LA LM E RM RA
29. Brush your teeth	LA LM E RM RA
30. Write	LA LM E RM RA
31. Hold a fork when eating	LA LM E RM RA
32. Pick up a piece of paper	LA LM E RM RA
33. Open a door	LA LM E RM RA
34. Hold a knife when cutting	LA LM E RM RA
35. Wash your face	LA LM E RM RA
36. Open a can of soft drink	LA LM E RM RA
37. Comb or brush your hair	LA LM E RM RA
38. Open a dresser drawer	LA LM E RM RA
39. Hold a heavy object	LA LM E RM RA
40. Unscrew a tight jar cap	LA LM E RM RA
41. Throw a ball	LA LM E RM RA
42. Hammer a nail	LA LM E RM RA
43. Screw the top on a bottle	LA LM E RM RA
44. Point with	LA LM E RM RA
45. Have the greatest strength	LA LM E RM RA
46. Turn on a light	LA LM E RM RA
47. Hold scissors when cutting	LA LM E RM RA
48. Feel how smooth something was	LA LM E RM RA
49. Cover your mouth when coughing	LA LM E RM RA

Table 2
Scores for the Dean Laterality Preference Schedule–Adult

Dean Laterality Preference Schedule	Male[1]		Female[2]	
	$\bar{X}$	SD	$\bar{X}$	SD
I (General hand)	25.56	11.92	21.49	8.54
II (Visual guided motor)	41.08	12.15	37.46	11.72
III (Eye)	11.69	5.94	10.46	4.03
IV (Ear)	12.23	2.94	11.56	3.38
V (Strength)	10.13	3.89	8.49	3.10
VI (Foot Use)	9.33	1.84	8.46	1.68

[1]n = 125; $\bar{X}$ CA = 23.41
[2]n = 131; $\bar{X}$ CA = 22.94

Table 3
Items of the Dean Laterality Preference Schedule comprising each Factor

Factor I	Factor II	Factor III	Factor IV	Factor V	Factor VI
General Laterality	Visually Guided Activity	Visual	Auditory	Strength	Foot Use
Items 12	Items 16	Items 1	Items 6	Items 36	Items 11
20	17	2	7	39	13
25	18	3	8	40	15
26	19	4	9	43	14
28	21	5	10	45	
29	22				
30	23				
31	24				
34	27				
37	32				
41	33				
42	35				
47	38				
	44				
	46				
	48				
	49				

GROOVED PEGBOARD

Description

The grooved pegboard is a manipulative dexterity task. The unit consists of 25 holes with randomly positioned slots. Pegs, which have a key along one side, must be rotated to match the hole before they can be inserted. This test requires more complex visuomotor co-ordination than most pegboards.

Equipment Supplier

Lafayette Instruments, Box 1279, Lafayette, Indiana 47902, U.S.A.

Administration

Patients are seated at a table with the pegboard directly in front of them. The board is at the distant end of the table with the peg tray closest to the patient. The test is explained as follows: "This is the pegboard test. The goal is to see how quickly and accurately you can work with your hands. Each peg has a 'key' on one side which will fit into a groove on the hole when the peg is turned the right way".

[*Demonstrate by filling the top row.*]

"When I say 'go', begin here (with the top left hole for the right hand or the top right hole for the left hand) and place the pegs in the holes as quickly as you can using only one hand. Fill each row from this side to this side–"

[*Indicate that, for the right, the holes are filled from left to right, and from right to left for the left hand side.*]

"–before doing the next row. Do not miss any holes".

The dominant hand is tested first, and then the non-dominant hand. Only one peg must be picked up at a time. Keep a count of the number of pegs dropped while timing the task. Only one trial is given for each hand without a practice session. A trial may be terminated after five minutes.

Scoring

Record the time taken to complete the task for each hand. Also, record the number of pegs dropped for each hand. The patient should be told not to pick up any dropped pegs since this slows results. There are ample additional pegs on the board to pick up.

Scores for the Grooved Pegboard Test*

The table below contains adult norms for the grooved pegboard test in the form of means and standard deviations. However, Golden's (1978) motor testing interpretations involving differential comparisons between the left and right hand are more useful than group norms. Intra-individual comparisons are also equally applicable to children.

*Adapted from: Swiercinsky, D. P. *Manual for the adult neuropsychological evaluation.* Springfield, Ill.: Charles C. Thomas, 1978.

Grooved Pegboard Test Scores

Population	Right Hand	Left Hand
	Mean and SD	Mean and SD
Psychiatric	83 sec. ± 38	84 sec. ± 40
Brain damaged	115 sec. ± 78	122 sec. ± 84

FINGER TAPPING TEST

Description

The finger tapping test is a measure of finger agility. It consists of a tapping key with a device for recording the number of taps.

Equipment Supplier

Ralph M. Reitan, Neuropsychological Laboratory, 1338 E. Edison, Tucson, Arizona 85719, U.S.A.

Administration

Patients are seated at a table with the finger tapper directly in front of them. The test is explained as follows: "This is the finger tapping test. The goal is to see how quickly you can tap. Place your arm and hand in a comfortable position and without moving your wrist or arm see how quickly you can tap on the key with your index finger".

[*Demonstrate the correct position and give the patient a ten second practice session.*]

"Please remember to allow the key to come all the way up and push it all the way down otherwise the number on the dial won't change. When I say 'go', tap as fast as you can. Stop when I tell you to".

The dominant hand is tested first, followed by the non-dominant hand. The number of times patients can tap in 10 seconds is recorded. Five consecutive trials are needed within five taps of each other. However, discontinue after 10 attempts. A brief rest period (approximately 20 seconds) between trials is recommended. All trials with the dominant hand need to be completed before testing the other hand.

Some patients may move the whole hand instead of merely the index finger. If this problem occurs the patient should be corrected and the trial can be repeated.

Scoring

Calculate the mean number of taps for five consecutive trials within a five point range for each hand. Use the five consecutive trials with the smallest range if no five consecutive trials are within five taps.

Scores for the Finger Tapping Test*

Dodrill (1978) compares the performance of normal adults to three groups of brain damaged individuals (right hemisphere, left hemisphere, and both cerebral hemispheres) and uses a control group as a basis for comparison and that simultaneously considers the relative performances of each hand on each task. As with other sensory motor tasks, significantly more impairment on one hand as opposed to the other implies the involvement of the contralateral hemisphere (Golden, 1978). Such intra-individual comparisons are equally applicable to both adults and children. Spreen and Gaddes (1969) provide group norms for children.

Finger Tapping Test Scores

Population	Right Hand	Left Hand
	Mean and SD	Mean and SD
Control group	53 taps/10 sec. ± 6	50 taps/10 sec. ± 5
Right damage	42 taps/10 sec. ± 9	31 taps/10 sec. ± 14
Left damage	37 taps/10 sec. ± 17	39 taps/10 sec. ± 11
Bilateral damage	40 taps/10 sec. ± 11	35 taps/10 sec. ± 10

HAND DYNAMOMETER

Description

The hand dynamometer is a measure of grip strength. The most preferred device may be adjusted to the size of the patient's hands and can record up to 100 kilograms.

Equipment Supplier

Stoeltine Company, 1350 S. Kostner Avenue, Chicago, Illinois 60623, U.S.A. (or other rehabilitation suppliers).

*Adapted from: Dodrill, C. B. The hand dynamometer as a neuropsychological measure. *Journal of Consulting and Clinical Psychology*, 1978, *48:* 1432.

Administration

The patient is asked to stand up and the test is explained as follows: "This dynamometer will measure your grip strength. Take it in your hand, point it downward, keep it away from your body and squeeze it as hard as you can".

[*Demonstrate the correct procedure*].

Two trials are given in alternating fashion for each hand starting with the dominant hand. If the two trials differ by more than five kilograms, more trials are given until two trials within five kilograms are obtained.

Scoring

Obtain the average of the two trials (within a range of five kilograms) for each hand.

Scores on the Smedley Hand Dynanometer*

Dodrill (1978) compares the performance of normal adults to three groups of brain damaged individuals (right hemisphere, left hemisphere, and both hemispheres). Golden's (1978) motor interpretations involving differential comparisons between the left and right hand should also be used. These intra-individual comparisons are equally applicable to children. Spreen and Gaddes (1969) provide group norms for children.

Hand Dynamometer Test Scores

Population	Right Hand	Left Hand
	Mean and SD	Mean and SD
Control group	48 kg ± 13	45kg ± 12
Right damage	34kg ± 12	21kg ± 15
Left damage	31kg ± 17	37kg ± 13
Bilateral damage	36kg ± 9	32kg ± 12

SPEECH-SOUNDS PERCEPTION TEST

Description

The speech-sounds perception test (SSPT) is a measure of ability to differentiate between similar sounding nonsense syllables containing the double

*Adapted from: Dodrill, C. B. The hand dynamometer as a neuropsychological measure. *Journal of Consulting and Clinical Psychology*, 1978, *48:* 1432–1435.

vowels 'ee' in the middle of the syllable with various consonants at the beginning and conclusion of each syllable. The items heard on tape must be matched with the written form of the syllable presented in multiple choice form. It requires a reading grade level of at least 4.5 (as measured by the wide range achievement test) for valid completion.

Equipment Supplier

The cassette tape may be purchased from: Ralph M. Reitan, Neuropsychological Laboratory, 1338 E. Edison, Tucson, Arizona 85719, U.S.A. A cassette player, answer sheet (which comes with the tape) and pencil are also required.

Administration

Reitan's tape contains 60 items. However, only the first 30 items need to be administered. This short form of the SSPT may be substituted for the complete version when evaluating both neurological and psychiatric patients without influencing diagnostic accuracy (Ryan, *et al.*, 1982).

Patients are seated at a table in good acoustic surroundings with a cassette player set at an appropriate volume. The answer sheet and pencil are placed in front of them.

The test is explained as follows: "You will hear a voice on tape saying 'the first word is . . .' and then it will say one of the four nonsense words on the first line of the answer sheet".

[*Point to the first set of options.*]

"The voice will then say 'the second word is . . .' and then it will say one of the four nonsense words on the second line of the answer sheet".

[*Point to the second set of options.*]

"You will have to listen carefully and pick out the word said and draw a line beneath it. If you make an error, cross it out and then draw a line under the word you want. I will now play a sample. Don't underline anything, just listen to it and point to the word you think is said".

[*Sample of 1, 2 and 3 are played and if there are no problems in comprehension, and the volume is loud enough, the examination may begin.*]

"We can now start. This time underline the word that you hear. If you are not sure, you may guess".

Once testing begins, no more help can be given. If the patient is obviously too slow to keep up with the tape, it may be turned off after each item. However, this fact must be noted during test interpretation.

Scoring

The score is the total number incorrect out of 30. A scoring key is provided with the tape.

Adult and Children's Speech–Sounds Perception Test: Short Form

The children's version of the speech-sounds perception test is applicable from ages nine to 14 years. The correct choices are italicized. A cut-off score of six errors on short forms of the test may be classified as outside the normal limits.

Adult Scoring Forms

Series A	**Series B**	**Series C**
1. theeks zeeks *theets* zeets	1. peem beem *peen* been	1. deeld *deel* beeld beel
2. weech yeech *weej* yeej	2. theez *theerz* feez feerz	2. weev heev *weef* heef
3. leeg bleeg *leeng* bleeng	3. sheesh *sheez* zeesh zeez	3. tjee fee *theer* feer
4. peez *peest* teez teest	4. veef weef *veeth* weeth	4. neeld *neel* meeld meel
5. freeb fleeb *freep* fleep	5. theel feel *theeld* feeld	5. seed zeed *seet* zeet
6. pleeb preeb *pleed* preed	6. peet *peent* beet beent	6. yeeg *yeek* heeg heek
7. seek *seech* sheek sheech	7. treep *treeb* teep teeb	7. meen *meem* neen neem
8. neek *neenk* meek meenk	8. steets speets *steeks* speeks	8. theerd *theer* teerd teer
8. wheech heech *wheesh* heesh	9. beert *beerd* peert peerd	9. heez wheez *heev* wheev
10. preet *preekt* peet peekt	10. sheed zeed *sheend* zeend	10. neep teep *neet* teet

Children's Scoring Forms

Series A	**Series B**	**Series C**
1. *theets* theeks zeets	1. beem peem *peen*	1. beel deeld *deel*
2. yeej weech *weej*	2. *theerz* theez feerz	2. *weef* weev heef
3. bleeng leeg *leeng*	3. *sheez* sheesh zeez	3. feer thee *theer*
4. teest peez *peest*	4. weeth veef *veeth*	4. meel neeld *neel*
5. freeb *freep* fleep	5. feeld *theeld* theel	5. zeet seed *seet*
6. preed *pleed* pleeb	6. *peent* peet beent	6. *yeek* yeeg heek
7. seek *seech* sheech	7. treep *treeb* teeb	7. neem *meem* meen
8. meenk *neenk* neek	8. speeks steets *steeks*	8. theerd *theer* teer
9. heesh wheech *wheesh*	9. *beerd* beert peerd	9. *heev* heez wheev
10. preet *preekt* peekt	10. zeend sheed *sheend*	10. *neet* neep teet

SEASHORE RHYTHM TEST

Description

The seashore rhythm test is a measure of the auditory perception for rhythmical patterns. Thirty pairs of rhythmical patterns are presented on tape and the patient must discriminate between them being either the same or different.

Equipment Supplier

The cassette tape may be purchased from: Ralph M. Reitan, Neuropsychological Laboratory, 1338 E. Edison, Tucson, Arizona 85719, U.S.A. A cassette player, answer sheet (which comes with the tape), and pencil are also required.

Administration

Patients are seated at a table in good acoustic surroundings with a cassette player set at an appropriate volume. An answer sheet and pencil are placed in front of the patient. The test is explained as follows: "You will hear two rhythmic patterns, one after the other. You must tell whether the two patterns are the same or different. If they are the same, place an S in the correct space in the answer sheet. If they are different place a D. Listen to a sample so that you can understand what to do."

If patients understand the instructions (and the volume is appropriate) the tape is restarted and the 30 items presented.

It is helpful to caution patients that the items are presented at a fast rate and that it is important to jot down the answers quickly. If patients cannot cope with the standard administration it may be clinically informative to slow the pace by stopping the cassette player after each presentation and waiting for their response. However, all such departures from standardized administration need to be noted.

Scoring

The responses are scored by counting the total number of correct answers under standard administration. A scoring key is provided with the tape.

Seashore Rhythm Test Key and Ranked Score Conversion Table*

Trites' (1977) rhythm key contains a list of correct responses. After the total number of correct answers is counted, this raw score is converted to a rank score using the ranked score conversion table.

*Adapted from: Trites, R. L. *Neuropsychological test manual.* Ontario: Lafayette Instrument Co., 1977.

Rhythm Key

	A	B	C
1	S	S	D
2	D	D	S
3	S	S	S
4	D	D	D
5	S	D	S
6	D	D	D
7	S	S	S
8	D	D	D
9	D	S	D
10	S	S	S

Add up the total number of correct answers. The clinically significant score for both children and adults is judged to be less than 26 correct. Borderline impairment is shown with scores between 21 and 25 correct responses; mild impairment is shown with scores between the 16 to 20 range; and severe impairment is noted when there are only 15 or less correct answers.

FACE HAND TEST

Description

The face hand test monitors the ability to recognize light tactile input.

Equipment Needed

Cotton balls.

Administration

The patient is seated at a table opposite to the clinician. The test is explained as follows: "Put your hands on the table palms down. I am going to touch either your hand—"

[*Touch the middle of the back of the right hand lightly with a cotton ball.*]

"—or your face."

[*Touch the middle of the left cheek.*]

"Tell me which one has been touched after your eyes are closed."

Without telling the patient of the occasional presentation of simultaneous stimulation, randomly touch the right hand, left cheek and both simultaneously. Continue this until stimuli have been applied simultaneously to both the cheek and hand four times. Repeat this procedure by touching the left hand, right cheek and both simultaneously.

Scoring

The total number of errors is recorded in the order that they occurred. Patients need to state that they have been touched on the face and the hand in order to be correct for simultaneous stimulation. Record the actual incorrect response. For example, if the subjects do not recognize that they were touched on the hand during the third round of the "right hand–left face" simultaneous stimulation trial, the error would be recorded as follows:

					TOTAL ERRORS	
RH - LF			X(H)		RH - LF	1
LH - RF					LH - RF	0

Smith and Centofani (1979) supply a commercially available manual on the administration, scoring and interpretation of this version of the face hand test.

FINGER AGNOSIA

Description

Finger agnosia is an impairment in specific digital recognition. Testing requires patients to recognize light tactile stimulation applied randomly to the fingers.

Equipment Needed

Pencil with rubber end.

Administration

Patients are seated at a table opposite to the clinician. The test is explained as follows: "Put your right (dominant) hand on the table, palm down with the fingers comfortably spread apart. I am now going to number your fingers beginning with the thumb. Your thumb is number one, two, three, four and five".

Touch the patient's thumb with the rubber end of the pencil, followed by each finger respectively. The fingers are lightly touched on the middle phalange. Once a finger labelling system has been established, ask patients to close their eyes. "I will now touch one of your fingers and you are to tell me by number which finger you feel was touched". The patient's fingers are touched four times, each in a random order. However, two adjacent fingers are not stimulated right after the other. Repeat this procedure with the non-dominant hand.

This test is designed to monitor digital recognition rather than the use of linguistic labels to identify the sources of stimulation. Consequently, if patients cannot learn the number system, they are allowed to report in other ways (for example, naming or pointing to the finger touched with the other hand).

Scoring

The total number of errors is recorded in the order that they occur for each hand. Record the actual incorrect response. For example, if on the right hand trial, the subject responded "two" the third time finger four was touched, the error would be noted as follows:

FINGER AGNOSIA

	1				2				3				4				5			
RIGHT															2					
LEFT																				

TOTAL ERRORS : R 1

L 0

GRAPHAESTHESIA

Description

Graphaesthesia requires the recognition of symbols traced on the fingertips without the use of vision and translating this knowledge into a spoken response.

Equipment Needed

Pencil.

Administraton

Patients are seated at a table opposite to the clinician. The test is explained as follows: "Put your right (dominant) hand on the table with the palm up. I am going to write some numbers on your fingertips with a pencil. First, I will write the numbers three, four, five, and six on the palm of your hand so that you know how I write each number. You will notice that the numbers are upside down since I am facing you. Now close your eyes and let us begin". Write a number in random order on each of the patients' fingertips and ask them to say what was written. Run four trials per finger with stimulation being completed for each of the five fingers before the next trial is administered. Repeat this procedure with the non-dominant hand.

Scoring

The total number of errors is recorded in the order that they occur for each hand. Record the actual incorrect response. For example, if, on the right hand trial, the subject responded incorrectly the third time finger four was stimulated the error would be noted as follows:

GRAPHAESTHESIA

RIGHT	1					2					3					4			X		5				
LEFT	1					2					3					4					5				

TOTAL ERRORS : R 1
L 0

TACTILE FORM RECOGNITION TEST

Description

The tactile form recognition test requires the identification of geometric shapes by touch alone (stereognosis). Testing for astereognosis is also routine in comprehensive neurological examinations.

Equipment Needed

Small plastic tokens (square, triangle, circle and cross). These shapes may be obtained in most preschool toy shops.

Administration

The patient is seated at a table opposite to the clinician. The test is explained as follows: "Put your right (dominant) hand on the table palm up. I am going to place an object in your hand and I want you to tell me what shape it is by feeling it with that hand only. Now close your eyes and let us begin".

The following small plastic shapes are then presented: square; triangle; circle; and cross. Repeat this procedure with the non-dominant hand.

Scoring

Record the number of errors for each hand. Note the degree of difficulty patients have when manipulating the objects.

TRAIL MAKING TEST: PART B

Description

The trail making test ("trails B") monitors planning ability as well as visuomotor speed and concentration. It consists of randomly printed circles that are either numbered or lettered. The patient draws a connecting line alternating between numbers and letters. There are versions for both adults and children. The adult version consists of 25 circles either numbered from 1 to 13 or lettered "A" to "L". The version for children has circles from 1 to 8 and letters from "A" to "G".

Equipment Supplier

Ralph M. Reitan, Neuropsychology Laboratory, 1338 E. Edison, Tucson, Arizona 85719, U.S.A.

Administration

Patients are seated at a table with the "trails B" sample in front of them and given a pencil. The test is explained as follows: "On this page are some numbers and letters. Commence at number one and draw a line from 1 to A, A to 2, 2 to B, B to 3, 3 to C, and so on, until you reach the end.

[*Point out each circle in the correct order while explaining the test.*]

"Remember, first you have a number, followed by a letter. Connect the circles as fast as you can without taking the pencil off the page".

If the sample is correctly performed the "trails B" test page is presented. Patients are again told to connect the circles in the appropriate order. The beginning and the end of the sequence are pointed out. Timing is begun as soon as patients start attending to the task. If patients make an error it is immediately pointed out and they are urged to continue the sequence without delay. Some patients may not be able to understand what is required of them despite rehearsals on the sample. Others may not know the alphabet. With such patients, testing is discontinued. Assessment is also terminated if patients require more than five minutes to complete the protocol.

Scoring

Record the time taken to complete the task together with the number of errors.

Adult and Children's Trail Making Test: Part B

The table below contains age-corrected scores from normal adult subjects in the form of percentile ranks.

Adult Trail Making Test (Part B) Test Scores (in Seconds)*

	Age (Years)				
Percentile	20-39	40-49	50-59	60-69	70-79
90	45	49	55	64	79
75	55	57	75	89	132
50	69	78	98	119	196
25	94	100	135	172	292
10	129	151	177	282	450

The 25th percentile is the cut-off point that is mildly suggestive of brain damage. Scores from the 10th percentile and below are moderately suggestive of brain damage.

The table below contains age-corrected norms for the children's version of the trail making test (part B) in the form of means and standard deviations. Scores that are two standard deviations outside the mean may be treated as clinically significant.

*Adapted from: Davies, A. D. Measures of mental deterioration in aging and brain damage. In S. S. Chown & K. F. Reigel (Eds), *Interdisciplinary topics in gerontology,* Vol. 1. Basel: S. Karger, 1968.

Children's Trail Making Test (Part B) Test Scores (in seconds)[†]

Age	Male		Female	
	Mean	SD	Mean	SD
8	78	35	72	39
9	58	22	51	15
10	52	15	43	15
11	43	20	41	12
12	40	13	34	11
13	40	26	31	7

BENTON VISUAL RETENTION TEST

Description

The Benton visual retention test monitors visual construction skills, visual memory and visual perception. The test requires the reproduction of a series of geometric figures. The subject must draw the design from memory after the card has been exposed for varying periods of time (five to 10 seconds). Three equivalent forms and four modes of administration are available.

Equipment Supplier

Psychological Corporation, 304 East 45th Street, New York, New York 10017, U.S.A.

Administration and Scoring

The test is administered and scored as described in Benton's manual (1974). It caters both for adults and children and provides an objective scoring system with normative data which make allowance for intelligence and age. Added qualitative information may be obtained by evaluating the type of errors patients make (for example, omissions of a peripheral figure, distortions, and perseverations).

REY-OSTERRIETH COMPLEX FIGURE TEST (COPY)

Description

The test is designed to monitor perceptual functioning, visual memory and higher planning functions. Patients are presented with a reproduction of Rey's complex figure and are asked to copy it while the clinician times them.

[†]Adapted from: Spreen, O., and Gaddes, W. H. Developmental norms for 15 neuropsychological tests age 6 to 15. *Cortex*, 1969, *5:* 171-191.

As patients complete each section, a different coloured pencil is given to them and the order of the colours is recorded. Approximately six coloured pencils are required. These serve as documentation for the type of strategy used. After this task is completed, patients' copies are removed and three minutes are allowed to elapse. They are then asked to reproduce the figure from memory while their effort is timed again.

Lezak's (1976) text contains a full scale reproduction of the Rey–Osterreith complex figure which may be used for testing purposes. Administration procedures, normative scoring criteria and interpretation of results are also dealt with in Lezak's (1976) review. Visser's (1980) manual also contains a cardboard reproduction.

Scoring Technique for the Rey–Osterrieth Complex Figure Test*

Units	Score (copy)	Score (memory)
1. Cross upper left corner, outside of rectangle		
2. Large rectangle		
3. Diagonal cross		
4. Horizontal midline of 2		
5. Vertical midline		
6. Small rectangle, within 2 to the left		
7. Small segment above 6		
8. Small parallel lines within 2, upper left		
9. Triangle above 2 upper right		
10. Small vertical line within 2, below 9		
11. Circle with three dots within 2		
12. Five parallel lines with 2 crossing 3, lower right		
13. Sides of triangle attached to 2 on right		
14. Diamond attached to 13		
15. Vertical line within triangle 13 parallel to right vertical of 2		
16. Horizontal line within 13, continuing 4 to right		
17. Cross attached to low centre		
18. Square attached to 2, lower left		
TOTAL		

Scoring

Consider each of the 18 units separately. Estimate the accuracy of each unit and its relative position within the whole of the design. For each unit count as follows:

Correct	Placed properly	2 points
	Placed poorly	1 point
Distorted or incomplete but recognizable	Placed properly	1 point
	Placed poorly	½ point
Absent or not recognizable		0 points
Maximum		36 points

*Adapted from: Lezak, M. D. *Neuropsychological assessment.* New York: Oxford University Press, 1976.

APHASIA LANGUAGE PERFORMANCE SCALES (ALPS)

Description

The ALPS monitors language ability in a comprehensive yet cost-efficient way. It assesses receptive skills (listening and reading) and expressive abilities (talking and writing), thus yielding four discrete subscales.

Equipment Supplier

Pinnacle Press, P.O. Box 1122, Murfreesboro, Tennessee 37130, U.S.A.

Administration and Scoring

The test is administered and scored as described in the ALPS commercially available manual (Keenan and Brassell, 1975).

CONTROLLED WORD ASSOCIATION TEST

Description

The controlled word association test measures verbal fluency and consists of three word naming trials using the letters F, A and S in that order. Patients are asked to say as many words as they can think of which begin with the designated letter, omitting proper nouns, numbers, and the same word with a different suffix.

Equipment Needed

Pencil and paper for examiner's use only.

Administration

The test is explained as follows: "I want to see how many words you can say beginning with a certain letter in one minute. Don't say proper nouns or numbers or the same word with a different ending. The letter is F, begin!" If patients have difficulty in understanding the task it can be explained with examples, using a non-designated letter. After the first (F) trial has been completed the A and S trials are administered. The examiner keeps a record of patients' verbal responses by writing them down.

Scoring

The total number of all correct words pronounced during the three one-minute trials is recorded. This sum is then adjusted for age, sex and education and it may be then converted into percentile scores.

Adjustment Formula and Conversion Table for the Controlled Word Association Test*

Adjustment Formula: Male

Years of Schooling	Age (Years) 25-54	55-59	60-64
9 or less	+14	+15	+17
9-11	+ 6	+ 7	+ 9
12-15	+ 4	+ 5	+ 7
16+	—	+ 1	+ 3

Adjustment Formula: Female

Years of Schooling	Age (Years) 25-54	55-59	60-64
9 or less	+9	+10	+12
9-11	+6	+ 7	+ 9
12-15	+4	+ 5	+ 7
16+	—	+ 1	+ 3

The total of all correct words pronounced during the three one-minute trials is recorded. This sum is then adjusted for age, sex and education and then converted into percentile rankings by consulting a table of norms.

Percentile Ranked Conversion Table

Adjusted Scores	Percentile Range
54-62	95+
51-53	90-94
49-50	85-89
46-48	80-84
44-45	75-79
43	70-74
41-42	65-69
40	60-64
38-39	55-59
37	50-54
36	45-49
35	40-44
34	35-39
33	30-34
31-32	25-29
29-30	20-24
27-28	15-19
25-26	10-14
24	5- 9
23 and below	4 and below

*Adapted from: Lezak, M. D. *Neuropsychological assessment.* New York: Oxford University Press, 1976.

MODIFIED WECHSLER MEMORY SCALE (WMS)

Description

Goodglass and Kaplan (1979) report that while no published test covers all the clinically significant aspects of memory, the Wechsler memory scale (WMS) has proved to be a popular, useful and sensitive instrument. It combines a survey of orientation and sustained attention with a new learning for both visual and verbal information. An alternate form, Wechsler memory scale Form II, is available for retesting.

Equipment Supplier

Psychological Corporation, 304 East 45th Street, New York, New York 10017, U.S.A.

Administration and Scoring

The test is administered and scored as described in the commercially available manual by Wechsler and Stone, 1973. It is also recommended that Russell's (1975) multiple scoring method be used as well. This modification of the WMS requires patients to recall two subtests (logical memory; and visual reproduction) after 30 minutes' delay.

Other testing not involved with memory may be done during this interval. Russell's (1975) scoring method yields the following six independent memory scales: verbal short-term; verbal long-term; verbal per cent retained; figural short-term; figural long-term; and figural per cent retained.

REY–OSTERRIETH COMPLEX FIGURE TEST (RECALL)

For details of the Rey–Osterrieth complex figure test see the previous discussion on page 103. After the figure has been copied, patients are asked to recall and reproduce it three minutes later.

WALTON–BLACK MODIFIED NEW WORD LEARNING TEST

Description

This is a task for the acquisition of new verbal information. It was designed to assist in the differentiation of patients with organic brain disease from those with functional disorders. Lishman (1978) provides a detailed review of the test and states that it is probably one of the most reliable instruments for such purposes.

Equipment Needed

Pencil and paper for examiner's use only.

Administration

A vocabulary test of ascending difficulty is administered (such as the subtest on the Wechsler adult intelligence scales [WAIS]) until the patient is unable to give the meanings of 10 consecutive words. (If the number of missed words resulting from the WAIS subtest is insufficient for testing, the Terman Merrill test may be used). Once a catalogue of 10 unknown words is obtained and listed on paper (for the examiner's use only) the test is explained as follows: "I want to see how quickly you can learn the meaning of new words. I have a list of words you missed on the vocabulary test. I will go through the list and tell you the meaning of the words. Immediately after this, I will test you to see if you know what these words mean. Please concentrate, we will now begin".

The procedure is repeated until the patient can give a correct explanation for any six of the 10 words. At each trial the exact wording of the definition is changed in order to avoid rote learning. Lishman (1978) described an easier version of this test for elderly depressed patients (synonym learning test). The same, rather than varied definitions, are given for each presentation.

Scoring

A record is kept of the number of correct words for each trial. Normal (non-organic brain damage) performance is judged to be the ability to learn six new words by the fifth trial. Norms are also available (Walton and Black, 1957).

WECHSLER INTELLIGENCE SCALES

Description

The Wechsler adult intelligence scales–revised (WAIS–R) and the Wechsler intelligence scale for children–revised (WISC–R) are recognized as well constructed and standardized tests which remain the best available measures of intellectual functioning.

Equipment Supplier

Psychological Corporation, 304 East 45th Street, New York, New York 10017, U.S.A.

Administration and Scoring

The WAIS–R is administered and scored as described in Wechsler's (1981) manual. The WISC–R is covered in Wechsler's 1974 manual.

WIDE RANGE ACHIEVEMENT TEST

Description

The wide range achievement test (WRAT) monitors educational achievement in reading arithmetic and spelling from kindergarten to college level. The reading test monitors word recognition and not comprehension since it focuses upon coding rather than semantic skills.

Equipment Supplier

Psychological Corporation, 304 East 45th Street, New York, New York 10017, U.S.A.

Administration and Scoring

The test is administered and scored as described in the manual by Jastak and Jastak (1978). Large print and Braille editions are available for the blind and partially blind.

STROOP COLOUR–WORD TEST

Description

This test monitors the capacity to maintain a uniform course of action independent of intruding stimuli. It requires patients to demonstrate flexibility by shifting their perceptual set to adapt to changing situations.

Equipment Needed, Administration and Scoring

No commercial version of the test is available throughout the world, but Golden (1979) describes a standardized form which may be easily constructed. His instructions are: "The Stroop test consists of three 8½ by 11 [inch—21.6 x 27.9 cm] pages. Each page consists of five columns of 20 items. Each item on page one is one of these words: Red, Green, or Blue. The words are repeated in a largely random order. Page two consists of 100 items, as does page one, but each item is the sequence X X X X. On this page, each X X X X is printed in red, green, or blue ink. Page three consists of the words on page one printed in the colours on page two, with the limitation that a word and the colour it is printed in may not match. Thus the word red may appear in blue or green ink, green appear in red or blue ink, and blue in red or green ink" (Golden, 1979:145–146).

On page one, patients are asked to read down each column as fast as possible, pronouncing the words contained there. On page two, the same procedure is followed, but patients are instructed to name the colour of the X X X Xs. On page three, patients are asked to name the colour of the ink the word is printed in rather than the word itself. The time limit is 45 seconds per page. The score is the total number of items correctly finished within the time limit on each page. Golden (1976) provides norms for the interpretation of results.

Means and Standard Deviations for the Stroop Colour–Word Test*

The table below shows the norms for the performance of 540 normal high school and college students on the Stroop test. Golden's interpretations† are discussed above.

Adult Percentile Norms

Test	Percentile			
Trial	25	50	75	100
Copy	31	32	34	36
Memory	18	22	27	35

Page	Mean	Standard Deviation
1. Word	99.6	18.9
2. Colour	72.2	15.7
3. Colour-word	46.3	9.8

PERSONALITY ORGANIZATION

Individual psychologists have their own preferred modes of assessing personality functioning, and so it may be presumptuous for others to recommend certain tests in this area. However, the Minnesota multiphasic personality inventory (MMPI) remains the most popular standardized test

*Adapted from: Golden, C. J. Identification of brain disorders by the Stroop color and word test. *Journal of Clinical Psychology,* 1976, *32:* 654–658.

†Golden, C. J. *Clinical interpretation of objective psychological tests.* New York: Grune & Stratton, 1979.

of personality in the world. It is so well known that it requires no further description here. This self-report instrument is cost-efficient as it does not require the clinician to administer it. The manual is obtainable from: Psychological Corporation, 304 East 45th Street, New York, New York 10017, U.S.A.

The MMPI is eminently computer-compatible and the marketing of programs for use with the MMPI scores has become a thriving industry. A particularly comprehensive automated process is the "Minnesota Report", from the original publisher of the MMPI. This is available from NCS Interpretive Scoring Systems, P.O. Box 1416B, Minneapolis, Minnesota 55440, U.S.A.

There are virtually as many modes of assessing the personality functioning of children as for adults. We favour a behavioural check list approach yielding a profile similar to that described by Edelbrock and Achenbach (1980). The child behaviour checklist is constructed to monitor the behavioural problems and abilities of children aged 4 to 16 years, as reported by their parents or guardians, in a standardized format. The checklist can be self-administered or administered by an interviewer.

Responses to the checklist are entered on the social competence and behaviour problem scales of the child behaviour profile. Separate editions of the profile are standardized at age ranges 4–5 years, 6–11 years, and 12–16 years for both boys and girls. The profile can be scored using either a computer program or hand scoring forms.

The child behaviour checklist and child behaviour profile, together with either hand-scoring templates or a 9-track, 800 bpi tape of computer entry and scoring program, are available at cost price from: Thomas M. Achenbach, Child, Adolescent, Family and Community Psychiatry, University of Vermont, 1 South Prospect Street, Burlington, Vermont 05401, U.S.A.

In Commonwealth countries local distributors supply many of the tests listed above as available from North American addresses.

Errors in judgement must occur in the practice of an art which consists largely in balancing probabilities.

William Ostler

6 Clinical Interpretation

THIS CHAPTER discusses the challenging task of the processing, integration and interpretation of the accumulated data base. Chapter 7 outlines the practical task of communicating test findings in the form of a neuropsychological assessment case report. The rest of this volume deals with the assessment of more specific subpopulations (children, medico-legal and psychiatric patients) with samples of actual clinical reports.

This chapter deals with the following material: warnings prior to attempting to interpret test results; a description of functional categories; the interpretation of single tests cross-indexed to these functional categories; the application of multiple inferential methods to test results; and test interpretation within the context of known organic brain syndromes. Any mention of "hit rates" during discussions of individual tests does not imply that a single test can be used in isolation. Rather, it is an attempt to convey the relative sensitivity of such a measure to cerebral dysfunction.

Before discussing data processing, it must be pointed out that a skilful interpretation of a diverse data base composed of the patient's history, medical records, qualitative behavioural observations and quantitative test scores cannot be abstractly conveyed by reading any book or attending a single workshop. Rather, this is a function of extended academic preparation in the behavioural and neurosciences together with a period of apprenticeship under clinical supervision during which the apprentice is exposed to patients with cerebral dysfunction.

Most clinical psychologists already have the psychometric background to learn the process of administration of neuropsychological tests with ease. The clinical interpretation process involves the integration of test results with the known facts of cerebral functioning. Thus, the more knowledge that generalist psychologists can gain of the central nervous system and the associated neuropathological processes, the more value they will be able to extract from their test findings.

Patient characteristics also need to be taken into consideration before specific attempts are made to interpret test results as a matter of routine. Knowledge of a patient's premorbid level of performance serves as a baseline which gives meaning to test results. Finlayson, *et al.* (1977) found that educational level had a significant effect on Halstead–Reitan test battery scores. Also, certain occupations may reinforce the overlearning of specific skills which can cause misleading test results. For example, instrument workers and accountants may develop a different pattern of strengths for fine motor co-ordination tasks and calculating skills because of the nature of their daily work.

It is well known that sensory-motor and cognitive skills tend to decline with increasing age. Consequently, age related norms are necessary for valid test interpretation. Unfortunately, many tests have inadequate norms for people in the sixth decade of life onwards. This often results in an over-diagnosis of brain damage for geriatric patients. Golden's (1978) review of literature on the effects of aging reports that the pattern of scores seen in brain-damaged patients is similar in younger and older adults. Thus when older patients are assessed it is more significant to look for discrepancies between test score patterns than to merely note the level of performance.

An increasing number of studies suggest that the sex variable is more important than previously thought in clinical psychology. For example, McGlone and Kertesz (1973) state that brain damage in males leads to greater functional asymmetry, especially in visuo-spatial skills, than in females. Witelson (1976) has demonstrated that boys perform right hemisphere related tactual–spatial tests better than girls. Unless certain tests monitoring areas with demonstrated sex differences have sex related norms their validity must remain in doubt. When there is deficient standardization more reliance must be placed upon clinical interpretation.

With regard to functional categories, Obrzut (1981) recommends a developmental paradigm as a strategy for structuring test data from the relatively simple to the more complex. Thinking in terms of functional categories facilitates the cross-indexing of tests to such categories within a framework based upon a hierarchy of information processing/learning. Conceptualizations of a hierarchy of learning reinforce attempts to "assess wide-range cerebral coverage of the central nervous system" (Obrzut, 1981:251). This developmental tradition can be traced directly to the contributions of Hughlings Jackson a century ago and serves as the rationale for the tabling of the adult and adolescent test batteries described in this volume.

MOTOR FUNCTIONING

The quality of motor functioning has long been recognized in neurology as an indicator of brain damage. More than 35 years ago Halstead (1947) showed that an evaluation of voluntary motor functioning contributed to the identification of cognitive deterioration. Reaction time studies demonstrate that both simple and choice reactions are slowed in approximately 45 per cent of non-psychotic individuals with cerebral dysfunction (Dee and Van Allen, 1973). The research of Stott, *et al.* (1972) provides a strong case for viewing motor testing as a relatively independent measure of neural dysfunction easily available for observation and virtually uncontaminated by cognitive and cultural factors. Another important reason for motor testing is to elicit independent measures of lateral ability.

It has been consistently demonstrated that discrepancies in performance between the two hands are related to the relative capacities of the two cerebral hemispheres. However, persons with unilateral brain disease also demonstrate slowing in the hand on the unaffected side of the body (Benton and Joynt, 1959). Thus, tests of motor speed, strength and co-ordination have proved to be sensitive to the quality of cerebral functioning, regardless of the locus of cerebral lesion. Comparison of performance efficiency of one hand relative to the other is often indicative of the hemispherical locus of the lesion when unilateral disease is involved. If lateral skills discrepancies exist in conjunction with deficits in higher cognitive functions, they become more significant clinically.

The evaluation of motor differences involves making an allowance for a better performance for the dominant hand relative to the non-dominant hand. If the dominant hand performs more poorly than the non-dominant hand on motor tasks this is suggestive of damage to the contralateral hemisphere. However, performance in the non-dominant hand must be more significantly impaired than the expected difference before impairment of the non-dominant hemisphere is suspected. A poor bilateral motor performance may indicate diffuse cerebral involvement.

Christensen's (1979) translation of Luria's neuropsychological investigation lists the following divisions of the cerebral cortex affecting motor functioning:

1. Basal areas influencing muscle power and tone.
2. Post-central areas responsible for kinaesthetic control.
3. Parieto-occipital divisions responsible for visuomotor co-ordination.
4. Pre-motor divisions influence the dynamic organization of movement and the frontal systems are associated with discrimination and control.

Lesions in specific areas may disrupt motor functioning dependent upon the integrity of these zones. Tests assessing motor functioning tend to monitor the integrity of the motor cortex. Impaired motor functioning is most likely to occur with pre-central lesions.

Although left-hand and right-hand functioning are commonly accepted indicators of laterality of cortical impairment, it is important to investigate other possible hypostheses during the structured neuropsychological interview. For example, peripheral motor and sensory damage, like that which occurs in spinal cord injuries, cannot cause deficits in cognitive skills, but the results of all tests with sensory motor components may be significantly influenced by such impairments. It is the role of the neurologist to rule out primary motor impairments not associated with cerebral dysfunction. Finally, it should be noted that sensory-motor tasks are easily susceptible to fluctuations in motivation and attention.

Lateral Dominance Investigation (Laterality Preference Schedule)

Since authorities unanimously recommend that the dominant hand should be tested first during all sensory-motor examinations, it is important to establish lateral dominance at the beginning of a neuropsychological investigation. Once lateral dominance has been established, results of motor testing and other more complex cognitive skills may begin to be more meaningfully interpreted. However, such interpretations must be made with caution.

Each cerebral hemisphere serves relatively independent cognitive functions. Since Hughlings Jackson's (1874) classic paper ("On the duality of the brain"), the recognition that language functions are associated with the left hemisphere has popularized the concept of cerebral dominance. Dean (1982) notes that although the concept of cerebral dominance originally referred to hemispheric dominance for language, modern conceptualizations of cerebral dominance imply more comprehensive control functions.

Motor functioning of either side of the body is controlled by the contralateral hemisphere of the brain (that is, the left hemisphere controls the right side and the right hemisphere controls the left side of the body). Current opinion views lateral preference as part of a continuum rather than as a discrete classification (Dean, 1982). Hence, although language functions may be controlled by the left hemisphere and visuo-spatial skills by the right side of the brain, both functions are continuous and can have varying degrees of lateralization (Whitaker and Ojemann, 1977).

Dean's (1982) multifactor laterality preference schedule reflects this view of lateral dominance as a continuum. It is a more sophisticated method of assessing lateral preference patterns, together with their neuropsychological implications, than the gross right handed–left handed dichotomy.

Handwriting preference is an inadequate measure of cerebral lateralization since there is no hard evidence relating handedness to the degree of lateralization (Rasmussen and Milner, 1975). The sodium amytal technique described by Branch, *et al.* (1964) has demonstrated that the majority of the population (95 per cent of normal right handed people and over 60 per cent of normal left handed people) have verbal functions represented in the left hemisphere with visuo-spatial skills in the right. Within this statistical dichotomy, lateral dominance remains on a continuum in the individual. Left handed patients and patients in whom there is mixed dominance pose additional problems of interpretation. For example, when language dominance is less completely lateralized, speech may be more diffusely represented in the brain. If vital surgical procedures are being considered in such patients, it is unlikely that a psychologist's lateral dominance investigation or other probability modes will be totally relied upon. Neurosurgery departments utilize the sodium amytal technique to conclusively determine dominance in a specific individual. This method allows for any individual differences in brain organization.

Many investigators have studied the potential relationship of learning disability with laterality, but findings remain inconclusive. Kinsbourne and Hiscock (1981) plausibly resolve the paradox between the fact of left-handedness being associated with cognitive pathology, whilst left-handers in the general population are cognitively intact, as follows: "since the baseline population of left-handers is relatively small, the pathological left-handers will constitute a substantial proportion of left-handers relative to the pathological right-handers, whose number will be miniscule among the vast right-handed population" (Kinsbourne and Hiscock, 1981: 144). However, Dean (1981) notes that, as lateral preference patterns become more mixed, results on a number of personality dimensions become more pathological.

A review of cerebral lateralization and cognitive development by Kinsbourne and Hiscock (1981) discredits the traditional concepts of hemispheric equipotentiality and progressive lateralization. Brain function appears to be lateralized from birth. Thus it is unlikely that learning disabilities are due to a retardation in the alleged lateralization process. Consequently, any deviant cerebral organization existing in children with learning disability has probably been present at an extremely early age and will continue in adulthood. Besides these developmental anomalies, some children also acquire pathological left-handedness and associated cerebral dysfunction due to early brain insult.

Grooved Pegboard

The grooved pegboard allows comparison of the dominant hand with the non-dominant hand on a manipulative dexterity task involving visuomotor co-ordination. As with other motor tasks, such as finger tapping and grip strength, significantly more impairment in one hand as opposed to the other implies the involvement of the contralateral hemisphere. Such differential comparisons of an individual's performance are more valid for lateralization purposes than the simple noting of performance levels. This is fortunate as available norms are inadequate for geriatric patients. Trites (1977) provided age curved norms (from 5 to 55 years) standardized from data for 2000 patients and found this to be of considerable help in evaluating lateralized brain damage.

Concerning the interpretation of clinical significance for motor testing, Reitan (1966) and Golden (1978) recommend the following guidelines:

1. The non-dominant hand may be generally expected to be 10 per cent less efficient than the dominant hand.
2. If the dominant hand is not 5 per cent or more efficient than the non-dominant hand this raises the possibility of dominant hemisphere impairment.
3. If the dominant hand is less efficient than the non-dominant hand, this is a strong indication of dominant hemisphere damage.
4. If the performance of the non-dominant hand is 20 per cent or more below that of the dominant hand this suggests non-dominant hemisphere dysfunction.
5. Bilateral slowing may be indicative of diffuse brain damage.

Finger Tapping Test

The finger tapping test is a measure of finger agility that is dependent upon motor speed. It also requires fine motor control and kinaesthetic ability. Since lateralized lesions can result in a significant drop in the tapping rate of the contralateral hand, the same rationale that was applied to the interpretation of the grooved pegboard above can be used for fingertapping. However, since the left hemisphere is associated with general co-ordination, bilateral tapping deficiencies may be specifically indicative of damage to this hemisphere (Golden, 1981b). Decrements for finger tapping may be associated with damage to the motor strip area. Disturbance of sensory feedback due to parietal lobe damage may also retard performance (Golden, 1978).

Most adult norms suggest that intact subjects average 50 taps per 10-second trial for their dominant hand and 45 taps for their non-dominant hand (Dodrill, 1978. Spreen and Gaddes (1969) supply norms for children on both a finger tapper with an electric counter and a manual counter key. Further norms for age and hand dominance are also available from Trites (1977).

Hand Dynamometer

The hand dynamometer measures the motor strength of the upper extremities. Dodrill (1978) reports that this simple test discriminates between normal and brain-damaged patients, and between lateralized lesions, as well or better than more complex neuropsychological tests (for example, the tactual performance test). The same guidelines that apply to the interpretation of the grooved pegboard and the finger tapping test can be applied to grip strength.

Norms for adults and children on the Smedley hand dynamometer are supplied by Dodrill (1978) and Spreen and Gaddes (1969).

AUDITORY PERCEPTUAL FUNCTIONING

Kimura's (1967) study of brain asymmetry suggests that the verbal and non-verbal elements of auditory perception are functionally independent. Milner (1962) further demonstrated that defects in the recognition of speech in the absence of a hearing impairment were indicative of a lesion involving the dominant hemisphere whereas impairments in non-verbal auditory perception (for example, music) indicated a lesion of the right temporal lobe.

Interpreting sensory discrepancies is relatively simpler than assessing motor differences as healthy individuals have equivalent sensory abilities on the right and left sides of the body. Any impairment of one side in comparison to the other may be suggestive of injury to the hemisphere contralateral to the deficient side. This guideline may be used for the assessment of auditory, tactile and visual abilities.

The parietal lobes are concerned with the integration of auditory, tactile and visual input. Damage to either parietal lobe will usually result in sensory deficits in the contralateral side of the body. Unlike motor deficits where pre-central lesions predominate, specific sensory impairments tend to occur with post-central lesions.

Swiercinsky (1978) has advised that, since the contralateral manifestation of auditory sensation is less extensive than for tactile and visual input, tasks such as the rhythm test may be administered simultaneously to both ears. Since inferences about hemispheric impairment are difficult to make through the auditory channel there seems no clinical advantage in assessing differences in the auditory acuity of the right ear relative to the left during routine testing.

Speech–Sounds Perception Test

The speech–sounds perception test (SSPT) monitors the auditory ability to discriminate phonemes and to equate them to their printed verbal symbols. Inadequate performance may be suggestive of damage to either temporal lobe, but with a higher probability of left hemisphere involvement.

Extremely poor performance is highly suggestive of left-temporal-lobe dysfunction (Golden, 1981b). Comparisons of relative abilities on the SSPT and the seashore rhythm test are helpful in differentiating between left and right hemisphere dysfunction. The SSPT provides a criterion for assessing receptive language ability.

A cut off score of six errors on the short form of the SSPT is recommended as being outside the normal limits by Ryan, *et al.* (1982). Spreen and Gaddes (1969) supply norms for children on Reitan's revised version of the adult's test for subjects below 15 years of age.

Seashore Rhythm Test

The seashore rhythm test monitors auditory perception for non-verbal rhythmical patterns. Besides requiring intact rhythmic abilities it also tests the ability to maintain sustained concentration. This prerequisite for sustained concentration gives it a hit rate of 82 per cent in identifying patients with cerebral dysfunction. The hit rate drops to 70 per cent if an acute psychiatric control group is included (Golden, 1981b). Milner's study (1962) suggests that it monitors the integrity of right temporal lobe functioning.

Norms are available from a wide variety of sources (of which one example is Trites, 1977).

TACTILE PERCEPTUAL FUNCTIONING

Disturbances of somatic sensation frequently represent the principal manifestations of nervous system disease. A complete understanding of these sensory disorders is outside the competency of most psychologists as it requires a knowledge of applied anatomy, physiology and the use of special tests designed to indicate the nature of the disordered function and its locality. Nevertheless, some simple screening procedures which are clinically relevant in the localization of brain lesions may be recommended. Such elementary screening items may be highly indicative of brain damage and rarely miss either patients with thought disorder or patients with peripheral neurological involvement. Consequently, mistakes on screening tests should be viewed quite seriously (Golden, *et al.,* 1980).

Tactile perceptual functioning tests identify deficits in touch perception and are quite sensitive to parietal lobe damage. Stimuli may be administered unilaterally and bilaterally by touch to both hands and by hand-to-face.

When lateralized deficits in the perception of tactile sensation occur, contralateral central neural impairments may be inferred. Reliable suppressions resulting from double simultaneous stimulation are usually clinically significant. Goldstein (1974) recommends that when suppressions do appear, tests should be repeated in order to establish whether the suppression is real or merely an artefact of administration. Sensory-perceptual testing is greatly influenced by the degree of motivation and concentration of the patient together with the presence of peripheral injuries.

Tactile perceptual functioning somehow influences a broad range of ostensibly independent more complex cognitive abilities (motor, visuo-spatial, language and memory processes). Both brain damaged children and intact children with relatively better tactile perceptual skills than respective brain damaged and normal control subjects did better on a battery of 10 cognitive tests (Boll, *et al.,* 1977).

Face Hand Test

When light touch stimuli are applied simultaneously to the cheek and the hand, patients with brain damage often report only one of the stimuli, or, if reporting both, may perceive one of them occurring on another area of the body. Errors can result on both sides of the body unlike the phenomena of contralateral extinction in the case of parietal lobe disease. Also, the mistakes usually concern the more peripheral stimulus (that is, the stimulus to the hand is usually extinguished or misperceived). Bender (1977) has done much to popularize this test.

Lishman's (1978) review of the validity of the face hand test showed that it can distinguish between organic and functional disorder, and that it compares favourably with other more complex techniques. Cognitively intact subjects may make initial errors on this test, but, as stimuli are repeated, the errors tend to cease. By the tenth trial, nearly all individuals correctly perceive stimuli and continue to perform correctly. Patients with functional psychiatric illnesses perform in the normal pattern. In contrast, 90 per cent of patients with diffuse brain damage persist with errors of extinction or displacement as long as testing continues. Consequently, errors of perseveration in an adult are strongly indicative of organic brain damage (Lishman, 1978).

Finger Agnosia

Finger agnosia is an impairment in specific digital recognition after tactile stimulation. Since normal individuals perform tactile sensitivity tests without errors it must be emphasized that, as a general rule, any mistakes on these tasks may be viewed as pathognomonic. Strub and Black (1979) state that finger agnosia errors may be likened to right–left orientation in that it may be developmental in nature or result from either diffuse or focal brain damage. Lesions are usually in the dominant hemisphere, particularly in the parieto-occipital area. The inability to recognize a finger when it is stimulated is generally worse on the side contralateral to the injury.

Bilateral deficits are frequent in cases of left parietal damage. Right parietal damage tends not to cause bilateral deficits. Scores for two sides of the body should differ by three or more errors before lateralization can be inferred (Golden, 1981b).

Graphaesthesia

Graphaesthesia (finger number writing) is reputedly more sensitive to cerebral dysfunction than finger agnosia. Thus it may be indicative of lesions not only in the parietal lobes but also in anterior frontal areas (Golden, 1981b). Results showing three or more errors on one hand relative to the other suggest lateralization to the contralateral hemisphere.

Tactile Form Recognition Test

The tactile form recognition test monitors the ability to identify geometric shapes by touch alone. It is performed by normal subjects without errors. Consequently, even one mistake may be clinically significant. As for most tactile perceptual disabilities, poor performance in one hand relative to the other is suggestive of lateralized parietal lobe damage (Obrzut, 1981).

VISUO–SPATIAL FUNCTIONING

The accurate evaluation of visual acuity, sensitivity, and perimetry, and knowing how to classify specific ophthalmological impairments, is a time consuming and complex speciality. It is not a practical activity for most psychologists to attempt to duplicate what ophthalmologists and neurologists do better. This is especially so as such information is usually readily available from the medical data base. The visuo-spatial functions closer to the psychologist's area of competency are the monitoring of such abilities as spatial perceptual analysis, visuomotor tracking and visual memory processes.

Tests which monitor visuo-spatial functioning generally lateralize to the right hemisphere in the absence of language disorders (Hecaen and Albert, 1978). This correlation is so strong that during the early years of neuropsychological testing (when the unitary concept of brain functioning was prevalent) single step screening devices consisted of one basic, visuo-spatial test (for example, the Bender–Gestalt or the Benton visual retention test). It is now recognized that the visuo-spatial tasks merely tap one facet of brain functioning. Thus inadequate performance of such tasks may rule in the presence of an acquired impairment of cognitive function, but correct completion does not necessarily rule out the possibility of brain damage. Absence of evidence is not evidence of absence (Teuber's dictum). This example emphasizes the necessity of making interpretations only within the context of a comprehensive sampling of the patient's neuropsychological strengths and deficits.

In general, however, perceptual disorders are highly indicative of cerebral dysfunction. The more complex learning skills are dependent upon the integrity of perceptual organization. Visuo-spatial functioning is a complex skill overlapping with cognitive and memory processes. Consequently, it is quite difficult, if not impossible, to relate visuo-spatial test items directly to focal structural impairments of the brain since most "visuo-spatial" tests also have motor and memory components.

Cerebral dysfunction can result in a wide variety of visuo-spatial impairments. Lezak (1976) reports that patients with left hemisphere lesions may ignore the right side of a line when reading, whereas right hemisphere lesions more commonly cause unilateral spatial neglect of the left side. Also, right cerebral damage produces the more significant impairments involving paper and pencil drawings of familiar objects and geometric designs than does left hemisphere damage.

Benton (1981) reports that visuo-perceptive and visuo-constructive functioning in patients with brain disease has been operationally studied in the following ways: identification of hidden figures; discrimination of complex patterns; facial recognition; inkblot interpretation; block design construction; stick arranging; copying designs; three-dimensional block construction; and visuo-spatial judgement. The above tests have proved useful indicators of the presence of cerebral dysfunction. An evaluation of the qualitative and quantitative aspects of language performance levels together with comparisons between the other modalities (language and intellectual functions) may contribute to the localization of the lesion.

Visuo-spatial tests are less dependent on educational and cultural background than verbal tasks. This section will focus upon testing for impairments in processing non-verbal stimuli. Deficits in the visual perception of written verbal material will be discussed under the category dealing with reading skills.

Trail Making Test: Part B

The trail making test: part B is a general monitor of visuomotor and visual-sequencing skills. It requires motor speed, basic spatial skills, counting ability, mastery of the alphabet, concentration and flexible planning ability. Consequently it is likely to be affected by cerebral dysfunction in many locations. Horton (1979) states that it is sensitive to both lateralized and non-lateralized lesions and has proved to have virtually as high a hit rate as the entire HRNTB. Gordon (1978) investigated the effectiveness of the test in discriminating between brain damaged and pseudoneurological subjects and obtained an overall hit rate of 87 per cent.

The relationship between part A and part B of the test has not been shown to be clinically useful for lateralization purposes, despite earlier claims. Consequently, no benefit is gained by administering part A, especially since part B has superior hit rates as a diagnostic indicator.

Davies (1968) supplies age-related norms in the form of percentiles for adults. Spreen and Gaddes (1969) supply children's norms on Reitan's intermediate (children's) version of the test.

Horton (1979) suggests that the 25th percentile be used as a cut-off point for scores mildly suggestive of brain damage. The 10th percentile may be used for a cut-off point for scores moderately suggestive of brain damage.

Boll and Reitan (1973) have documented that trail making performance is significantly correlated with IQ. Unfortunately, norms corrected for intelligence do not exist yet. However, Horton (1979) advised that a poor performance on trails by a patient with above average IQ may be viewed as a discrepant result and thus suggestive of cerebral dysfunction. A good performance by a patient with a superior IQ does not necessarily rule out brain damage.

Goldstein and Neuringer (1966) found that qualitative signs were important when differentiating between organic and functional disorders. Patients with organic disorders were less likely to exhibit bizarre behaviour during testing whereas patients with functional disorders were more likely to produce error-free performances. Additionally, schizophrenic patients tended to give up more easily.

Benton Visual Retention Test

The Benton visual retention test is sensitive to visual inattention, visual memory, spatial organization and visuo-constructive skills. Like other visuo-constructive tests, it is more sensitive to diffuse impairments and right hemisphere lesions than to left hemisphere dysfunction. Patients with right parieto-occipital lesions tend to perform most poorly. Golden's review (1979) states that it is more effective than other drawing tests in discriminating between normal, brain damaged and psychiatric patients (hit rates of 80 to 90 per cent for control subjects and 60 to 70 per cent for organic patients).

Memory deficits may be differentiated from perceptual deficits by allowing patients to copy the designs while the card is in front of them. Benton (1974) reports that the perceptuomotor components of the visual retention test are associated with right hemisphere functioning, whereas the memory component is not. Errors on simple drawings lateralize to the right hemisphere. More complex drawings may be performed poorly by both right and left hemisphere damaged patients. The former tend to exhibit disruptions in spatial arrangement whereas the latter reproduce simplified figures whilst retaining adequate spatial orientation.

Benton (1968) reports that the performance of patients with frontal lobe lesions differs according to the side of the injury. Patients with bilateral damage average 4.6 errors. Those with right-sided injuries average 3.5 errors. Those with left-sided lesions have an average of 1.0 errors, which falls within normal limits.

Benton's (1974) manual covers diagnostic interpretation in great detail. The possible determinants of defective performance are discussed for schizophrenic, depressed and "simulating" patients and the literature on localization of lesions is reviewed.

The manual provides an objective scoring system. There is useful interpretation of subjects' performance on the basis of an "expected score" appropriate for their age and assumed premorbid intellectual functioning. A score which is three points above the "expected score" is considered to raise the question of an acquired impairment of cognitive functioning. A score which is four points above the "expected score" suggests such impairment. Finally, a score which is five or more points above the "expected score" is strong indication of such impairment.

Added qualitative information may be obtained by analysing the type of errors the patient makes. Guidelines for such qualitative analysis are clearly presented and students are encouraged to master them. For example, an understanding of the omission of peripheral figures, rotational and size errors can be a very significant addition to the data base.

This test's three equivalent forms, four possible modes of administration, and availability of quantitative norms for both children and adults, together with qualitative guidelines, exemplifies the flexible standards which creators of new tests should attempt to emulate.

Rey–Osterrieth Complex Figure Test (Copy)

The complexity of the figure in this test precludes verbal coding. Thus, it is more likely to tap the visuo-spatial modality than simpler patterns. For example, if patients were asked to reproduce a triangular figure, they might verbally encode information by naming the shape of a triangle, and thus display less reliance on non-verbal cues.

A comparison of differences between the copying and recall parts of the test may help to differentiate perceptual, visual memory and higher planning function problems from each other. Walsh (1978) emphasizes that the complex figure test has regional significance for the frontal lobe. Patients with frontal lobe lesions appear to perform poorly on this test because of impairment in planning, regulating and checking programmes of action.

Lezak's work (1976) contains an excellent coverage of the normative scoring criteria and interpretation of results. Guidelines to the qualitative analysis of the patient's strategy in performance of the test are also discussed. Lezak (1976) notes that, in general, there is a larger disparity between the copy scores and the memory scores of patients with cerebral dysfunction relative to the scores for normal subjects.

Recently, Visser (1980) produced a revised manual of the complex figure test which includes a cardboard reproduction of the actual figure. He defines his instrument as a test, developed for the assessment of cerebral dysfunction, which involves the restructuring of behaviour. An analysis of drawing sequences is used to discriminate brain-damaged patients from intact individuals by means of objective scoring procedures. The test may be viewed as an objective measure of the extent of fragmentation (piecemeal approach) which comes to light during a copying task. Visser's (1980) revision does not require reproduction from memory during testing. Relations with neurological and psychological variables are discussed.

Both the interpretive schemes covered by Lezak (1976) and Visser (1980) are contributions not only to clinical testing but also to information processing theory.

LANGUAGE ABILITY

After sensory-motor and visuo-spatial functioning have been evaluated it is recommended that the first complex cognitive category to be assessed should be language. Language is of crucial significance for many other cognitive abilities. A severe language impairment may make it impossible to continue the valid assessment of other higher intellectual functions. In fact, Goodglass and Kaplan (1979) claim that an inability to perform adequately on the WAIS and the Wechsler memory scale may serve as a screening procedure for aphasia. For example, aphasic word-finding difficulties will impair performance in all of the verbal subtests of the WAIS.

Disorders of language are extremely handicapping because speech functions as a basic requirement of interpersonal relationships. The clinical assessment of language disorders helps to clarify the relationship between psychological functions and the anatomy and physiology of the cerebrum. Language skills are intermediate between the well localized sensory motor functions and the more complex cognitive functions, such as fantasy and abstract thinking, which cannot be localized (Mohr and Adams, 1980). Thus, tasks such as the SSPT monitor both auditory perceptual functioning and receptive language ability.

Unlike most other localized neurophysiological patterns (which are organized according to a bilateral and symmetrical plan), the evolution of both speech and manual skills occurs in relationship to neurophysiological pathways located in one cerebral hemisphere (Mohr and Adams, 1980). While tests monitoring visuo-spatial functioning generally lateralize to the right hemisphere, tests of verbal function reflect left hemisphere involvement. Language impairments have been well researched and their evaluation facilitates the localization of lesions within the dominant hemisphere (Strub and Black, 1979).

Studies of right handed aphasic patients have identified the posterior language area as the cortical zone basically concerned with the comprehension of spoken speech. Traditionally, this has been referred to as Wernicke's area. Patients with lesions in this area are commonly called receptive aphasics because their major difficulty is comprehending spoken language.

The anterior language area is concerned with language production. Within the anterior language area, Brodmann's area 44 is known as Broca's area. Patients with damage to the anterior area are commonly called expressive aphasics because of their difficulty in generating language.

In a succinct review of the clinical implications of language impairments Strub and Black (1979) point out some problems in the use of the term "expressive aphasia". Since all aphasics exhibit some type of abnormal language expression there is a tendency to mistakenly classify all aphasia as "expressive aphasia". Consequently, Strub and Black (1979) prefer to use a categorization system, based upon classic anatomical patterns, which facilitates correct localization of lesions. They classify language impairments into the following categories: global aphasia; conduction aphasia; anomic aphasia; transcortical aphasia; pure word deafness; articulation disturbances; alexia; agraphia; psychotic language; and non-organic speech and language disorders.

It is of great clinical advantage for students of neuropsychology to immerse themselves in the voluminous literature on language disorders. This facilitates the recognition of pertinent qualitative symptoms during testing. Raw data from the results of quantitative language tests alone cannot hope to reveal sufficient information. Gross aphasia is difficult to overlook, although less experienced clinicians sometimes have been known to classify paraphasic speech, mistakenly, as a symptom of psychosis or dementia.

Children with multiple articulation disorders have the greatest difficulty with tests which consider sensory receptive functions. This is suggestive of left hemisphere dysfunction (Frisch and Handler, 1974). The most sensitive indicators of left hemisphere dysfunction include reading disability (dyslexia), writing disability (dysgraphia), inability to name objects (dysnomia), and difficulty in recognizing numbers and letters (visual letter and number dysgnosia). Other left hemisphere signs, such as calculating disability (dyscalculia), spelling disability (spelling dyspraxia) and right-left disorientation (Golden, 1981b), may also indicate damage to the right hemisphere.

Many problems of interpretation occur during language evaluation. For example, because of the potential for bilateral language representation in the left handed patient the standard classification systems are less useful than they are for right handed patients with left hemisphere lesions. It is also difficult to classify the language status of the patient with an acute lesion. These injuries result in maximal language disruption and are often accompanied by disorientation. Patients with undiagnosed impairments often present with speech dysfunction and tend to perform poorly when given quantitative language tests. Finally, there are brain damaged patients without dysphasic signs.

Language tests are strongly reflective of educational background, and this must be taken into account during interpretation of results. In contrast to adults, inadequate language performance by children does not have the same definitive localizing significance although it remains suggestive of brain damage (Benton, 1981).

The comprehensive evaluation of language requires an assessment of the following functions: spontaneous speech; comprehension; ability to repeat spoken language; word finding; reading; writing; and spelling. The tests outlined in this section monitor receptive skills (listening and reading) and expressive ability (talking, writing and word finding fluency). A more educationally oriented approach to reading and spelling will be discussed in the section dealing with intellectual functions directly related to scholastic performance. Spontaneous speech may be screened clinically. During both the structured neuropsychological interview and quantitative testing the clinician should be alert to any evidence of dysarthria (specific disorders of articulation wherein basic grammar and word choice is intact), dysprosody (interruption of speech melody) and specific aphasic errors of grammar and word finding.

Aphasia Language Performance Scales

This global screening test is sensitive to both receptive disabilities (listening and reading) and expressive disorders (talking and writing). The manual gives detailed guidelines for interpretation of the four discrete subscales involved (Keenan and Brassell, 1975). Test items can identify dysarthria, alexia, apraxia, anomia, and other language disorders. The aphasia language performance scales (ALPS), in conjunction with clinical interviewing, the speech-sounds perception test, and word finding fluency test described below, serves as a normally comprehensive monitor of language ability. If more specialized assessment is required a speech pathologist may be consulted.

Controlled Word Association Test

Lesions of Broca's area are commonly associated with deficits in verbal fluency. The controlled word association test is an excellent measure of word finding fluency. Lezak (1976) supplies a table of norms adjusted to age, sex and education expressed as percentile ranks. As with most other neuropsychological tests, scores which fall below one standard deviation from the mean begin to have clinical significance. The 25th percentile is a useful cut-off point which is mildly suggestive of brain damage. The 10th percentile may be viewed as being moderately suggestive of cerebral dysfunction.

MEMORY PROCESSES

Memory impairments, particularly deficits in recent memory, are the most frequent initial complaints presenting in the early stages of the organic brain syndromes. Consequently, comprehensive memory assessment is perhaps the most important diagnostic indicator in assessing cerebral dysfunction. Since memory is involved in all mental activities it is also the cognitive function most easily tested. Unfortunately, because of such widespread involvement in the thinking processes, impairments of memory can be extremely incapacitating both vocationally and socially.

Strub and Black (1979) describe memory as a hierarchical process with distinct neuroanatomical substrates. Because different organic illnesses may result in various types of memory impairment involving a relatively specific neuronal system, detailed memory testing can frequently result in both a clinical and an anatomical diagnosis. Limbic areas and temporal lobes appear to be quite susceptible to structural and vascular damage which is manifested in the form of memory impairment. Strub and Black (1979) state that almost all patients with pre-senile and senile dementia exhibit early memory problems.

Benton (1981) describes memory as a comprehensive modality with the ability to retain all types of material over different periods of time and involving different types of responses. Performance on memory tests may vary according to the sensory category involved (auditory versus visual), the form of material to be remembered (verbal versus non-verbal) and the type of response required (recognition versus reproduction). Benton (1981) advises the use of discrete memory tests which can be specifically compared against each other in the above manner.

Similarly, Christensen (1979) emphasizes that memory disturbances can be of a general type (for example, the Korsakoff syndrome) or a partial type affecting a specific modality (for example, impairment of verbal or visual recall). All levels of coding may be disrupted or the deficit can be limited to one level only (for example, the basic or relatively higher intellectual processes). Therefore, a thorough evaluation requires the independent assessment of immediate, short-term, recent and remote memory together with the capacity to learn new information across both verbal and visual modalities. An assessment of all levels of memory coding across modalities assists in the localization of lesions.

It is convenient to discriminate between immediate memory, short-term memory, recent memory and remote memory. Immediate memory is associated only with the registration of information whereas other types of memory involve data storage over time.

Immediate memory is commonly assessed by digit repetition and reversal (auditory) and memory-for-designs (visual) tasks. The latter test has been found to be more sensitive to cerebral dysfunction than the former (Sterne, 1969).

Deficits on visual memory tests are associated with right hemisphere lesions. In contrast, persons with left hemisphere lesions demonstrate more significant deficits on auditory–verbal memory tasks with potentially inconsistent performance in visual items. Immediate memory may be disrupted by damage to the primary sensory cortex. Patients with impairments of immediate memory are either inattentive, aphasic, demented or they suffer from a specific dysfunction of the sensory system under evaluation (Strub and Black, 1979).

Short-term and recent memory are imprecise terms which are used inconsistently. Short-term memory is commonly evaluated by monitoring retention of information after brief presentation (10 seconds to 10 minutes later). Recent memory is often operationally defined as the retention of information 30 minutes after brief presentation, but it may also refer to a time span measuring months. Recent memory deficits are often exemplified in impaired temporal orientation. However, impaired orientation for person or place is rare in non-psychotic organic brain syndromes (Benton, 1981). Milner (1954) reports that recent memory and the ability to learn new information can be impaired by damage to the hippocampi or the mamillary bodies/medial thalamic nuclei. Although a bilateral lesion appears to be required for a profound memory disturbance, unilateral dominant temporal lobe damage may decrease verbal learning while non-dominant temporal lobe lesions are more associated with visual memory deficits.

Remote memory is relatively impervious to limbic damage, but it can be impaired by widespread cortical deterioration. Patients suffering from cortical atrophy (for example, Alzheimer's disease) exhibit remote memory disturbance. If remote memory is intensively assessed with specialized techniques (questionnaires on public figures and important events) deficient recall may be as great for the oldest and most remote material as it is for less remote events (Benton, 1981). Consequently, such findings dispute the popular belief that remote memory is relatively immune to the effects of brain damage.

As many patients with memory deficits have a tendency to deny their problems and to confabulate, a valid assessment of memory processes may require the substantiation of questions asked by the examiner by a source other than the patient. When patients' performance on memory tasks is not discrepant with their results on other neuropsychological tests it raises the probability that their memory processes are intact.

Impairment of concentration inherently disrupts memory processes, and hence learning ability. There is some evidence that variable concentration is associated with abnormal electroencephalographic results in epileptic patients (Prechtl, *et al.,* 1961).

Poor performance on memory tests needs careful interpretation as not all memory impairments have an organic aetiology. Adequate performance on memory tests requires sustained attention. Consequently, patients with non-organic impairments of attention (that is, some neurotic and psychotic patients) will perform poorly. It is important to spend time in establishing rapport with and relaxing anxious patients before testing. Sometimes, severely depressed patients are tragically misdiagnosed as having dementia. An important point to note about depressed patients is that they are unlikely to show any other cognitive deficits than those related to psychomotor retardation (pseudodementia).

This section concentrates on tests monitoring recent memory (modified Wechsler memory scale) and capacity to learn new information (Rey complex figure and the Walton–Black). The evaluation of immediate and remote memory is catered for in the subtests of the Wechsler intelligence scales and the Benton visual retention test.

Modified Wechsler Memory Scale

There is some redundancy in administering the whole Wechsler memory scale (WMS) because many of the results it produces overlap with other items in the battery. However, it is useful to calculate a "memory quotient" since it is highly correlated with the IQ. Discrepancies of more than 15 points between a patient's memory quotient and IQ raise the possibility of an organically related memory impairment (Wechsler and Stone, 1973). In order to save time, results from the WAIS digit span may be used in preference to doing this item again on the WMS. Results from the orientation section of the structured neuropsychological interview may also be transposed when calculating the memory quotient.

However, specific memory tests are more useful than a composite "memory quotient" score. Russell's (1975) modification of the WMS serves this purpose yielding six independent memory scales and allows multiple comparisons across modalities. A comparison of performance on the verbal (short-term; long-term; and per cent retained) relative to figural (short-term; long-term; and per cent retained) scales has lateralization significance. Verbal and non-verbal components of memory may be differentiated. The former are associated with dominant (left) hemisphere functioning whereas the latter lateralize to the non-dominant (right) hemisphere.

Such modifications of the WMS make it useful for adolescents and children since intrapersonal verbal *v.* figural comparisons obviate the need for well validated group norms, which until recently have been unavailable for children. Age corrected adult norms are contained in the manual by Wechsler and Stone (1973). Hulicka (1966) provides a more extensive set of norms. Further interpretive standard scores for selected subtests of the WMS are provided by Osborne and Davis (1978).

Rey–Osterrieth Complex Figure Test (Recall)

For further information on this test see Rey–Osterrieth complex figure test described under the interpretation of visuo-spatial functioning category in this chapter. After the figure has been copied, the patient is asked to recall and to reproduce it three minutes later. Appropriate interpretations are well covered in Lezak (1976). Percentile norms for accuracy scores on copy and memory trials are available in Lezak (1976). This makes the complex figure test results amenable to computerized interpretation and thus compatible with the rest of the data base.

Walton–Black Modified New Word Learning Test

A variety of tests requiring patients to learn the meaning of unfamiliar words is available. Such tests use a standard word list and differ only in the number of the words to be learned (Walton and Black, 1957; Savage, 1970).

Inability to acquire new information efficiently is highly correlated with the extent of cerebral dysfunction. Lishman (1978) reports that the Walton–Black is an excellent means of monitoring the acquisition of new verbal information and extremely effective in differentiating patients with organic brain disease from those with functional disorders. Inability to learn six new words by the fifth trial is judged to be outside the normal limits. Quantitative norms are also available (Walton and Black, 1957).

Performance on the Walton–Black may be diagnostically contrasted with new visual–figural learning tests (Benton visual retention test; figural subtests of the modified WMS; and Rey complex figure). Such comparisons are suggestive of the information processing efficiency of the left hemisphere relative to the right.

HIGHER COGNITIVE PROCESSES

Strub and Black (1979) emphasize that attention, language and memory are the basic cognitive processes which serve as the foundation for the development of higher intellectual skills. These basic processes are necessary, but not sufficient in themselves for the execution of higher order intellectual abilities.

Unlike language, the higher cognitive processes are not well localized and are most likely diffusely represented in the cortex. Consequently, care must be taken in interpreting these complex functions. Teuber (1964) concludes that posterior lesions are more debilitating to intellect than frontal ones. Strub and Black (1979) report that dominant hemisphere lesions often disrupt verbal reasoning and abstraction. Critchley (1953) states that impaired calculating ability may result from lesions that are bilateral or unilateral in either the right or left hemisphere.

Because the higher cognitive processes involve the most advanced stages of intellectual functioning they are frequently vulnerable to neurological disease. Consequently their assessment often reveals the early effects of cerebral dysfunction before the more basic functions of attention, language and memory show deterioration (Strub and Black, 1979). Deterioration in intellectual functioning is often the first sign of an organic brain syndrome (for example, Alzheimer's disease). Such cognitive impairments can be potentially devastating.

Patients' capacity to adapt to their environment is dependent upon the integrity of their higher cognitive processes. Thus an evaluation of these processes is needed for a meaningful interpretation of interpersonal, educational and vocational prognosis. An intellectual assessment attempts to evaluate the highest level of cortical functioning–that which is abstract and symbolic. It reflects the ability to solve problems by manipulating verbal and non-verbal symbols (Obrzut, 1981).

This section surveys tests which monitor abstract reasoning and complex problem solving (Wechsler intelligence scales), cognitive flexibility (Stroop colour–word test) as well as a diagnostic measure of educational achievement (wide range achievement test [WRAT]).

Results of such tests are more meaningfully interpreted if an adequate estimate of premorbid intelligence can be made to serve as a baseline. Premorbid educational, vocational and socioeconomic levels, together with a history of recreational activities, are useful indicators. Educational achievement tests, such as the WRAT, together with subtests for which the results are relatively unaffected by brain damage (for example, vocabulary level) are further supportive data. Finally, various statistical techniques such as Mahan's (1979) converted residual technique for the prediction of premorbid intelligence represent a more systematic approach to formulating premorbid baseline levels.

Wechsler Intelligence Scales

It is not possible to review the voluminous literature on the Wechsler adult intelligence scale–revised (WAIS–R) and the Wechsler intelligence scale for children–revised (WISC–R). The relationship of Wechsler subtest patterns to cerebral dysfunction has generated sufficient data to furnish a library confined solely to this topic. Matarazzo (1980) and Zimmerman and Woo-Sam (1973) provide a detailed study of the clinical interpretation of the WAIS. Kaufman (1979) comprehensively covers intelligence testing with the WISC–R. Selected comments concerning the Wechsler scales are made below. Most remarks are equally applicable to both the WAIS and the WISC–R.

Intelligence tests were not originally created to reflect neurological or developmental paradigms. However, the subtests composing intelligence test batteries have been operationally related to sub-cortical, cortical and hemispheric specialization functioning (Obrzut, 1981).

Despite this relationship between information processing (as measured by the WICS–R) and the cerebral cortex, it is inappropriate to localize any specific type of neurological impairment in children solely on the basis of WISC–R results (Obrzut, 1981). The WISC–R is better perceived as one of many tools contributing to a description of how information is being processed by a specific child in order to facilitate coherent remediation.

Noting that WAIS scores are strongly related to cerebral dysfunction, McFie (1975) lists the following WAIS patterns as being correlated with various types of localized lesions in adults: left frontal lesions are associated with a deficit in digit span without loss in the verbal IQ; right frontal lesions are correlated with poor picture arrangement; left temporal lesions result in low similarities and digit span; right temporal injuries are associated with a deficit in picture arrangement; left parietal lesions may cause deterioration on arithmetic, digit span and block design; right parietal lesions may disrupt block design and picture arrangement; and diffuse brain damage usually causes deterioration in the results of most of the subtests sensitive to brain lesions (block design, arithmetic, digit symbol and digit span).

Russell's (1979) pattern analysis of the WAIS is less ambitious and thus less prone to error than McFie's highly localized orientation (1975). Russell asserts that there is no single pattern for all types of brain damage on the WAIS, although the deterioration pattern is fairly common. In this pattern, information, comprehension and vocabulary are relatively unaffected whereas digit symbol, block design, picture arrangement and object assembly tend to deteriorate. This pattern seems to be characteristic of patients with degenerative conditions (for example, Alzheimer's disease). Right hemisphere damage gives almost the same profile as that shown by diffuse degenerative damage. This suggests that block design, object assembly and picture arrangement are tests which are also strongly indicative of right hemisphere damage. Left hemisphere damage does not appear to produce a differential pattern since all the subtests tend to be relatively depressed.

Goodglass and Kaplan (1979) similarly note that the WAIS consists of subtests which monitor established knowledge (vocabulary, comprehension, and information) relatively resistant to organic impairment and of other subtests (block design, arithmetic, digit symbol, and similarities) which involve new learning or problem solving reputedly more susceptible to impairment. Consequently, any discrepancies between these categories of operation may be significant clinically. The vocabulary subtest is particularly useful for interpretive purposes in that it is the best indicator of premorbid functioning.

A comparison of a patient's actual IQ score corrected for age with the expected score corrected for age (as reflected by persons with a similar educational and cultural background) has theoretical diagnostic significance. IQ scores which are below those expected may suggest either a developmental or an acquired impairment of cognitive functioning. However, this technique results in a moderate degree of mistaken classification as many patients with well documented brain damage do not show any signs of intellectual deterioration as measured by the WAIS (Benton, 1981).

The full scale IQ score has proved to be accurate in predicting educational achievement. This makes it useful for establishing a baseline against which other neuropsychological test scores may be interpreted. The verbal IQ and performance IQ scores are less useful clinically as there is much overlap in what they measure. Consequently, discrepancies between verbal and performance scores are less significant than previously believed. Kaufman

(1979) cites evidence that hemisphere differences tend to be more related to the method of processing stimuli than to a left–right dichotomy. Verbal–performance differences may need to exceed 20 IQ points before they become clinically significant. A discrepancy of four scaled points between any two subtests is also usually accepted as clinically significant (Lezak, 1976).

Residual deficits in attention may be studied in children by using the freedom from distractibility quotient (Kaufman, 1979). This is derived from the WISC by applying the following formula:

arithmetic + *digit span* + *coding (scaled scores)* x 2.2 + 34

A quotient of 85 or less falls at or below the 16th percentile and may be regarded as outside the normal limits. Low quotients reflect a deficiency in capacities such as attention to external visual and auditory stimuli, concentration and other low-level processing functions.

It seems appropriate to reiterate that the information and digit span subtests contribute to the monitoring of memory processes. The information subtest represent remote (long-term) memory, which is resistant to limbic damage but which may deteriorate with widespread cortical damage. The digit span subtest represents immediate memory which is generally vulnerable to brain impairment. It is particularly disturbed by damage to the primary sensory or motor cortex. Goodglass and Kaplan (1979) state that a difference of more than two digits between the forward and backward section of this subtest is strongly indicative of cerebral dysfunction.

Wide Range Achievement Test

The wide range achievement test (WRAT) is a useful addition to attempts in estimating premorbid functioning as it is a well standardized test of educational achievement and correlates well with IQ. Consequently, large discrepancies (10 points or more) between WRAT and IQ standard scores may be clinically significant.

If the IQ is significantly higher the examiner might consider the possibility that the individual is performing below expectations. If the educational achievement is higher, the examiner should consider over-achievement or the possibility of cerebral dysfunction.

As educational achievement standard scores may be relatively unaffected by many forms of brain damage, there will usually be a difference between the WRAT scores and the results of other neuropsychological tests which are more easily depressed by brain injury.

The reading and spelling subtests contribute to a comprehensive evaluation of language coding skills. Golden (1979) states that reading impairment may be associated with the temporal–occipital injuries in the left hemisphere.

Lezak (1976) reports that patients with left hemisphere lesions may have word recognition problems on the right side of the page, whereas those with right hemisphere injuries may ignore the left side of the page. Luria (1980) notes that parietal–occipital lesions may be characterized by an inability to spell simple words.

Lezak (1976) describes the arithmetic subtest as being of sufficient variety to facilitate the identification of specific difficulties (for example, dyscalculia of the spatial type, a number or figure alexia, and loss of number concepts or basic operations). Golden (1979) suggests that deterioration in the ability to perform complex multiplication and subtraction problems may be associated with right hemisphere damage when all other mathematical skills are normal.

The WRAT manual (Jastak and Jastak, 1978) contains a succinct interpretation of learning disabilities and their remediation. Users must be cautioned that coding skills and comprehension are independent variables. The WRAT measures the former and is not concerned with reading comprehension or arithmetic reasoning. Also, WRAT standard scores, but not grade ratings, allow meaningful individual and group comparisons.

Stroop Colour–Word Test

Some patients with cerebral dysfunction are distractible, lack behavioural flexibility and experience problems in adapting their behaviour to meet the demands of new situations. The Stroop colour–word test measures the ability of a patient to maintain a uniform course of action in the face of interference. Golden (1979) states the Stroop test is able to accurately differentiate between normal, psychiatric and brain damaged patients. It appears to be particularly sensitive to frontal lobe dysfunction. As brain damage is difficult to document on the results of most other neuropsychological tests, this makes the Stroop particularly valuable.

The test comes in a three-page form and yields the following three scores: page 1, the number of words named within 45 seconds (word naming score); page 2, the number of colours named in 45 seconds (colour naming score); and page 3, the number of colour–words named in 45 seconds (colour–word naming score). Golden (1976) provides appropriate norms.

Comalli, *et al.* (1962) have studied the changes in performance on the Stroop test in patients aged from seven to 80 years and their data helps to understand the effects of aging upon peoples' performance of the Stroop. The norms which are available and corrected for age remain relatively underdeveloped, however.

Golden (1979) suggests the following interpretations for differential diagnosis:

1. On page 2 (colour naming score), normal patients complete 70 to 90 items, psychiatric patients complete 60 to 80 items, and brain damaged patients usually complete less than 60 items.
2. Adequate scores on pages 1 (word naming score) and 2 (colour naming score) together with a low score on page 3 (colour–word naming score) suggest frontal lobe lesions, particularly in the left hemisphere.
3. Normal scores on page 1 with low scores on pages 2 and 3 are associated with right hemisphere dysfunction.
4. Poor scores on all 3 pages are characterized by left hemisphere (non-frontal) injuries.
5. Equivalent scores on pages 2 and 3 suggest dyslexia as this pattern does not occur with literate adults. Consequently, if the score for page 3 is within 10 per cent of page 2, there is a probability of dyslexia as this suggests that the normal interference phenomenon has not eventuated.

PERSONALITY ORGANIZATION

An interpretation of personality organization is an integral aspect of neuropsychological assessment as the goal of such assessment is to obtain a comprehensive description of an individual's behaviour. Patients with brain damage frequently react with loss of control, disorganized thinking and behavioural disturbances. Conversely, a highly integrated premorbid personality together with an effective support system may modify the clinical state. Consequently, the significance of neuropsychological test scores is best interpreted within the context of the patient's "real-life" adaptive capacities. For example, a patient may obtain superior scores during formal structured neuropsychological testing but in actuality be significantly incapacitated in the unstructured milieu inherent in everyday living. An understanding of the patient's adaptive capacities facilitates a meaningful rehabilitation programme.

Some diseases which affect the brain may result in personality change as they are capable of directly influencing structures which mediate emotional behaviour. If a previously well adjusted individual who has no trace of family psychiatric history begins to lose their capacity to function effectively an organic brain syndrome may be suspected. Left hemisphere lesions causing aphasia often cause catastrophic reactions as patients can be devastated by the loss of their language abilities. In contrast, right hemisphere damage is more associated with reactions of indifference and neglect. Tumours in the septal region tend to produce rage. Bilateral temporal lobe dysfunction is characterized by placidity. Anterior temporal lobectomy may generate increased sexuality. Herpes simplex encephalitis destroys the orbitofrontal and anterior temporal regions. Such destruction of the limbic system may be expressed in the form of impulsivity, memory loss and depression. Lesions of the orbital, frontal areas are difficult to detect by using standard neuropsychological tests as abstraction abilities generally remain unimpaired. This illustrates the importance of knowledge of the emotional and behavioural sequellae of brain damage for differential diagnosis. However, the degree to which personality change is either a specific reaction to brain damage or a secondary result due to the stress entailed in the loss of previous cognitive abilities remains difficult to determine (Reitan, 1976).

An independent personality evaluation in conjunction with neuropsychological assessment may contribute to differential diagnosis. Simplistic either–or questions (for example, functional *v.* organic) need to be avoided as many psychiatric patients may have cerebral impairment as well as psychological conflicts (for example, chronic alcoholics with personality disorders). Conversely, most patients with brain damage exhibit some signs of emotional conflict, which is present because of their limitations.

The complex issue of the neuropsychological assessment of emotionally disturbed patients is dealt with in Chapter 9. Filskov and Leli (1981) note that there is no discrete "organic personality" type and conclude that when personality tests are used alone the results are unable to be used to discriminate between organic and psychiatric impairment. All available procedures fail in discriminating between organically impaired patients and process schizophrenics as these two groups of patients are probably inseparable and may even share similar cognitive deficits.

Despite the above difficulties, attempts should be made, first to determine the extent of cerebral dysfunction, if any, in a psychiatric patient followed by an evaluation of their emotional status. If possible, the interaction between organic deficits and psychological disturbance needs to be monitored. Before an organically determined personality change can be diagnosed, it must be clarified which changes in behaviour are secondary reactions to the consequences of brain damage.

Golden, *et al.* (1980) report that patients with mild neuroses or personality disorders will obtain scores on neuropsychological tests within the normal limits if they are without brain damage and co-operative. Lack of motivation, malingering, and the prospects for faking plausible neuropsychological deficits are difficult to document and will be discussed in Chapter 8.

The differential diagnosis of depression from dementia is complicated by the fact that mood, motivation and memory are functions closely associated with the integrity of the limbic system. Consequently, it is not unusual for a process which may produce alterations in mood to also disrupt intellectual functioning. A history of depression in the patient, or a family history of bipolar affective disorder, helps to rule out the hypothesis of dementia. Wells and Duncan (1980) provide excellent criteria for differentiating between dementia and pseudodementia. Golden (1981b) discusses some practical diagnostic steps in the use of neuropsychological test batteries with psychiatric patients.

A structured neuropsychological interview may serve as a qualitative screening technique for personality organization as it incorporates the data usually monitored in any mental status examination (the patient's physical appearance, personal and social history, and cognitive and emotional state).

In addition to the clinical impressions obtained from interviewing, it is the routine role of psychologists to utilize a wide variety of standardized personality tests. The choice of instruments is best left to the individual practitioner. The Minnesota multiphasic personality inventory has world wide popularity as a comprehensive screening procedure and can be safely recommended. If the patient's profile is suggestive of psychopathology on this test then their problems may be studied in more detail with other more specialized techniques. An increasingly popular instrument for children is the child behaviour checklist, which may also be recommended (Edelbrock and Achenbach, 1980).

Minnesota Multiphasic Personality Inventory (MMPI)

Golden (1979) provides a particularly succinct review on the administration, hand scoring and clinical interpretation of the MMPI, together with its advantages and disadvantages. Verbal comprehension must be at least at a low average level for the patient to produce a valid profile. Reitan (1976) states that localization of cerebral damage is not associated with certain MMPI profiles, despite claims to the contrary.

Automated administration and interpretation may replace the tediousness of hand scoring techniques and take advantage of the new electronic data processing technology. For example, the Minnesota Report is a computerized mode of tapping the massive volume of MMPI-related actuarial data which may be of help in the interpretation of the case at hand.

Arion II® teleprocessing through the means of an ordinary data communications terminal can place the Minnesota Report on a neuropsychologist's desk in the time it takes to place a phone call (Interpretive Scoring Systems, 1983). Inexpensive MMPI software, which can be used by anyone with access to a personal microcomputer (Apple or TRS-80), is also available.

Clearly, automated processes are designed to serve the user rather than to mechanically over-rule or replace clinical judgement. Automated profiles are best viewed as an aid during the testing of hypotheses. Final interpretations are directly related to clinical skill and experience. Best results are obtained when the MMPI profile is integrated with the rest of the data base (the patient's history, current physical and emotional status, results of the rest of the neuropsychological assessment, etc.). Ultimately, it is clinicians who must adjust their standardized data base to meet the needs of the individual patient.

The Child Behaviour Checklist

The child behaviour checklist yields a profile suggestive of behavioural problems and competencies. It can also be used to assess changes in reported behaviour over time (Edelbrock and Achenbach, 1980). The profile consists of social competence scales and behaviour problem scales. Although each scale has been given a descriptive label, the authors warn that diagnostic decisions must be made within the context of a patient's unique history and entire behavioural pattern rather than on scores for individual scales.

The child behaviour checklist may be hand scored or computer processed. There is also on-line access to scoring programs on the University of Vermont DEC2060 computer system. This enables individuals to enter their own raw data and obtain the scored data back on their own terminal. Unlike the MMPI, this new test has not yet accumulated the almost half a century of actuarial related data which are so helpful in automated interpretation.

MULTIPLE INFERENCE

Clinical interpretation is a logical step-wise process of accumulating data and inferring its relative significance. After the neuropsychological tests (cross-indexed to the functional categories) have been administered, scored and individually interpreted, the task of multiple inference may then begin. Such clinical inferences represent the initial step in a sequential method that involves the integration of the rest of the data base (history and presenting symptoms). This process should yield a comprehensive description of the patient which is both psychologically and neurologically meaningful.

One of Reitan's major contributions was the adaptation of neurological diagnostic techniques into multiple inference modes for the clinical interpretation of test battery scores (Reitan and Davison, 1974; Boll, 1978, 1981; Rourke, 1981; Selz, 1981; Golden, 1981b).

Multiple inferential techniques maximize the value of each test within a battery whilst at the same time compensating for any particular weakness in such tests. For example, weaknesses in group norms for certain sensory-motor tests in a geriatric population are of no practical consequence as comparison of the performance of the two sides of the body within an individual is a superior inferential approach to that of level of performance. Unfortunately, scientific publications are virtually totally based upon a single inferential method. This may be a major cause of the many controversies associated with the validity and reliability of test battery results which are of doubtful benefit (Boll and Reitan, 1972).

Selz (1981) gives a particularly clear summary of the four methods of inference as used in testing children. These are equally applicable to adults and are: monitoring the range of ability through examination of level of performance; pattern analysis of intratest and intertest performance scores; documentation of specific behavioural deficits (pathognomonic signs); and comparison of the relative efficiency of the two sides of the body (right–left differences).

Level of Performance

Monitoring the range of ability through examination of level of performance suggests a vertical dimension connoting varying degrees of adaptation in processing sensory-motor and cognitive data. The higher the level, the more adaptive the behaviour. This inferential technique compares an individual's performance with normative criteria. These comparisions provide obvious evidence of a patient's deficiencies in a measured ability relative to their reference group. As measures of level of performance rely upon normative data and are highly amenable to statistical manipulation, they have been widely used for academic research purposes. However, there are several difficulties with using level of performance scores in isolation.

Low scores may derive from many non-brain related factors, thus bringing about the classification of a large number of false positive results. Similar deficit levels may result from diverse brain-related conditions. For example, in the case of children, a low score may not be indicative of brain damage, but rather may reflect temporarily delayed maturation. Normal and abnormal levels of performance are statistical and psychometric concepts and are not necessarily synonymous with normal and abnormal cerebral functioning. Some patients have documented brain damage without significant deterioration in the psychometric level of performance (Smith, 1981). Consequently, the normative approach to level of performance should be used as a supplementary inferential technique and never as a strict guide to clinical interpretation *per se.*

Pattern of Performance

The pattern of intratest and intertest performance scores conveys more information than sole reliance upon an absolute level of performance. Such pattern analysis is also referred to as the differential score approach and has been very productive in the study of learning disabilities (Rourke, 1981). For example, identical full scale IQ summary scores may be derived from a combination of quite distinct neuropsychological abilities in individuals as revealed by their variable patterns of subscale scores.

Patients with cerebral dysfunction are often characterized by a profile of discrepant scores. Performance discrepancies within and between functional categories may have syndromal significance even though the absolute levels of each test performance may fall within the average range. However, normal and average are not clinically synonymous terms (Boll, 1981).

One of the well studied patterns of performance is the lateralizing signs configuration. When analysing test results it is useful to tabulate hemisphere–test relationships as well as the level of impairment. This suggests the degree to which one hemisphere is intact relative to the other.

Pattern analysis of test scores yields quantitative profiles of unique configurations of abilities and deficits which promise more accurate descriptions of subpopulations with clinical disease. Such an approach is computer compatible and capitalizes upon the ability of electronic data processing technology to compare test results involving a large number of variables (Knights and Stoddart, 1981).

Pathognomonic Signs

The search for specifically pathological behavioural deficits is as old as the history of medicine itself. Certain tests are designed in such a way that healthy persons should make few, if any, errors. Sensory-perceptual and language examinations are dependent upon the pathognomonic signs approach for their interpretation. For example, the aphasia language performance scales use items that can be easily performed by normal subjects. Consequently, failure is indicative of aphasia. Finger agnosia, graphaesthesia and the tactile form recognition test are other examples of techniques eliciting positive signs of neuropathology.

Such a presence–absence approach to data minimizes reliance upon quantification. Boll (1981) notes that the signs approach is designed to eliminate false positive results, thus making it prone to false negative results. A lack of pathognomonic signs does not guarantee absence of neuropsychological impairment. Comprehensive questions can only be answered by a comprehensive examination taking all the other modes of inference into account.

Right–Left Differences

Comparisons of the relative efficiency of the two sides of the body is a fundamental topic in neurology and has also proved to be a uniquely useful inferential technique during neuropsychological assessment. It is not influenced by the many non-brain related factors which can complicate test interpretation. Motivation, mood and educational level are unlikely to disrupt performance on one side of the body relative to the other. Thus right–left findings may be used to test hypotheses obtained from using other inferential methods when results are inconclusive.

Because sensory-motor functioning is primarily controlled by the contralateral hemisphere, consistently inadequate performance on one side of the body is indicative of impairment of the contralateral hemisphere. In children, inconsistent performance where one side is inadequate on some tests but the other side is deficient on other measures may be indicative of a mild disability related to uneven general cerebral maturation.

The best results are obtained by simultaneously using all modes of inference. A multiple inference approach has the potential to yield more detailed and useful clinical descriptions. The value of multiple inferential techniques is further increased by repeated testing of patients. This monitoring contributes further descriptions of the natural recovery and deterioration patterns in specific organic brain syndromes (Boll, 1978).

QUANTITATIVE SYNDROME ANALYSIS

Comparisons between the results of tests are the basis of multiple inferential techniques. These comparisons suggest quantitative test result patterns that are neuropsychologically meaningful and which may be coherently related to specific neurological syndromes. Awareness of the possible modes in which certain brain diseases influence test results depends as much upon knowledge of the underlying nature of such syndromes as on having a mastery of the nature of the tests being used. Meaningful measurement is facilitated by knowing what potential entity is to be measured.

Much has been written which relates the HRNTB and allied procedures to physical neurological signs, electroencephalographic studies and characteristic descriptions of various neurological subpopulations (Golden, 1978, 1981b; Boll, 1978; Selz and Reitan, 1979; Hevern, 1980). Golden (1981b) provides the best summary and empirically relates certain brain lesions to specific test battery signs. Test interpretations made within the context of known organic brain syndromes do not imply that complex functional cognitive systems can be easily localized in a specific cerebral area as these functional systems are distributed in a constellation of "co-operating zones of the cerebral cortex and subcortical structure" (Luria, 1979: 17). Rather, test battery signs associated with well defined organic syndromes may be interpreted as generalized quantitative descriptions of such cerebral dysfunctions.

Multiple inferential techniques facilitate the assignment of test findings into the following classifications: those falling within normal limits; those suggestive of left hemisphere involvement; those suggestive of right hemisphere involvement; potential indicators of anterior or posterior lesions; and those suggestive of a diffuse disorder. If a lesion is found to be lateralized it is sometimes possible to localize it within the appropriate hemisphere. Focal hypotheses may be tested by correlating test score patterns with the type of impairment which might be expected from the involvement of a particular part of the brain. Isolated test scores suggesting cerebral dysfunction are rarely meaningful. However, data approach significance, if consistent patterns emerge which may be coherently related to neurological syndromes.

Sometimes, it is also possible to identify the psychometric effects of various modes of cerebral dysfunction (for example, tumour *v.* stroke *v.* head injury) occurring within either the left or right hemisphere. Variables such as acuteness and chronicity also tend to produce characteristic quantitative profiles (Boll, 1981).

There is no one-to-one correlation between function and structure. Functions which can be pinpointed to one area of the brain involve other regions as well and some behaviours may be distributed throughout the whole brain. Taken with the warning that things are not as localized as previously thought, Golden's (1981b) generalizations concerning typical test battery signs suggestive of dysfunction in various cerebral lobes are selectively exemplified below. These constellations are likely to contain many exceptions in the individual patient and thus must serve as probability statements.

Left Frontal Lobe Signs

The identification of frontal lobe damage can be difficult. Lesions in the primary area of the left frontal lobe tend to disrupt the efficiency of the right hand on motor tasks. For example, relative differences between the hands on the finger tapping test and the hand dynamometer are suggestive of damage in the low-lateral surface of the motor strip. If there is significantly equal impairment of both hands, this may be indicative of either left hemisphere or diffuse brain damage as bilateral deficits can occur with left hemisphere lesions. Motor deficits may influence results on all performance subtests of the WAIS with the exception of picture completion as they disrupt manual skills.

Expressive language disabilities are associated with anterior brain damage, especially in the motor and premotor areas. Motor dysphasia and dysgraphia as screened by the talking and writing scales of the aphasia language performance scales, respectively, are associated with left secondary frontal and premotor lesions.

Patients with lesions confined solely to the left frontal area demonstrate a characteristic inability to structure and plan their behavior. Problem solving in new situations is impaired. Consequently, such tasks as the trail making test (part B), the Stroop colour–word test and the complex figure test, which all require both cognitive flexibility and conceptual structuring, tend to be performed poorly. However, global intelligence as measured by the WAIS appears to be relatively untouched by left prefrontal lesions. Frontal lobe damage is not generally associated with marked neuropsychological deficits but it can be characterized by lack of motivation, which is due to cortical tone disruption in some cases.

Right Frontal Lobe Signs

Lesions in the primary area of the right frontal lobe tend to disrupt the efficiency of the left hand on motor tasks (for example, impairments on the finger tapping test and the hand dynamometer). The right hemisphere has little ipsilateral representation of motor functioning. Thus motor deficits are almost solely confined to the left side of the body.

Poor performance on visual problem solving tasks such as the picture arrangement, picture completion, block design and object assembly subtests of the WAIS is commonly associated with right frontal lobe damage. Inadequate drawing ability due to right frontal lobe dysfunction indicates the disruption of spatial regulation rather than suggesting spatial perception deficits.

Left Temporal Lobe Signs

Patients with left temporal lobe damage often show signs of auditory perceptual deficits. Relative differences in performance of the speech sounds perception test (SSPT) and the seashore rhythm test may have lateralization significance. If results for the SSPT are poor compared with those for the seashore rhythm test, the probability of left hemisphere dysfunction is raised. Relatively less adequate results for the seashore rhythm test are suggestive of right temporal lobe damage. These must remain guarded probability statements since the seashore rhythm test has only a weak correlation with right cerebral damage and also relies greatly upon concentration span, thus making it sensitive to a wide variety of cerebral dysfunctions (Boll, 1978).

Left temporal lobe damage is highly disruptive for language ability and thus can result in poor performance on both the receptive and expressive subtests of the ALPS. Lesions of Broca's area are commonly associated with deficits in the controlled word association test (Lezak, 1976). Inadequate scores are also common on the digit symbol and similarities subtests of the WAIS (McFie, 1975). Also, poor results for tests generally sensitive to brain dysfunction are not unusual (examples of such tests are the trail making test part B, the Stroop colour–word test, the spelling and reading subtests of the WRAT, the verbal subtests of the WMS, and the Walton–Black modified new word learning test). Golden (1981b) suggests that dysfunction of the integrative auditory areas in the left temporal lobe may generate deficits in both immediate and auditory memory together with verbal conceptual ability.

Severe cognitive deficits are associated with psychiatric disturbance. Patients with left temporal lobe lesions often display highly pathological profiles on the MMPI.

Right Temporal Lobe Signs

Right temporal lobe impairment is more difficult to isolate than left temporal lobe damage. Auditory and visual deficits are produced by right temporal lobe lesions. As mentioned previously, results for the seashore rhythm test may be poor. A basic sensory loss and deficits in integration resulting from damage to primary or secondary areas also undermine visual analysis abilities. Thus the picture arrangement and object assembly subtests of the WAIS may return poor results. As lesions progressively move toward the parietal–occipital areas, spatial deficits such as constructional dyspraxia tend to predominate (Golden, 1978).

Damage confined solely to the right temporal lobe is characterized by a small cluster of specific neuropsychological deficits (auditory and visual deficits operationally monitored by the seashore rhythm test and the picture arrangement subtest).

Left Parieto–Occipital Signs

Parieto–occipital deficits are characterized by sensory-motor dysfunctions. Luria (1966) emphasized that proximity to the motor strip explains the disruption of motor abilities (for example, weakened grip strength). Also, slowed finger tapping may be due to inadequate sensory feedback.

Parietal lobe damage is characterized by the demonstration of pathognomonic signs on tactile perceptual functioning testing (the face hand test, finger agnosia, graphaesthesia, and the tactile form recognition test). Poor performance in one hand relative to the other is suggestive of lateralized parietal lobe damage. Bilateral motor and sensory deficits are frequent in left posterior parietal injuries (Golden, 1978).

Tactile suppression characterizes lesions in the sensory–projection area of the parietal lobes. Visual suppression is associated with occipital lobe lesions. Inadequate performance of the digit span, arithmetic and block design subtests of the WAIS is commonly associated with left parieto–occipital damage (McFie, 1975).

Deficits in the left–right differentiation due to lesions in the tertiary areas may cause reading, spelling, writing and arithmetic problems on the WRAT (dyslexia, dysgraphia and dyscalculia).

Right Parieto–Occipital Signs

Lesions in the primary and secondary areas of the right parieto–occipital region are characterized by sensory deficits on the left side of the body. These become evident through the performance of the tactile perceptual functioning tests. Motor deficits are less evident, which is not the case in left parieto–occipital lesions.

Tactile suppression on the left side of the body characterizes lesions in the sensory-projection area of the right parietal lobe. Left field visual suppression is associated with right occipital lobe lesions.

Parieto–occipital lesions in a more posterior position disrupt spatial abilities. For example, patients with right parieto–occipital lesions tend to perform the Benton visual retention test very poorly. Constructional dyspraxia is also common as measured by the block design subtest of the WAIS. Other visuo-spatial WAIS subtests may also be affected (object assembly, picture arrangement, and picture completion).

Diffuse Signs

By definition, diffuse injuries generally involve the whole brain or refer to deficits in multiple focal areas. Alzheimer's disease is a typically generalized diffuse disorder characterized by global deterioration in the results of most tests in the battery. Some diffuse disorders such as generalized atrophy may not demonstrate significant neuropsychological deficits. Perhaps this is because their gradual onset allows for readjustment of cerebral functioning (Golden, 1978).

Golden (1981b) describes psychometric signs for such varied non-generalized diffuse disorders (characterized by deficits in multiple focal areas) as multiple sclerosis, multiple metastatic tumours and head injuries with coup and contrecoup sequelae.

There is a high probability that the majority of tests in the battery may be affected by diffuse injuries. Thus it is difficult to isolate clearly differentiated test battery signs for various generalized disorders. Golden (1981b) recommends the use of a detailed medical history as a helpful mode of differentiation (for example, the age of onset in hydrocephalus is early, whereas it is late in Alzheimer's disease). Diffuse impairment is indicated in the following situations: generally low levels of performance on tests widely sensitive to cerebral dysfunction (for example, the trail making test, part B); the presence of bilateral signs where both hemispheres or the same lobes are impaired; and left and right contralateral signs where different tests elicit deficits in both hemispheres.

Disease Processes

If the clinician is aware of how certain lesions in various cerebral lobes may result in a characteristic constellation of test battery signs, a context in which to interpret a specific patient's actual test results is provided. Further knowledge of how cerebral disease processes influence the results of tests facilitates the monitoring of such diseases.

Golden (1981b) provides succinct psychometrically oriented process interpretations of the following diseases: brain tumours; abscesses; head trauma; cerebrovascular disorders; epilepsy; alcoholism; presenile dementias; Parkinson's disease; and multiple sclerosis. This approach adds to the quantitative description of subpopulations in terms of neuropsychological profiles. Such profile characteristics are influenced by lesion location, the disease process involved, chronicity, age of onset, lateral preference patterns, premorbid intelligence, motivation and the psychiatric status of the particular patient being tested.

An almost infinite variety of deficits is possible dependent upon the interaction of the above factors. For example, benign tumours produce less impaired profiles than those which are fast growing. Head injuries tend to result in a focal deficit area at the site of injury with a relatively more diffuse and serious deficit on the contrecoup side. Multiple sclerosis results in rather distinct HRNTB patterns which differentiate it from other forms of cerebral dysfunction and psychiatric disorders (Hevern, 1980). However, the evidence regarding the characteristic patterns of neuropsychological test performance for patients with Huntington's chorea, alcoholism and learning disability remains debatable (Hevern, 1980).

You write with ease to show your breeding, but easy writing's curst hard reading.

Sheridan

7 Neuropsychological Report Writing

Most psychologists are required to write reports from time to time. In this chapter we provide brief guidelines for neuropsychological report writing. Many legitimate styles exist for communicating test results, dependent upon preferences and the nature of the referral agency. Consequently, detailed and rigid recommendations are avoided. Some examples of entire reports are provided in Chapter 10.

It is beyond the scope of this manual to convey the practical skills involved in neuropsychological report writing. Many excellent texts about improving reporting style are available (Martin, 1972; Tallent, 1976; Hollis and Donn, 1980). Valid content is a function of clinical skill and experience. However, the following basic guidelines are of relevance.

1. There is a need to have a clear understanding of the specific referral questions. Any ambiguity needs to be clarified before testing proceeds.
2. It is necessary to have a knowledge of the appropriate tests which can parsimoniously answer the referral questions.
3. It is necessary to possess the skill to use the selected tests in order to elicit a valid data base which will elucidate the particular aspects of brain–behaviour at issue.
4. It is necessary to accumulate all other available pertinent medical records and social history in order that test scores are not interpreted within a vacuum. Efforts should be made to resolve any discrepancies within this plethora of information.
5. The most difficult task is to integrate the data base and derive valid interpretations from it. The patient's history, clinical symptoms and the quantitative test scores all need to be meaningfully integrated in order to estimate the probability of a neuropsychological deficit.

6. Significant findings should be coherently communicated in such a way as to meet the specific needs of the referral agency. A detailed knowledge of the nature of the organic brain syndromes is intrinsic to such a successful communication.
7. Neuropsychological reports contain confidential information and access to such reports should be carefully monitored.

CONTENT

The contents of a neuropsychological report vary according to the nature of the referral questions. The point of emphasis will logically focus upon the question being asked. For example, a specialized referral (as for a medico-legal report) has its own characteristic requirements. Medico-legal reports are dealt with separately in Chapter 8. The following subheadings are found in most reports: title page; history and behavioural observations; intellectual functioning; neuropsychological functioning; personality organization; diagnostic impression; comments; and appendix. This artificial, although clinically convenient, organizational structure helps the reader as well as the writer (Hollis and Donn, 1980).

Title Page

The title page of the report contains orienting data. It should give the patient's name and age, and the date of testing. A concise statement of the purpose of the evaluation and the referral source gives the reader a firm idea of the specific task involved. Finally, the tests used, listed according to functional categories, should be included to show the types of instruments upon which the evaluation was based.

History and Behavioural Observations

Under this subheading there is more focus upon the qualitative aspects of the evaluation. The information is basically derived from the structured neuropsychological interview. It gives the examiner an opportunity to establish rapport with the patient and to write down initial clinical impressions. These hypotheses can later be systematically tested during the process of integrating the history with the presenting symptomatology and the test scores.

It is useful to note the patient's general appearance, marital status, nationality, and other demographic data. For example, a Macedonian immigrant from a rural village and with limited English obviously requires a different testing strategy to that which would apply to a Harvard University graduate from an urban family background. A brief statement concerning the patient's current medical status, abstracted from the interview and previous medical records, gives a coherent direction to the evaluation.

A concise description of the present illness, with information on onset, duration and behavioural changes, provides valuable clues. Any previous condition, such as loss of consciousness that may have led to cerebral dysfunction, should be noted. It is also valuable to summarize the results of any available surgical or laboratory procedures which suggest brain damage (for example, any skull X-ray films, or computerized tomography scans).

An estimate of premorbid functioning at this stage serves as a baseline for judging the relative seriousness of the patient's problems. The patient's educational level, occupational history, reading level and recreational interests provide such a reference point.

A prime purpose of the interview is to gauge the patient's state of consciousness. Orientation, concentration span, and the extent of confused thinking readily become apparent during history taking.

The data base should be placed in context to allow its validity to be assessed. The patient's emotional status, extent of co-operation, motivation and interpersonal skills all influence their capacity to achieve maximal performance on the tests.

Finally, it may be advantageous to conclude the history by listing the patient's subjective complaints verbatim. The problem list should be compared with any pathognomonic signs or objective symptoms that are amenable to behavioural observation or which can be elicited during clinical examination (for example, tremor, slurring of speech, etc.).

Intellectual Functioning

When reporting test results we have found it more convenient to begin with higher cognitive processes by arbitrarily separating them from the other neuropsychological categories. The rationale for this is that many of the tests on the battery can only be interpreted within the context of an estimate of the premorbid intellectual level.

The comparison of the scaled scores on the Wechsler intelligence scales with the individual's performance on the wide range achievement test serves as a logical start for hypothesis testing. Normally, intellectual level and educational achievement are relatively well correlated. Thus, any discrepancies are often clinically significant. For example, when IQ is significantly higher than achievement test scores the probability of learning disability is increased.

Neuropsychological Functioning

The patient's performance in the following neuropsychological categories needs to be summarized: higher cognitive processes; motor functioning; auditory perceptual functioning; tactile perceptual functioning; visuo-spatial functioning; language ability; memory processes; and personality organization.

The body of the report should interpret, rather than list, raw data. It is not necessary, and can often be confusing, to scatter a maze of subtest scores throughout the body of the report. This quantitative data may be relegated to appendices. Many referral questions can be answered by describing the patient's abilities and deficits for the pertinent functional categories. If a qualitative analysis has also been undertaken, the nature of any documented deficits can also be elucidated.

Personality Organization

The ability to assess personality functioning is basic to the role of any clinical psychologist. It must be remembered to keep sight of the fact that the main thrust of neuropsychological testing is to monitor brain output. Thus, the description of personality organization should be succinct. It is useful to emphasize personality change and to monitor the adaptive capacities of the brain damaged patient.

Diagnostic Impression

Once the data base has been meaningfully integrated and interpreted, a profile of the patient's strengths and deficits emerges. If a diagnostic impression is to be formulated, this pattern needs to be compared with the characteristics of various organic brain syndromes.

Diagnosis can be a relatively simple procedure when test score patterns are suggestive of a well known syndrome or when the patient exhibits obvious organic signs and medical reports are available which unequivocally document neurological damage. It is routine diagnostic strategy to look for overlap between test scores, neurological symptoms and the medical history. Since an infinite variety of interactions can emerge from these complex variables, neuropsychological testing remains an interesting challenge. Any diagnostic statement must derive directly from supportive data cited within the body of the report itself.

Comments

Under the "comments" subheading should be included a summary of the major areas of intact functioning as well as impairment, the extent of disability and an explanation of the underlying nature of the deficit if this is known. When discussing the extent of disability it is common practice to categorize this as either mild, moderate, severe or profound. Also, it is practical to explain what the categories imply for the patient's daily functioning.

Since recovery from brain injury varies greatly with the individual patient, it is difficult to formulate an accurate prognosis. Knowledge of the nature and extent of damage, together with the results of tests of memory, is the best available prognostic guide. Clinical experience suggests that, in the majority of cases, the greatest amount of recovery occurs within six months of injury, slowly reaching the maximum level after 24 months. The patient's premorbid level of functioning and motivation are other important factors which influence progress. Unfortunately, there are few long-term studies of recovery. Therefore little is known concerning the restitution of function after brain damage.

The neuropsychological report should attempt to provide some guidelines for the patient's future management. A comprehensive profile of the patient's strengths and deficits facilitates the formulation of a coherent rehabilitation programme. It encourages an individual treatment plan wherein specific interventions can be cross-indexed to pertinent problems elicited by the results of the tests. A typical strategy that may be recommended is to retrain the patient in specific skills where possible, compensate for any deficits and to capitalize upon the patient's strengths.

Appendices

The final pages of the neuropsychological report may include appendices containing the quantitative data which document the normative evidence upon which the diagnostic impressions are based. These add objective support to the examiner's more qualitative clinical observations.

Quantifying the data base in a standardized manner where possible is the essence of the scientific method. It allows for a meaningful review of work and its replication and permits colleagues to come to their own conclusions. This is particularly important for student supervision, peer review and follow-up for medico-legal and research purposes.

A quantitative profile of a patient's abilities and deficits may be formulated after the conclusion of test administration. Such information is amenable to pattern analysis and aids the examiner in the interpretation of the data base. The presence of normative guidelines is particularly valuable for students as it provides discipline for their clinical thinking.

Finally, a standardized appendix containing a list of tests which parallels the order on the title page serves as a check. While testing, the examiner may find it useful to record test scores in the appropriate spaces provided.

DISCUSSION

The neuropsychological report is the practical end result of the assessment process. No interpretation of neuropsychological functioning is complete without estimating the effect that a particular psychometric deficit may have on a patient's adaptation to real life. It should also be noted whether the patient has developed any compensatory mechanisms to cope with specific deficits. Such interpretive statements need to be carefully and responsibly phrased as they may directly influence the future management of a patient. The neuropsychological report becomes a permanent record which may be consulted by numerous other people throughout the patient's life.

The philosophical and theoretical assumptions of the author inevitably influence the report, either consciously or unconsciously. Thus, a periodic clarification of the author's basic assumptions and biases concerning brain–behaviour relationships facilitates communication. Whilst examining others, psychologists should also be examining themselves.

Tallent (1976) reported on problems which might arise with general psychological report writing and this work is equally applicable to neuropsychological assessment. A major criticism is that psychological reports too often have an improper emphasis and hence do not meet the specific needs of the referral source. The antidote is to avoid writing to please oneself. Instead, consider the practical purpose the report is expected to have for those requesting such a document. Such considerations help develop a more appropriate content.

The accuracy of interpretations of test data depends upon the psychologist's skill and experience. Deficient interpretations may derive from personal bias, writing to please the referral source, overspeculation, exceeding the level of one's competency, reporting broad generalizations which apply to all patients, and making contradictory statements. If equivocal data are present, an attempt should be made to resolve such contradictions, and conclusions should be clearly stated. It is not possible, nor desirable, to communicate every potential interpretation within the data base. Rather, interpretations should be appropriately focused upon referral questions. Interpretations should be selected on the basis of the degree to which they elucidate the patient's major problems. The inclusion of trivial or unnecessarily confusing interpretations undermines the value of the rest of the report.

Referral sources often criticize psychological reports on the basis of problems with the author's personal attitude and orientation. Common complaints concern reports that are deemed too dogmatic, overly theoretical, pedantic or impractical by neglecting rehabilitation issues. Such criticism may be overcome, at least partially, by improving communications between the author and the user (Hollis and Donn, 1980). If the author and the referral source establish a working interpersonal relationship, most assessment problems can be anticipated and misunderstandings resolved.

Exceedingly late reports, such as those received after a patient has already been discharged from hospital, are a particular source of irritation. Advances in electronic data processing technology assist in cost-efficiency. Those who use computer-compatible tests must accept that computerized interpretations are not intended to serve as the final report. Rather, they are a series of hypotheses which require further clarification from other clinical sources. It is a good policy to reinterpret and rewrite the generalizations from the computer report in order to make it a more accurate reflection of a specific patient coping in a unique situation.

Problems in literary communications can plague all who commit pen to paper. Beginners may find it necessary to prepare a rough draft and then rewrite it, checking such factors as clarity and conciseness of language, correct grammar, adequate communication style, logic of interpretations, and so on. Rambling reports are no more useful than the presentation of raw, disorganized data. Unduly lengthy reports tend to be ignored; length is not necessarily correlated with quality. The level of presentations should meet the capacities of the primary reader, but report writers should be aware that secondary readers may also refer to the report (secondary readers may be supporting team members, allied professions, etc.). A descriptive analysis of behaviour is preferable to theoretical jargon. Hollis and Donn (1980) provide detailed instructions for improving psychological writing style.

Perhaps the major challenge in neuropsychological assessment lies as much in the inherent nature of the discipline as in the fallibilities of the report writer. It is a truism that brain–behaviour relationships are exceedingly complex. Also, unresolved issues in the neurosciences and personality functioning remain, as exemplified by the proliferation of competing theories and applied strategies. For example, there is no consensus concerning the units of measurement to be used during quantified assessments.

In conclusion, the best mode of obtaining familiarity with a variety of reporting styles is to review samples of the work of more experienced colleagues. Improvement will come if the better features of the work of other clinicians are incorporated into one's own reports. It is also valuable to request feedback from referral sources and other colleagues concerning the utility of one's reports. The improvement of reporting style is a continuing educational experience which also upgrades the diagnostic skills of the author concerned, as well as enlightening readers.

Report writing can be a time consuming burden. The challenge is to reduce writing time as much as possible without comprising the quality of the report. Preprinted forms with a standardized format make report writing easier and faster (Hollis and Donn, 1980). An example of a worksheet, in the form of a topical outline with appropriate spaces for entering pertinent neuropsychological data, is contained in Appendix 1.3. Such preprinted forms provide a matrix for describing patients, save much repetitious writing for the psychologist, and serve as reminders for not omitting pertinent neuropsychological issues. Secretaries can easily type a final report from these preprinted worksheets. Preprinted forms are cost-efficient tools provided they are not overstructured or used mechanically to the extent that they discourage individuality and flexibility in report writing (Hollis and Donn, 1980). Clinicians should use their initiative to change the preprinted worksheets in any way they choose to.

The safety of the people shall be the highest law.
Cicero

8
Clinical Neuropsychology and the Law

THIS CHAPTER discusses the relationship of clinical neuropsychology to forensic medicine. It is important to do so for there is a high probability that the reports of any psychologist who accepts referrals for neuropsychological assessment will be subpoenaed.

The following forensic issues are reviewed: the legal framework within which neuropsychologists legitimately function; and contributions neuropsychologists may make towards answering basic medico-legal questions such as the nature, extent and duration of a potentially compensatable cognitive deficit. Finally, some elementary forensic principles are illustrated using severe head injury, minor head injury (post-traumatic syndrome) and pseudo-head injury (malingering) as examples.

It is hoped that this discussion will help neuropsychologists better meet the specific referral needs of lawyers. The ability of neuropsychologists to elucidate the nature, extent and duration of neuropsychological deficits can facilitate the lawyer's attempts to gain optimum justice for their litigating clients. This collaboration reinforces productive relationships between these disciplines.

During the last 20 years the relationship between psychology and the law has become increasingly productive throughout the world. For example, the role of the forensic neuropsychologist has expanded since the U.S. Court of Appeals for the District of Columbia circuit found, in 1962, that competent psychologists qualified as expert witnesses on mental disorders. Interdisciplinary collaboration is manifested by the profusion of international journals and annual conferences and formalized through the existence of accreditation boards in forensic psychology in certain countries. Winick's (1981) review of the forensic psychology literature comes to the conclusion that the relations between these areas have become substantive enough for recognition as a discipline. This speciality has already developed a fair degree of knowledge as exemplified by *The Role of the Forensic Psychologist* (Cooke, 1980).

Clinical neuropsychologists have an important social responsibility to contribute to the forensic sciences (Russell, 1981). Courts increasingly depend upon the testimony of neuropsychologists in cases where compensatable events are alleged to have caused neuropsychological deficits. Neuropsychological assessments are regarded as practical contributions to the advancement of forensic medicine.

The significance of forensic neuropsychology is magnified by its tradition of involvement with broad social concerns. Referral sources are as infinite as the scope of such social concerns in both developed and developing countries. To list all sources of potentially compensatable neuropsychological deficits would require a voluminous text confined to this topic alone. However, some representative topics may be briefly listed below.

Methylmercuric salts, as do many other industrial toxins, have many destructive effects on the nervous system. For example, in Minamata, Japan, an industrial effluent was noted to cause cerebellar ataxia and cortical blindness (Rustam, 1975). The surrounding population, affected on a large scale by permanent damage to the nervous system, initiated successful mass litigation for substantial compensation.

Medical malpractice, in particular where surgery and drugs are concerned, is a source of iatrogenic brain dysfunction with its inevitable personal and socioeconomic sequelae.

The significance of forensic neuropsychology is further dramatized by the World Safety Organization's (1981) estimate that one of every 10 hospital beds is occupied by a road accident victim. Industrial accidents are also responsible for a large number of head injuries which have medico-legal implications. Payments for third party insurance have increased dramatically over recent years as the number of motor vehicle and industrial accidents has also increased. Compensation payments have often exceeded one million dollars in individual cases of gross brain damage.

It is recognized that not all potentially compensatable neuropsychological deficits are traumatic in origin. However, for the purpose of brevity this chapter will rely exclusively upon examples of alleged head injury to illustrate some elementary medico-legal principles. This delineation allows a more detailed and controlled discussion of forensic concerns pertinent to the functions of non-specialist clinical psychologists.

Clinical neuropsychology's collaboration with the forensic sciences is not limited to the applied area. The collaboration extends to basic research as well. For example, Yeudall, *et al.* (1981) report that the significantly higher levels of neuropsychological deficits found in people who have many criminal convictions are not merely accompaniments of their criminal careers or unrelated ramifications of their psychosocial milieu but in many instances are antecedent and contributory to the cause and continuation of criminal activity. The writers have also been intrigued by the extent to which specific learning disabilities are elicited during routine testing of the prison population. Unfortunately, such provocative research issues are beyond the scope of this practical workbook of neuropsychological assessment.

THE LEGAL FRAMEWORK

McMahon and Satz (1981) emphasize that, with the exception of malpractice suits, neuropsychologists cannot assist the liability phase of proceedings (that is, whether or not a given event occurred and whether a certain individual was responsible for that event). Despite this, neuropsychologists may make significant contributions both in the criminal and civil spheres of law.

Criminal Law

Within criminal law, neuropsychological assessment routinely deals with such issues as an individual's competency to stand trial and the state of their cerebral functions at the time of the offence. In the author's experience, lawyers are increasingly requesting evaluations of an individual's intellectual capacity to understand the legal implications of their record of interview. This is particularly so for the migrant population.

Civil Law

McMahon and Satz (1981) warn that the courts are reluctant to accept evidence of brain damage as sole grounds for defence. If the courts did not have this attitude, virtually all chronic alcoholics would have some degree of legal incompetence. Cognitive deterioration must be proved to be profound before diminished responsibility is conceded. Moreover, the concept of insanity as a defence is a contentious issue and there have been bewildering changes in guidelines. Consequently, the most productive interaction between neuropsychology and the law has traditionally been within the civil sphere.

A significant proportion of industrial and motor vehicle accidents are responsible for compensatable head injuries and their neuropsychological sequelae. Justice in the courts depends upon able advocacy. Lawyers are increasingly aware of the fact that comprehensive assessment of an individual with head injuries should include a functional evaluation (for example, a neuropsychological assessment) as well as evidence of structural damage (for example, skull X-ray films).

A related issue is that of consultation. Lawyers may profit by requesting second opinions from independent neuropsychologists if they are not satisifed with the medico-legal reports they may receive from allied professions (for example, psychiatrists, neurologists, or even other neuropsychologists).

BASIC MEDICO-LEGAL QUESTIONS

For the lawyer, the most valuable contents of the neuropsychological assessment are the following:

1. The history obtained.
2. The patient's condition when examined by the clinician.
3. The relationship between the patient's injuries and their present condition.
4. Are the patient's complaints genuine?
5. The diagnosis and/or nature of the disability.
6. The extent of the disability.
7. The prognosis and/or the duration of disability.
8. Recommendations for further treatment.

The history the clinician obtains from the patient may be quite subjective. The phenomenological data are significant in that they inform lawyers how their clients experience the situation. Individual differences are important as the legal interest is in what is happening to a specific person rather than how a theoretical majority might react to a particular accident. Consequently, it is useful to list that patient's problems verbatim under "history and behavioural observations". It is also important to note whether the patient has had any previous or subsequent head injuries or psychiatric problems that may be unrelated to their compensation claim. It is preferable to note any treatment, including surgery, the patient has had, together with reactions. The neuropsychological evaluation of the patient's condition serves as the objective section of the report ("intellectual functioning", "neuropsychological functioning" and "personality organization" headings). This may contrast with the patient's subjective perception of their problems.

Essentially the courts are attempting to estimate the "before and after" picture in order to award compensation. This requires careful estimates of the premorbid level of functioning followed by a convincing documentation of the current nature and extent of the patient's disabilities. When considering a profile of neuropsychological deficits the courts demand an interpretation of the technical data so that it is possible to comprehend what these deficits mean for every day functioning (personal, social, vocational and general quality of life). For example, if an architect has been found to have a mild visuo-spatial difficulty together with a moderate impairment of recent memory, examples of how this influences the architect's work efficiency, and hence his professional future, should be given to the lawyer. This non-technical data may be elaborated upon under "comments".

The most difficult and vital thing to do is to elucidate the relationship between the patient's injuries and their present condition. Aetiology is often multifactorial and may be influenced by an infinite number of elements. For example, an individual may be predisposed to cerebral disease which may then be precipitated by a head injury. If the patient's complaints are directly attributable to an accident then this causative link should be clearly documented. Indirectly related problems (for example, emotional response to the frustrations of a cognitive deficit) also need to be explained. It must be remembered that predisposing factors do not inherently excuse a defendant. Under tort law the defendant must "take his victim as he finds him" (that is, the "cracked vase" principle).

The validity of the patient's complaints can be a complex diagnostic issue and will be later discussed under malingering.

The most important contribution a neuropsychologist can make to legal matters is to give a full description of the nature, extent and duration of disability.

The Nature and Extent of Disability

The sensitivity of neuropsychological techniques is favourably compared to neurological diagnostic procedures by Crockett, *et al.* (1981). This comparison exemplifies the unique contribution that neuropsychological techniques may make in elucidating the nature and extent of disability. Essentially, the two procedures supplement each other. Their relationship is discussed in Chapter 9.

Neurological diagnostic procedures supply structural evidence of head injury. They cannot easily give direct information concerning the functional severity of brain damage (Hayward, 1980). Neuropsychology's functional orientation is extremely valuable in litigation as the prime concern is the extent to which the plaintiff's lifestyle is disrupted.

Often neuropsychological procedures are able to document the nature and extent of cognitive dysfunction when the results of physical neurological examination and laboratory techniques are negative (Broe, 1979). Thus, legal colleagues may be assured that neuropsychological testing is strongly established as a valid and reliable technique.

The examiner's diagnostic impression is a succinct statement of the final decision on the nature of the patient's disease or distress. However, the extent of disability, in terms of restrictions to be placed upon a person's future earning capacity, requires detailed elaboration as it is of interest to all parties involved in litigation. This requires wide range testing in order to establish a comprehensive profile of neuropsychological strengths and deficits. Such a profile of a client's current status may then be contrasted with estimates of their premorbid level of functioning. Loss is best assessed in terms of discrepancies from previous abilities. School records, employment history and the use of special neuropsychological tests which are relatively less affected by brain damage are routinely used as indicators of premorbid level. Individuals and their families also differ in how they adapt to similar injuries and stresses. This must be estimated together with the degree of motivation for rehabilitation.

The Duration of Disability

After the nature, extent and immediate effects of cerebral dysfunction have been determined, the probable long-term consequences of any neuropsychological deficits should be estimated. The prognosis for head injuries can never be formulated with finaliy and is most safely phrased as a guarded probability statement. However, a knowledge of the research on recovery rates applied to the individual patient is the basis for any qualified prognostic statement. Some statistics concerning recovery rates are provided in the sections below which deal with the medico-legal aspects of head injury. Lawyers often pressure clinicians to state the exact proportion of loss of cerebral function together with the specific duration of such disabilities. However, such exactitude cannot be achieved when evaluating organic brain syndromes.

Any recommendations for further treatment may be included under "prognosis". Such recommendations should detail the specific interventions which may facilitate the patient's rehabilitation, the probability of success and the costs involved, if known.

When organizing their briefs, lawyers should be aware that, in patients with significant head injuries, most recovery occurs within six months of injury and then slowly tends to reach a maximum level after 24 months. Consequently, it is ideal to arrange a neuropsychological assessment as soon as possible after an accident, with a re-evaluation just before attempted court settlement. The availability of data recorded at two different times provides a base-line against which the patient's recovery rate can be monitored. Questions concerning long-term prognosis for head injury cannot be realistically answered until at least 18 months have elapsed after such injury.

MEDICO-LEGAL REPORTING STYLE

The style to be used with forensic neuropsychological reports does not differ essentially from routine psychological report writing. The legal system has as much respect for the scientific method as is shown in clinical practice. Consequently, the same standards of objectivity, reproducibility, parsimony, adequate documentation and confining comments to the level of competency apply.

It is the responsibility of every lawyer to be the best possible advocate for their client. The role of the neuropsychologist must not be confused with such advocacy as it is the aim of the neuropsychologist to develop a more detached perspective without investment in the outcome of any case. Thus, reporting style should be as formal and neutral as possible.

Conclusions should derive directly from a careful evaluation and interpretation of the available data base. Objectivity and reproducibility are enhanced by documenting the types of instruments upon which an evaluation is based. It is customary to list the tests used on the title page of the report. An appendix at the conclusion of the report is helpful in revealing the quantitative test results from which clinical interpretations are derived.

The law of parsimony recommends that data should not be elaborated upon beyond a point necessary to support conclusions. Lawyers appreciate a succinct report which avoids discussion of extraneous theoretical issues which may do damage by provoking inconsistencies. Also, in order for neuropsychological reports to be better understood by the intelligent layperson, psychological jargon should be kept to a minimum.

The nature of the adversary system, upon which litigation is based, ensures that all reports will be read with judicious scepticism and every statement must be able to withstand rigorous cross-examination. Consequently, acceptable medico-legal report writing style requires adequate documentation throughout. This emphasizes the importance of establishing a valid and comprehensive data base which includes areas of intact functioning as well as deficit functioning. As justice depends so much upon the skilled presentation of available evidence, readers of reports should be led through a convincing process of reasoning which clarifies how test results reflect a specific patient's condition. Opinions should be seen to derive logically from available data. It is an advantage to summarize the data supporting each opinion in a separate "conclusions" section of the report. Speculative clinical intuition is unacceptable and may be avoided by staying within the bounds of the data base.

Opinions need to be stated clearly. Doubts must also be documented. If an adequate data base cannot be obtained, this should be stated. Anything which compromises validity (for example, testing ethnic minorities, the use of an interpreter, etc.) should be acknowledged. If the diagnosis is uncertain, it is better to concede this. A doubtful diagnostic statement drawn from an incomplete data base discredits the whole value of a report.

Perhaps the most common source of legal objection to reports is when a neuropsychologist without medical qualification is judged to have exceeded their area of competence. Competency is difficult to delineate as neuropsychology is at the interface between the neurosciences and the behavioural sciences. The psychologist needs to have the ability to contrast medical testimony with neuropsychological testimony. Thus, it is more appropriate to express findings in terms of the functional aspects of the brain's output rather than to elaborate upon gross structural or anatomical issues. For example, it is more acceptable to state that an acquired impairment of cognitive function exists and that it is exemplified by a deficit in auditory perceptual functioning, rather than to say that brain damage has occurred and that the lesion is located in the superior portion of the right temporal lobe. Both statements may imply the same things but the former is more palatable from a psychologist, whereas the latter seems to fit more closely the accepted role of a neurologist. Some conservative judges are particularly sensitive to diagnostic statements emanating from psychologists as they perceive the role of diagnosis to be exclusively the domain of a physician.

It is fortunate for neuropsychology that litigation is oriented more functionally than structurally. It is preferable to elucidate the patient's level of functioning and quality of life than to hypothesize the location of a specific lesion, or to show overconcern with diagnostic categories.

Lawyers will encounter two differing approaches commonly used in neuropsychological assessment. One strategy employs a standardized test battery whereas the other emphasizes an inductive approach in which hypotheses are formulated and tested. Luria and Majovsky (1977) reviewed the advantages and disadvantages of both these paradigms by contrasting the quantitatively oriented Halstead–Reitan (1969) and Luria's (1980) qualitative syndrome analysis scheme. Both have established their usefulness in clinical neuropsychology. Luria's orientation has made significant contributions in rehabilitation settings whereas the standard battery approach has been more compatible with the medico-legal context.

Courts readily recognize the limitations inherent in anything suggestive of intuitive clinical method. Objectivity is compromised when any examiner relies overly upon an intuitive, creative strategy. This unstructured approach may be useful in purely clinical and rehabilitative settings with correct medical back-up, but such a lack of structure maximizes subjectivity and makes medico-legal documentation and replication difficult. Qualitative schemes, when used alone, tend to undermine the very elements of reliability and objectivity that characterize the contributions of psychologists to neuropsychological assessment in particular, and the behavioural sciences in general. Inductively oriented qualitative approaches are awkward to write about objectively. Also, clinical intuition does not readily withstand cross-examination, no matter what reputation the expert witness has. Consequently, lawyers should note carefully the reporting style of their neuropsychological consultants and ensure that it is compatible with the local forensic context. Ziskin (1981) deals in detail with how to cope with psychological testimony.

HEAD INJURY: MEDICO-LEGAL ASPECTS

Most head injuries that occur in peacetime are of the closed type and involve acceleration and deceleration of the brain within its bony compartments. Most closed head injuries of significance result in sudden loss of consciousness (Wells and Duncan, 1980). When unaccompanied by other neurological deficits and followed by complete recovery, the condition is called cerebral concussion. Cerebral contusion and cerebral laceration can either resolve or show up as focal deficits. Frontal lobe damage is extremely common in motor vehicle accidents (Golden, *et al.,* 1983). Levin, *et al.* (1982) provide a comprehensive review of literature on the neuropsychological consequences of head injuries.

The following factors determine the consequence of head injuries:

1. The severity of the injury—usually, the more severe the neurological picture revealed by the initial assessment, the worse the prognosis.
2. Changes that have occurred since the accident—generally, extent of recovery is related to the time taken before objective evidence of improvement can be seen. Thus, a quick early recovery is more likely to progress to complete recovery than one in which no improvement is seen for several days or more.
3. Characteristics of the victim—for example, Hayward (1980) reports that children have the potential to recover from injuries that would be fatal to adults. In contrast, elderly patients are less able to survive moderate/severe head trauma as the complications associated with prolonged bed rest take their toll. Such trauma may also exacerbate pre-existing cognitive deterioration.
4. Association with other injuries—for example, chest injuries may cause hypoxia which can aggravate cerebral oedema; cerebral fat embolism from fractures has also been known to be implicated in cognitive dysfunction.

Wells and Duncan (1980) recommend the duration of post-traumatic amnesia as a good measure of the severity of head injury. In persons whose periods of post-traumatic amnesia are 24 hours or less, total intellectual reintegration may be expected in the majority of patients. With individuals in whom the post-traumatic amnesia lasts for more than 24 hours, residual intellectual deficits are far more common. It must also be remembered that the amount of recovery is likely to be unpredictable in the individual patient.

The medico-legal aspects of head injury may be conveniently reviewed under the following subheadings: severe head injury; mild head injury (the post-traumatic syndrome); and pseudo-head injury (malingering). A brief review of the neuropsychological literature may be useful to lawyers so that they can better understand the prognostic opinions of their consultants, and in the overall planning of their suits.

Severe Head Injury

Knowledge of what types of changes to expect after severe head injury facilitates assessment. First, there are intellectual changes. Miller (1979) warns that, despite the fact that IQ scores may show significant improvement, it is probable that severe head injury inevitably results in some degree of permanent functional impairment. Second, most victims sustain some relatively stable and long-term memory impairments which may vary in degree. The incidence of memory impairment seems to be related to post-traumatic amnesia duration. Third, a wide range of other functional disturbances is common (for example, epilepsy, aphasic disabilities, and motor and visuospatial impairments).

Awareness of research on the likely outcome for severe head injuries facilitates the formulation of a realistic prognosis. Unfortunately, Miller's (1979) review suggests that outcome is poor. Of those people who had been in a coma of at least six hours' duration (but excluding those who die within the first six hours of injury), approximatey 50 per cent had died six months later. Of those patients still alive, one third to one half failed to reach a reasonable level of adjustment. The greatest proportion of recovery occurs within six months of injury and then slowly reaches a maximum level after 24 months. There is some controversy about whether or not there is a tendency for head injury victims to be more susceptible to intellectual deterioration in later years. For example, it has been reported that progressive dementing disease has not been documented as a result of head injury except in boxers who are exposed to repeated trauma (Wells and Duncan, 1980). It has been recommended that if progressive dementia appears after head injury, it should be assumed to have antedated the trauma but to have been undiagnosed.

Faster recovery tends to occur with injuries in motor and sensory areas than with injuries affecting higher cognitive functions (Golden, *et al.,* 1983).

Mild Head Injury (the Post-Traumatic Syndrome)

Head injuries have a number of psychiatric sequelae. Some types of personality changes appear to be unrelated to either the extent or the severity of brain damage. In fact, the post-traumatic syndrome is unusual in patients with severe head injury, but it is present in 40 per cent of traumatized patients who do not suffer loss of consciousness (Miller, 1966). Moreover, Wells and Duncan (1980) observed that virtually identical symptoms (except for the location of pain) are seen after trauma which does not involve the head at all.

For diagnostic purposes it is useful to remember that the incidence of retrograde amnesia tends to resolve as recovery proceeds. Miller (1966) claimed that a component of prolonged retrograde amnesia suggests functional rather than organic aetiology. However, the extent of post-traumatic amnesia may or may not recede with recovery.

The post-traumatic syndrome has many synonyms (compensation, accident or litigation neurosis; functional overlay; and abnormal illness behaviour). It is a popular, albeit controversial, diagnosis in litigation and is a well known complication of a relatively minor injury.

The patient with post-traumatic syndrome presents with a considerable number of varied and transient pseudoneurological complaints for which there is no objective physical basis. Lloyd (1980) states that compensation neurosis is characterized by severe subjective complaints which are intractable to treatment and occur within the context of the gain–blame oriented medico-legal process.

It occurs mainly in adult non-professional males, 80 per cent of whom develop many of the following symptoms within two months of a relatively minor head injury: headache; anxiety; dizziness; excessive fatigue; intolerance to noise; sleep disturbance; marital or sexual dysfunction; mild intellectual deficits; and ingrained conviction of unfitness for work.

A review of research on the post-traumatic syndrome by Wells and Duncan (1980) suggests that there are no neurological deficits in most of these patients and that the acute symptoms are thought to be non-specific effects of the trauma. In most patients, the symptoms resolve. However, in a significant minority, such symptoms persist and are accompanied by added problems such as chronic depression, anhedonia, insomnia, obsessions and phobias. The longer the neurosis persists the worse the prognosis. Seventy-five per cent of affected patients return to work within one year. Repeated clinical assessments and legal delays reinforce symptomatology. Financial settlement does not necessarily lead to symptom resolution and up to 20 per cent of patients remain disabled. Forty per cent may retain some degree of symptomatology.

Such a clinical picture does not fit any of the recognized organic brain syndromes. Thus, the results of neurological examination, electroencephalography and computerized tomography are usually within normal limits. Examination of mental status often shows an uncooperative patient who is irritable, demanding, anxious and depressed. Performance during neuropsychological testing is often inconsistent. There appears to be a vague impairment which does not fit the recognized organic brain syndromes. Also, there is often a discrepancy between interview behaviour, which will be adequate, and performance on formal tests, which will be inadequate.

Some researchers believe that the syndrome has a physical basis with a gross psychogenic elaboration superimposed. Powerful psychosomatic forces may be impinging upon the patient whose reactions may be viewed as a coping mechanism as adjustment is made to a stressful situation. However, there is little evidence in favour of an organic aetiology as the syndrome is grossly discrepant with the extent of neuropathological damage which might even generously be calculated (Wells and Duncan, 1980).

Wells and Duncan (1980) also admit that although the evidence does not support the hypothesis of an organic aetiology, the evidence suggesting a psychogenic basis is also equivocal. For example, there is no evidence that most individuals suffering from the post-traumatic syndrome were premorbidly neurotic. Consequently, a comprehensive understanding of the post-traumatic syndrome remains unavailable.

There is no evidence that psychiatric treatment is effective for the post-traumatic syndrome, even when the patient is co-operative and there is no secondary gain (Wells and Duncan, 1980). Lloyd (1980) also acknowledges that the condition is resistant to treatment. However, he recommends that an early and clear communication be given about the extent of the injury and that the patient be encouraged to return to work as soon as possible. Supportive psychotherapy may also be applied.

Pseudo-Head Injury (Malingering)

This section focuses upon research concerning the exaggeration of neuropsychological deficits. However, the general conclusions about malingering below may also apply to cases feigning other types of injuries.

The very nature of the medico-legal process whereby disability is compensated and recovery penalized ensures that malingering must exist. However, the available research literature does not contain consistent statistics. Lloyd (1980) reported that only a small proportion of compensation neurosis cases are thought to be malingering. In contrast, a controversial Australian Medical Association survey (1981), which later proved to be based upon the files of a single surgeon, claimed that nearly half of all compensation cases involve persons who are either faking or grossly exaggerating their disability. Locke (1981) claimed that only five per cent of compensation cases are malingering, and that these cases are responsible for 50 per cent of the costs of litigation. Most studies confirm that people who were on compensation took longer to get better.

Clinicians attempt to make a distinction between malingering and hysterical neurosis as a matter of routine. Lawyers are particularly interested in making this differentiation as it may decide the outcome of the case.

Malingering is an unpopular diagnosis and a heavy burden of proof falls upon the accuser. Ellard (1970) admitted that it is almost impossible to make an unequivocal diagnosis of malingering and advised caution. When an individual consciously feigns symptoms which are under voluntary control for financial gain they are traditionally classified as a malingerer. If a person's symptomatology is allegedly generated unconsciously in order to meet some emotional need then this is generally viewed as a neurotic process (that is, neurotics tend to unconsciously deceive themselves for secondary emotional gain whilst malingerers tend to consciously deceive others for primary financial gain).

However, differential diagnosis is rarely clear-cut. Symptom exaggeration also includes a conscious component despite the presence of objective disability. Thus, the patient's motivation for playing the sick role can operate at different gradients of consciousness. Medical sociology also suggests that cultural differences exist in the perception of pain and the sick role may be an honourable and functional one within the context of an extended family. Some clinicians believe that the persistent malingerer is inherently emotionally disturbed and may play the sick role so well that they become a captive of it. Such a self-fulfilling prophecy is succinctly illustrated in the Torah:

> And if a man is lame, blind and halting,
> and he feigns one of these—he will
> become one of these.

In contrast, Gorman (1982) asserts that malingering is not a mental disorder but an act which is distinguished from a legal or mental status. Failure to distinguish act from status accounts for many of the differences in definitions. Gorman defines malingering as the fraudulent simulation or exaggeration of physical or mental disease in order to obtain money or drugs, or to evade duty or criminal responsibility. Malingering may be seen in apparently normal children, students, test subjects, spouses and adults. It may also coexist with antisocial personality disorders, factitious disorders (for example, the Ganser syndrome and the Münchausen syndrome), hysterias, traumatic neuroses and other psychiatric disorders.

The research of Heaton, *et al.,* (1978) on malingering suggests that the prospects for faking believable deficits when undergoing neuropsychological testing can be quite good. Malingering is still difficult to detect, but more guidelines are being formulated. For example, although malingerers may show significant abnormalities on testing, their neuropsychological profiles differ from those produced by patients with genuine head injury (Heaton, *et al.,* 1978). Malingerers performed sensory-motor tests especially poorly and displayed a greater range and degree of apparent personality dysfunction on the Minnesota multiphasic personality inventory.

Lezak (1976) described a useful battery of tests for dissimulation. Ostensibly, these tests appear difficult, but they are rarely failed by any except the most profoundly brain damaged patients. Bash and Alpert (1980) provided a promising set of objective tests for computing a malingering score. This was based upon a system of approximate answers.

Finally, the DSM III of the American Psychiatric Association (1980) stresses the following features associated with malingering: medico-legal context of presentation; contradictions and inconsistencies in the patient's history and test results, especially when sub-tests are repeated; uncooperative and evasive attitude; symptomatology inconsistent with known neuropsychological syndromes; severe disability after trivial injury; delay between accident and onset of symptoms (period of meditation); and presence of antisocial personality disorder and/drug dependence.

Examiners must also be alert for paradoxical, yet not unusual, cases wherein individuals tend to underestimate their objective deficits. Such patients may deny their disabilities because of difficulties in accepting their limitations. There are others who are so disoriented that they are not aware of their neuropsychological status.

It is a better policy to create a testing environment where maximal performance is reinforced and malingering is minimized rather than be faced with attempts to detect this difficult entity. Heaton and Heaton (1981) advise that patients involved in litigation should be subtly oriented at the first sign of lack of co-operation as follows: the tests are sensitive enough to detect even the mildest of their problems thus exaggeration serves no purpose; it is also possible to identify the minority of persons who may not do their best since some of the tests are not influenced by brain damage; unfortunately if patients do not do their best such an attitude must be documented for the court and their test results then cannot be used to their advantage: and the examiner hopes that they will be able to report to the court that the patient was totally co-operative and that the test results are valid. Such information should be communicated in a friendly and supportive manner.

Finally, it is imperative to appreciate the extent to which the adversary nature of litigation may be disruptive to normal clinician–patient relationships. Such a process reinforces the plaintiff's perception that any clinician retained by an insurance company would be potentially biased. Therefore great skill is required to facilitate co-operation and to establish rapport under such conditions. High professional standards and the ability to communicate real empathy for the litigant's difficult situation helps to protect the patient and raises the possibility of obtaining valid test results.

I have often amused myself with thinking how different a place London is to different people. They, whose narrow minds are contracted to the consideration of some one particular pursuit, view it only through that medium. A politician thinks of it merely as the seat of government in its different departments; a grazier, as a vast market for cattle; a mercantile man, as a place where a prodigious deal of business is done upon 'Change; a dramatick enthusiast, as the grand scale of theatrical entertainments; a man of pleasure as an assemblage of taverns, and the great emporium for ladies of easy virtue. But the intellectual man is struck with it, as comprehending the whole of human life in all its variety, the contemplation of which is inexhaustible.

Boswell

9 Clinical Neuropsychology and Medicine

THE EVALUATION and management of patients with organic brain disease are interdisciplinary responsibilities. Therefore, it is important that neuropsychologists working with these clients appreciate the basic approaches and skills of colleagues in the related disciplines of paediatrics, neurology and psychiatry if they are to make a meaningful contribution to clinical practice. The aim of this chapter is to introduce the concerns of neurology and psychiatry to psychologists in order to facilitate communication between the various disciplines.

NEUROPSYCHOLOGY AND THE DEVELOPMENTAL DISORDERS OF CHILDHOOD

Psychologists assessing children obviously must be aware of basic developmental issues if they are to appreciate the significance of their test findings. Age related neuropathological and psychological processes influenced by brain lesions are always difficult to interpret and the valid application of neurobehavioural principles in children is a relatively undeveloped area in clinical neuropsychology. Analogies from adult practice are not particularly helpful as children use different cognitive strategies to those chosen by adults. A voluminous literature exists concerning baseline studies of neuropsychological development in normal children with which all persons involved in assessing children should be acquainted (Klonoff and Low, 1974).

There are important distinctions to be made between the neuropathology of children and adults. First, many of the common adult conditions occur very rarely in childhood (dementia and alcoholism, for example). Second, adult organic reactions indicate loss or alteration of cerebral function in a previously mature individual. In contrast, the organic reactions of early childhood occur before the establishment of certain cognitive functions and in fact prevent continued normal development (Rutter, 1982). Third, the immature brain has a limited mode of expression. Learning disabilities and attention deficits are found in many apparently heterogeneous childhood disorders.

A widely held, but simplistic, view is that brain lesions in young children are invariably associated with a better prognosis than in adults because the immature brain is allegedly more "plastic". Satz and Fletcher (1981) cite contradictory evidence which suggests that immature organs are in fact more susceptible to damage than mature ones, especially at the period of their most rapid growth which is under two years of age where the brain is concerned. Young children, for example, have a greater probability of intellectual deterioration after suffering meningoencephalitis than do older children (Rutter, 1982).

Hypotheses of recovery should differentiate restoration of function from mere reorganization of function. In the case of reorganization, distinctions must be drawn between psychological changes reflecting compensation for previously learned behavioural repertoires and actual neurophysiological changes. It is true that the earlier the brain damage the greater the extent of reorganization of the neuronal connections influencing behaviour (Van Hof, 1981). In that sense the immature brain is indeed more plastic. However, Rutter (1982) cogently emphasizes that such "rewiring" does not necessarily imply recovery of function. Rather, the development of anomalous neuronal connections may even be disruptive to functioning.

Similarly, the effects of unilateral lesions on more specific functions may be less damaging when these occur at an early age. Lenneberg (1967) reports that recovery of speech after unilateral brain damage is greater in children injured before the age of four years than in older children. There is greater potential for the right hemisphere to "take over" language abilities following left hemisphere damage. Such greater potential for recovery in the immature brain based upon interhemispheric "transfer" has only been noted in unilateral lesions and is unlikely to apply to "transfer" within a single hemisphere (Rutter, 1982).

The impact of brain damage is related to the cognitive developmental stage attained by the child. Thus brain damage in early childhood may retard the learning of reading and mathematical skills which have not yet been established. In the older child, brain damage is less likely to undermine already well established skills (Rutter, 1982).

Rutter (1982) castigates the tendency to introduce dubious assumptions of organic aetiology without neuropathological evidence. Popular terms such as minimal brain dysfunction (MBD) and hyperkinesis are symptomatic labels which actually refer to behavioural patterns and in which brain damage has been inferred but not satisfactorily demonstrated. Rie and Rie (1980) emphasize that the unitary MBD concept lacks precise definition, has an implausible theoretical base and suggests a confusing range of heterogeneous symptomatology.

Another major yet controversial concern of paediatric neuropsychology is that of specific cognitive deficit or learning disability. It is recognized that a variety of motivational psychosocial factors may be involved in educational underachievement. However, Orton (1961) asserts that the so-called emotional factors are unimportant as a primary cause of reading failure or other form of specific learning disability. Benton (1979) states that one of the major research tasks of clinical neuropsychology is the identification of the neurological correlates of specific learning disabilities.

According to Denckla (1979) specific learning disability is to mental retardation in children as aphasia is to dementia in adults. Although such analogies have heuristic value, there does not appear to be any easy transition from paediatric to adult neuropsychology. Rutter (1982) suggests that it is unlikely that focal structural deficits will be identified as the aetiological factor in most specific developmental disorders.

Strub and Black (1981) assert that learning disability has a primary organic aetiology that is manifested as an alteration in the child's developmental process as opposed to being the consequence of an acquired cerebral lesion. Nearly one out of every six children in the United States has symptoms of learning disabilities (Pirozzollo and Campanella, 1981). The frequency and social impact of these disorders make them extremely important.

The concept of specific learning disability implying a processing disorder of organic aetiology is controversial as the basic problem of precise definition remains. Terms such as specific learning disability, dyslexia and developmental aphasia are conceded to be ambiguous and based upon circular reasoning. As in the concept of MBD, the aetiology of learning disabilities remains unknown. Brain dysfunction is presumed, but not conclusively demonstrated.

It is uncertain whether the cerebral "dysfunction" in disabled learners should be viewed merely as a variation of normal development or as evidence of an underlying deficit. Satz and Van Nostrand (1973) suggest "maturational lag" as a possible explanation for many instances of neuropsychological dysfunction in this context. The brain-related skills that are impaired in children with learning disabilities are not the same for all of this population. Maturational lag may manifest itself in a variety of forms according to age. Young dyslexic patients, for example, may have been more susceptible to a delay in conceptual linguistic abilities. Also, since similar performance deficits in reading, spelling and arithmetic may be the result of different patterns of brain related strengths and deficits, it is not valid to think in terms of the general characteristics of children with learning disabilities. Rourke and Gates (1981) note some difficulties with the "maturational lag" hypothesis as an increasing discrepancy between age-expected reading level and actual reading performance becomes evident as reading-disabled children become older.

Neuropsychological research suggests that there are two main types of reading disabilities, an auditory–linguistic type and a less common visual–spatial form. The former type is characterized by difficulty in learning the phonological clues that interpret the speech code and hence produces an inability to appreciate the relationships between visual form and the sound of words. Children with visual-spatial dyslexia seem to have adequate language development but cannot learn the visuo-spatial requirements upon which reading depends (Pirozzolla and Campanella, 1981). Dyslexic children with audiophonological problems are reported to have a better reading prognosis than those with visuo-spatial deficits. On the other hand visuo-spatial deficits may be expressed as reversal errors and are associated with right–left confusion, more generalized learning difficulties and clinical symptoms of neurological abnormality (Shankweiler, 1963).

A movement away from thinking in terms of general characteristics and towards identifying meaningful subtypes of learning disorders has resulted from the work of neuropsychological laboratories. Rourke's (1981) team emphasizes a neuropsychological deficit approach to the assessment and remediation of learning-disabled children which encourages further subtype classification research. Satz and his associates found that the three variables that most successfully predicted eventual reading achievement were alphabet recitation, a test for finger localization and a visual recognition–discrimination task (Satz, *et al.*, 1978). Most studies suggest that the continued presence of neuropsychological deficits in children with reading disabilities is related to persistent reading underachievement. Similar assessment procedures have great potential in contributing to the meaningful description and operational definition of specific learning disabilities together with facilitating a better understanding of their aetiology, treatment and prognosis.

Another seminal area of research in paediatric neuropsychology is the identification of the psychological sequelae of brain damage in children. Rutter's (1981) review of the empirical evidence concludes that brain damage causes a greatly increased risk of both cognitive impairment and psychiatric disorder. This heightened susceptibility is related to the severity of cerebral dysfunction. The behavioural sequelae do not appear to be strongly influenced by the locus of injury and there appear to be few specific intellectual or behavioural sequelae of brain damage. The relationship between brain injury and social disinhibition is an exception to this rule.

European researchers are doing valuable work in establishing an interface between cognitive psychology and neuropsychology. For example, British investigators such as Patterson (1981) have facilitated neuropsychological approaches to the study of reading.

Concerning remediation, Benton (1979) concludes that sensorimotor techniques such as visuo-perceptual training are ineffective. The best, widely available sourcebook of practical, although sometimes speculative, techniques for reading remediation is that by Valett (1980). His detailed lesson plans, cross-indexed to specific problems, are neuropsychologically based and primarily follow Luria's perspective.

A particularly creative contribution to assessment and rehabilitation in paediatric neuropsychology has been Feuerstein's (1979, 1980) learning potential assessment device (LPAD) with its associated intervention programme for cognitive modification. Conventional testing monitors current level of performance. However, the LPAD attempts to assess a child's potential ability to learn. This dynamic strategy tests the individual during the process of learning and the results then serve as a basis for cognitive modification. Such a test-training test "process" approach facilitates the dual role of tester and teacher. Feuerstein's strategy is based on Piaget's work and uses a learning-to-learn approach. Children are taught step-by-step to focus their attention on significant environmental events and ideas in order to modify their cognitive abilities. These methods challenge the critical period of development theory and suggest the possibility of modifying cognitive strategies at least as late as adolescence. However, it is still too early to conclude whether Feuerstein's revolutionary assessment strategy can fulfill its promise and make a lasting contribution to clinical neuropsychology.

PAEDIATRIC ASSESSMENT

The basic rationale used in the assessment of adults may also be applied to the neuropsychological assessment of children. The test battery should review a wide range of adaptive abilities through a variety of modalities and should be interpreted using multiple inference methods such as level of performance, pattern analysis, pathognomonic signs and comparisons of performance on the two sides of the body. Test administration and interpretation are discussed in previous chapters in relation to the adult battery. In addition, developmental issues need to be considered together with the appropriate age-related norms before reaching an overall assessment.

The most popular test batteries for children derive from modifications of the Halstead–Reitan procedures by Ralph Reitan and his associates in the 1950s (Reitan and Davison, 1974). The correct name for the test battery used in children aged from nine to 15 years is the Halstead neuropsychological test battery for children and allied procedures. The test battery for children has been reported to be as valid an instrument as is the adult Halstead–Reitan procedures (Boll, 1978).

The battery includes the following tests, not all of which need necessarily be used: (i) lateral dominance examination; (ii) finger tapping test; (iii) grip strength test (dynamometer); (iv) speech–sounds perception test; (v) seashore rhythm test; (vi) tests from the Reitan–Kløve sensory–perceptual examination; (vii) tactual performance test; (viii) children's version of the trail making test; (ix) aphasia screening test; (x) Wechsler intelligence scale for children—revised; (xi) wide range achievement test; and (xii) category test.

A further simplification of the Halstead neuropsychological test battery for children produced an instrument designed for the five to nine year old age group. This is technically named the Reitan–Indiana neuropsychological test battery for children and allied procedures. Again, validation studies reach adequate levels (Boll, 1978).

Most users of this battery include all or some of the following procedures: (i) lateral dominance examination; (ii) finger tapping test; (iii) grip strength test (dynamometer); (iv) adaptation of the Reitan–Klove sensory–perceptual examination; (v) tactual performance test; (vi) aphasia screening test; (vii) Wechsler intelligence scale for children—revised; (viii) wide range achievement test; and (ix) category test. Note that the speech–sounds perception test, the seashore rhythm test and the trail making test are deleted as they are deemed to be too complex for this young age group.

Currently, no suitable validated test battery exists for children under the age of five years.

Table 4 contains a list of tests cross-indexed to functional categories which adequately meet our criteria for a cost-efficient adolescent neuropsychological test battery. The result is a revision of the Halstead neuropsychological test battery for children (aged from nine to fifteen years). It was refined from the 1979–1983 Royal Prince Alfred Hospital cost-efficiency study (previously described) using the 12 to 16 year old age groups as subjects. The adolescent battery has considerable overlap with our adult neuropsychological test battery (Table 1).

Sensory-motor, visuo-spatial, language and higher cognitive functions

Table 4
Adolescent Neuropsychological Test Battery (1982/83)

Function Tested	Test Used
Motor functioning	Laterality preference schedule
	Grooved pegboard
	Finger tapping test
	Hand dynamometer
Auditory perceptual functioning	Speech–sounds perception test
	Seashore rhythm test
Tactile perceptual functioning	Face hand test
	Finger agnosia
	Graphaesthesia
	Tactile form recognition test
Visuo-spatial functioning	Trail making test (Part B)
	Benton visual retention test
	Rey–Osterrieth complex figure test (copy)
Language ability	Aphasia language performance scales
	Controlled word association test
Memory processes	Modified Wechsler memory scale
	Rey–Osterrieth complex figure test (recall)
	Walton–Black modified new word learning test
Higher cognitive processes	Wechsler intelligence scale for children—revised
	Wide range achievement test
	Stroop colour–word test
Personality organization	Child behaviour check list
	Neuropsychological structured interview

may be assessed by basically the same types of tests as used for adults. For example, the Wechsler intelligence scale and the trail making test have children's versions, including norms. As mentioned previously, well validated norms exist only for adults in respect to the Wechsler memory scale, but nevertheless the test is useful as adolescents tend to perform as well or better than adults on memory scales. A computerized Wechsler memory scale monitor has been advertised recently with norms for ages 10 to 90 (Clinician's Digest, 1151 Cheshire, Casper, Wy 82609, U.S.A.). We preferred a behavioural checklist yielding a profile as described by Achenbach and Edelbrock (1979) for assessing personality organization in children. A computerized version of this checklist is also available. Others may prefer the personality inventory for children (PIC) as described by Lachar and Gdowski (1979). The PIC is a 600 item rating scale (modelled after the MMPI) designed to generate personality profiles and diagnostic information for children and adolescents with behavioural disorders.

Our adolescent battery incorporates 10 of the 12 procedures from the Halstead neuropsychological test battery for children. The remaining two (category test, and the tactual performance test) are omitted in the interests of cost-efficiency.

It has been noted that children's "versions" of the Halstead category test do not measure frontal lobe skills, as for adults, but rather the "ability to memorize a complex pattern of results, or luck" (Golden, 1981:294). This example emphasizes the fact that although simpler versions of adult tests may be constructed for children, such tests do not necessarily measure the same cognitive processes in young children as in adults. Dawdy (1980) further warns that paediatric neuropsychology has its own unique modes of data interpretation. Consequently, caution must be exercised in using the adolescent battery in children below the age of 12 years. However, it is adequate for children as young as nine years of age, but the value of some of the tests tends to diminish progressively when subjects are aged less than the age of adolescence. Children below the age of nine years will be better assessed using the Reitan–Indiana neuropsychological test battery.

Omission of the category test and the tactual performance test allowed the additional fortification of the test battery with 10 allied procedures (grooved pegboard, Benton visual retention test, complex figure test, aphasia language performance scales, controlled word association test, Wechsler memory scale, Walton–Black, Stroop colour–word test, child behaviour check list, and neuropsychological structured interview). This adds a more detailed assessment of expressive language, memory processes and personality organization—modalities that are relatively neglected by the original Halstead–Reitan procedures. The deletion of the category test alone gives more than ample time for the inclusion of the above items. The rationale of such a revision together with validation issues has been previously discussed in detail in Chapter 3.

NEUROLOGY AND CLINICAL NEUROPSYCHOLOGY

Neurology is that branch of internal medicine which deals with the diagnosis and treatment of disease of the whole nervous system. It is related to neuroanatomy, neurophysiology and neuropathology. Consequently, its subject matter is broader in content than clinical neuropsychology. The latter is simply a system of psychology based on neurology and thus is primarily concerned with the functional aspects of brain–behaviour relationships. The ultimate meaning of neuropsychology's functionally oriented test results must be interpreted within the context of neurology's structural foundations.

THE NEUROLOGICAL APPROACH

The following problems not faced in other branches of internal medicine are inherent in neurological diagnosis (Adams, 1980):

A. The complexity of the nervous system, which in fact comprises many separate though integrated systems, generates an overwhelming number of possible clinical dysfunctions that must be elicited and interpreted.
B. The recognition of a specific syndrome suggests the presence of certain diseases to the exclusion of others, since the anatomical localization of the lesion assumes significance with reference to pathological states as certain diseases are known to influence certain areas and not others.
C. Two qualitatively differing levels of clinical data must be integrated—introspective phenomena reported by the patient, and objectively verifiable behavioural data.
D. Diseases of the brain tend to make the patient an unreliable historian. Thus, friends and family must be approached to obtain information about the disease process.

The detailed description of disease emphasizes anatomical diagnosis and the identification of related syndromes. This takes priority over aetiology. Consequently, neurological methods tend to proceed as follows:

1. The clinical data base is obtained from the patient's history and a comprehensive examination that includes a survey of all functions from the mental to the simplest of reflexes.
2. The clinical data pertinent to the presenting problem are interpreted in terms of neuroanatomy and physiology.
3. From such data, a syndrome is determined which points to the localization that best explains the observations that have been made (syndromal and anatomical diagnosis).
4. The history of the onset and course of the disease, the associated medical findings and laboratory data are then integrated.
5. Finally, an aetiological diagnosis is postulated from this information as well as the location of the disease process.

Because different illnesses may cause the same syndrome and any single disease may cause more than one syndrome, textbooks usually present the features of the various syndromes as well as discussing the types of disease. Common syndromal expressions can then be stressed when discussing any specific disease.

Despite the above approach, many neurological diseases cannot easily be diagnosed (Adams, 1980). The anatomical diagnosis may be established, but the aetiology may remain a mystery. Such vexing clinical problems may sometimes be solved by monitoring the condition of the patient over the passage of time.

THE NEUROLOGICAL EXAMINATION

As in all clinical work, a careful history precedes physical examination. A comprehensive neurological examination is then undertaken, followed by a thorough systems review (cardiovascular, respiratory, etc.) as many generalized diseases are accompanied by neurological manifestations.

A guiding principle of the neurological examination is that every function is abnormal until it is examined and found to be normal. Standard texts such as De Myer (1974) may be consulted as useful references on the techniques of the neurological examination.

The integrity of the sensory and motor functions of the 12 sets of cranial nerves is examined in great detail as specific dysfunctions are important in suggesting the location of abnormality. The peripheral motor system is examined to evaluate muscle bulk, tone, power, and coordination, and to test for the integrity of reflexes and for the occurrence of involuntary muscle movements. Such data facilitates inferences concerning the nature of central motor damage and the lateralization of lesions. A sensory examination assesses sensitivity to painful stimuli, touch, temperature, vibration sense, joint position sense, two-point discrimination, tactile localization, stereognosis and graphaesthesia. A comparison of functions of different sensory systems together with a comparison of motor functions yields further localization information.

A routine examination of the potentially normal nervous system contains the following typical headings (Mason and Swash, 1980): mental status; gait; cranial nerves; visual fields; fundi; motor; sensory; and general examination of the skull, spinal movements and posture. Any deviations from the norm provoke further detailed examination in the area concerned.

DIAGNOSTIC METHODS

The nature of a neurological disease often remains in doubt despite the taking of a careful history and physical examination. Laboratory tests may then be indicated.

Adams (1980) warns that laboratory techniques should normally follow rather than precede clinical case study as they are merely one phase of the clinical method. They should be used for the specific purpose of eliciting otherwise unavailable information necessary for the solution of the problem being studied. Some laboratory methods are expensive, time-consuming, and relatively painful or dangerous. They may require the admission of the patient to hospital and can generate needless confusion if the data are not interpreted expertly. As for any other tools, they have their unique contributions and limitations.

A selective survey of neurological diagnostic methods of interest to neuropsychologists is briefly mentioned below (Isselbacher, *et al.,* 1980): lumbar puncture and examination of the cerebrospinal fluid (CSF): radiological examination of skull and spine; electromyography (EMG); and electroencephalography (EEG).

Cerebrospinal Fluid Studies

Analysis of cerebrospinal fluid (CSF) is the only means of assessing the subarachnoid space without surgically opening the skull. Lumbar puncture is the usual procedure for obtaining samples of CSF. It carries a risk of introducing infection and further, if the CSF pressure is high, it increases the possibility of a fatal cerebellar or tentorial pressure cone. A sample of CSF can be obtained by lumbar puncture for cellular, chemical and bacteriological examination, to assist in treatment by introducing therapeutic substances into the subarachnoid space, and to inject air or opaque media for radiographic studies (encephalography).

Radiological Examination of Skull and Spine

Plain X-ray films of the skull and spine are an important aspect of the study of traumatic, spondylitic and neoplastic illnesses, but they are of less value in others. Of relatively more value in neurology are special radiological techniques which allow the visualization of most of the brain and spinal cord together with their vessels.

Cerebral angiography allows the intracranial blood vessels to become recordable by introducing radio-opaque substances through arteries in the neck. Air encephalography lets the ventricular system be shown through the injection of air by means of a lumbar or cisternal puncture. As they are invasive and dangerous, such procedures are used less frequently nowadays.

Computerized tomography (CT scan) is a new, non-invasive and low risk radiological procedure that has revolutionized diagnostic neurology. This technique measures the absorption by the brain, skull and CSF of over 30 000 2 to 4 mm X-ray beams and then produces a computer analysis which shows the ventricles, subarachnoid space and the major cisternal fissures and sulci in a number of horizontal planes. The method has greatly reduced the need for air encephalography and angiography. Its greatest value lies in identifying tumours, evaluating vascular accidents and head injuries, and locating various intracranial lesions together with brain atrophy.

Radioactive isotopes are regularly used for the direct radiological demonstration of tumours, inflammatory masses and vascular lesions. A radioisotopic compound is injected into one of the arteries and travels throughout the vascular system, including the brain. The brain surface is then scanned with a Geiger counter.

Electromyography

In electromyography (EMG), the electrical activity of muscles is monitored. Needle electrodes inserted into the muscle, or surface electrodes attached to the skin, record electrical activity. This is then amplified and displayed either as an auditory signal or as a visual signal on a cathode ray oscilloscope. Analysis of this electrical activity supplements the clinical study of the primary diseases of muscle (myopathies and dystrophies) and of lower motor neurone lesions (denervation).

Electroencephalography

Electroencephalography (EEG) is one of the most widely used neurological diagnostic methods for the study of cerebral disease. Electrodes applied to the scalp monitor small changes in electrical potential. After amplification these are recorded on paper. In addition to the resting record, a number of "activating procedures" are often carried out (for example, deep breathing, stroboscopic stimulation, etc.). Electroencephalography is particularly valuable in the investigation of epilepsy and for the localization of cerebral tumours. It is acknowledged to be a crude measure of underlying brain activity and it lacks diagnostic specificity.

Any one EEG record from an epileptic individual may be "normal". Hence, serial recordings frequently need to be sampled. Thus the report of a "normal" EEG does not necessarily rule out an epileptic process. On the other hand, "abnormal" records are obtained in approximately 18 per cent of persons who have no further evidence of neurological or psychiatric deficits, so the presence of an EEG abnormality does not necessarily imply pathology.

RELATION OF CLINICAL NEUROPSYCHOLOGY TO NEUROLOGY

Neurology and neuropsychology are both concerned with brain–behaviour relationships. They differ in their emphasis and methodology. Nevertheless, both disciplines rely upon clinical histories and observations, together with formal tests which provide the data base. Both also rely upon clinical inferences for diagnosing functional impairment before proceeding to infer structural damage. Hence the neurologist and neuropsychologist generate complementary, albeit different, sets of data for use in assessing brain dysfunction.

Clinical neurology studies the full range of the nervous system from discrete reflexes to complex behaviours for the purpose of diagnosis and treatment of neurological disease. The primary emphasis is upon identifying typical behaviour patterns generated by neuroanatomical subsystems, monitoring the patient's responses in relatively gross gradations, and noting significant aberrations or absence of such responses. The neurologist seeks clinical and laboratory evidence for structural nervous system pathology. From the patient's viewpoint, this tends to be a passive process as active co-operation is seldom required.

Clinical neuropsychology is more interested in the higher cognitive processes. The emphasis is upon monitoring the functional aspects of brain output via inferences from precisely scaled quantitative tests. For the patient, it tends to be an active procedure as it necessarily involves volition and considerable co-operation.

Neurology offers a structural perspective of the brain whereas neuropsychology complements this strictly organic view with a functional elaboration. Consequently, it is not surprising that there is a need for complementary data for the fulfilment of both disciplines.

A minority of clinical neuropsychologists rely solely upon qualitative syndrome analysis techniques. This restriction leads to an identity crisis. The practitioners involved are often accused of trying to be "junior neurologists" as they attempt to accomplish what neurologists do (syndromal and anatomical diagnosis). We believe there is a considerable disadvantage in the lack of mastery of quantitative assessment methodology by psychologists as this is a unique contribution of their discipline and categorically differentiates the field from the traditional approach of clinical neurology. Moreover, quantification of cognitive deficits remains the most popular neuropsychological referral requested by neurologists.

Neuropsychological assessment is most effective within the context of neurological procedures as both approaches complement each other. For an interpretation of psychometric data to be valid, it must take into account the medical condition of the patient, including behavioural response to drugs or surgery. An interpretation such as this, within the context of neurology's structural foundations, enriches the meaning of test results. For example, Walsh (1978) reports that the significance of computerized tomography for neuropsychology is the mapping of neurological lesions against which correlations with behavioural indices may be accomplished more meaningfully. Of course, a "one to one" correspondence can never be expected as brain structure does not correlate perfectly with complex human functions, despite clinically useful overlap.

The majority of referrals for neuropsychological assessment come from neurologists. These assessments contribute to the clarification of "soft" neurological signs, help differentiate between focal and diffuse, and functional or organic, deficits and generally facilitate estimates of the nature and extent of cognitive disabilities. Standardized tests administered at different times also precisely measure the patient's progress, be it towards deterioration or restitution of higher cognitive functions.

As a branch of internal medicine, neurology bases diagnosis and treatment upon the traditions of the medical model. This model has a necessarily acute perspective, especially in cases of life threatening illness, with an almost exclusive concern for quickly stabilizing the condition of the patient. After this aim has been accomplished, neurologists and rehabilitation physicians often refer brain damaged individuals to neuropsychologists for long term follow-up. The neuropsychological evaluation of the whole person (including both strengths and deficits) within the context of a "real life" environment facilitates ongoing remediation programmes. These programmes may be based upon compensating for cognitive dysfunctions and redesigning therapeutic environments to reinforce adaptive educational, vocational and social functioning. The patient's home environment, financial situation and cultural support system all need to be taken into account.

It is not possible to function optimally as a clinical neuropsychologist without developing an interest in the neurological literature, at least at an elementary level. In fact, such knowledge is the basis of a formal neuropsychological curriculum. Neurological tests monitor neurological conditions, thus it is an obvious advantage to be able to recognize the basic characteristics of organic brain syndromes.

Lack of understanding of the normal limits of central nervous system functioning results in an absence of criteria for recognizing characteristic signs of dysfunction when they occur. During the routine course of neuropsychological assessment one is continually confronted with medical records which contain the results of neurological examinations and associated laboratory findings. If one has a rudimentary grasp of the significance and limitations of such diagnostic procedures, this contributes to interpretation of the data base and also allows for the rational comparison of one's own neuropsychological test findings with available neurological reports. Further, the formulation of practical rehabilitation programmes is contingent upon knowledge of the functional capabilities of individual patients, given the nature and extent of their specific neurological deficits. This also requires a familiarity with the basic elements of behavioural neurology.

The sensitivity of neuropsychological techniques is favourably compared to neurological diagnostic procedures by Crockett, *et al.* (1981). It must be remembered that the reported accuracy of neurological techniques under special research conditions does not necessarily predict the actual rates obtained in clinical practice. Physical examinations (Stuss and Trites, 1977) and X-ray studies (Hayward, 1980), in particular, are often very inaccurate, and electroencephalographic findings, as already noted, may be most confusing. The more recent high technology methods are more reliable, but Davis, *et al.* (1976) claimed that in general terms, over all types of cerebral dysfunction, the accuracy range of neurological investigations ranges from 16% to 85% depending on the specific conditions under which the tests are performed.

Although computerized tomography has revolutionized diagnostic neurology, this new technique is unlikely to diminish the importance of neuropsychological testing. Computerized tomography demonstrates the photon absorption coefficients of the tissues examined, and does not document pathology *per se.* More important, an abnormal computerized tomography result, like any other radiological investigation, does not necessarily suggest the functional severity of brain injury, nor can it estimate the patient's potential for recovery (Hayward, 1980). On the other hand, "normal" results for computerized tomography do not necessarily rule out brain damage. Because of their location and small size some focal lesions may be undetected. Also, in some cases of dementia, alterations in brain function antedate brain atrophy by months or even years.

Neuropsychological techniques are often able to document cognitive defects when the results of physical neurological examination and laboratory tests are negative. Broe (1979) found that 43 per cent of head-injured persons who initially showed no significant neurological deficit on standard neurological examination (including computerized tomography) proved to have subtle but incapacitating organic deficits on follow-up neuropsychological testing. Hawkes and Pusakulich (1982) show the importance of neuropsychological assessment by reporting a case of recurring infiltrating astrocytoma in which computerized tomography was inconclusive while the condition of the patient was deteriorating. A review of literature concerning base rate of accuracy for diagnostic neurology and clinical neuropsychology (Crockett, *et al.,* 1981) shows that such results are not isolated findings.

A thorough evaluation of brain function is always an important diagnostic adjunct to monitor anatomical or physiological cerebral changes. Spreen and Benton (1965) documented that the proportion of accurate diagnosis of severity and laterality of brain damage ranged from 71 per cent to 90 per cent during neuropsychological testing and that these accuracy rates compared favourably with those reported for other neurodiagnostic techniques. Their results have been replicated and an accuracy rate of 89 per cent has been reported for neuropsychological batteries, compared with accuracy rates of 16 per cent for skull X-rays and 80 per cent for angiography (Filskov and Goldstein, 1974). Golden, *et al.* (1983) provide excellent guidelines for the neuropsychological assessment of various brain diseases. For example, these authors warn that it is impossible to document a seizure disorder on the basis of psychometric testing. Cognitive deficits may exist in the absence of epilepsy whilst epilepsy is often associated with a normal neuropsychological profile. Concerning tumours, the slow-growing variety may result in trivial cognitive deficits whereas rapidly growing tumours tend to cause poor performance on the whole test battery. During the assessment of cerebrovascular disorders a flexible battery is required in order to avoid underestimating residual strengths in a patient with sensory-motor and speech deficits. Patients with Parkinson's disease usually have more neuropsychological impairment than those with multiple sclerosis.

From the traditional medical perspective, clinical neuropsychology, as a specific system of psychology based upon a thorough knowledge of neurological structures, may appear a minor discipline. It is interesting that *Harrison's Principles of Internal Medicine* (Isselbacher, *et al.*, 1980) lists psychometry as one of many associated diagnostic methods in neurology. There is no doubt that neurology has developed varied and highly specialized methods for investigating nervous system disorder. However, as practically performed, the neurological examination is severely limited in techniques for assessing the higher cognitive functions. Walsh (1978) views the major contribution of neuropsychology as the provision of a methodology for evaluating uniquely human complex functions. Luria also expresses the relationship between neurological and neuropsychological investigations in terms of such a sophisticated contribution: "In this respect neuropsychology is merely the most complex and newest chapter of neurology and without this chapter modern clinical neurology will be unable to exist and develop" (Luria, 1973: 344).

Clinical neuropsychology also acts as an interface between psychiatry and neurology with the potential for reversing the schism between these disciplines. Benson (1981) notes that these previously related fields have been drifting apart with the resultant neglect of a large group of patients suffering behavioural problems of organic aetiology. Strub and Black (1981) assert that recent advances in genetics, pharmacology and neurochemistry provide increasing evidence that the major disorders of schizophrenia and manic depression do in fact have an organic aetiology. These promising findings can only increase the future role of clinical neuropsychology.

PSYCHIATRY AND CLINICAL NEUROPSYCHOLOGY

Psychiatry is that branch of clinical medicine which is concerned with the diagnosis and treatment of psychotic and neurotic illnesses, personality disorders and behavioural and emotional disturbances. Nemiah (1981: 1) describes modern psychiatry as an inexhaustible science, "a great brawling metropolis which has engulfed in its urban sprawl a host of arts and sciences". This rich diversity is well illustrated by Kaplan, *et al.* (1981), an eclectic work with a large number of different theoretical models, which is multidisciplinary and comprehensive in scope and has 236 contributors!

Psychiatry deals with variations and disorders of human behaviour. Its theoretical background derives from the biological sciences, neurology, psychology and the sociocultural disciplines.

Paradoxically, although psychiatry is a medical specialty, it is holistic in approach (the whole person having the disease and not just the disease itself) which provides a broad psychosocial view transcending traditional medicine. This holistic perspective emphasizes that the clinical manifestations of all illnesses, be they psychiatric or otherwise, are the result of three complex interacting variables—biological, psychological, and sociocultural. All these factors interact and influence the adaptation level of the individual.

As mentioned previously, the comprehensive assessment and treatment of patients who may have brain damage require the active participation of a wide variety of personnel from various disciplines. The patient can benefit from such interdisciplinary collaboration as long as the data base is responsibly integrated. Ultimately, one physician needs to be nominated to retain the final responsibility for making the crucial medical decisions concerning diagnosis, treatment and general care. Psychiatrists are admirably suited to take such responsibility by virtue of their undergraduate medical training and the broad psychosocial orientation derived from postgraduate education. This holistic biological and behavioural sciences education facilitates integrated assessment of the somatic, psychological and environmental forces which shape a person's illness.

THE PSYCHIATRIC APPROACH

The examination of psychiatric patients includes intensive interviewing, comprehensive history taking and analysis of mental status. The successful psychiatric interviewer requires a wide knowledge of the biological and behavioural sciences integrated with clinical experience. The interview is based upon a cogent awareness of psychopathology and psychodynamics and is designed to reveal the patient's personality strengths and deficits, including the degree of motivation for change. The paramount tools of the psychiatric interview are psychiatrists themselves. As experts on interpersonal relations, their goal is to evaluate the content and process of the verbal and non-verbal communications between themselves and the patient.

The basic aims of the psychiatric interview are to obtain a psychiatric history and perform a mental state examination. Psychiatrists, like all clinicians, rely upon a detailed history for diagnosis and planning of treatment. The standard approach is to elicit the following information: a description of the onset, duration and severity of the patient's presenting complaints in their own words; a review of past medical and psychosocial problems; and a description of the patient's present functioning.

The psychiatric history should yield a profile of the patient's individual personality traits, including strengths and deficits. Insight into the quality of the patient's relationships with significant others is particularly important information to obtain. Descriptions of patients, psychopathology and developmental history should all interrelate coherently. The patient's inner mental life needs to be related to their symptomatology and lifestyle. A knowledge of psychodynamics and developmental psychology helps to explain the continuing links between the past and present.

The mental state examination is designed to describe all the components of mental functioning involved in diagnostic classification. This technique "is the psychiatric equivalent of the medical specialist's physical examination" (Taylor, 1981:2). The routine mental state examination is most effective when describing the psychopathology of the neuroses and psychoses. Assessment of personality disorder is more easily derived from the patients' histories and the nature of their interaction with the psychiatrist. This requires an awareness of the complex facets of ego functioning.

The written mental status examination typically contains data structured as follows: (i) general description of the patient including mode of speech; (ii) documentation of mood, feelings and affects; (iii) screening for perceptual disturbance; (iv) evaluation of thought process (form of thinking); (v) noting the level of consciousness; (vi) evaluation of orientation; (vii) assessment of memory processes; (viii) estimation of capacity for impulse control; (ix) degree of social judgement; (x) degree of insight; and (xi) impression of the patient's reliability as a historian.

The results of the interview, history and mental state examination are integrated in a psychiatric report. Kaplan, *et al.* (1981) recommend the following outline:

A. A psychiatric history surveying all the developmental stages.

B. An indication of mental state derived from the sum total of the examiner's observations and impressions gained during the initial interview.
C. A request for further diagnostic studies if needed (for example, physical examination, computerized tomography, psychological testing, etc.).
D. A summary of positive findings (for example, mental symptoms, laboratory findings, and psychological test results);
E. The diagnosis, using an established system such as the American Psychiatric Association's *Diagnostic and Statistical Manual of Mental Disorders* (DSM-III).
F. The prognosis regarding the probable future course, extent and outcome of the illness, together with goals of therapy.
G. A psychodynamic formulation explaining the causes of the patient's disturbance, assessing the life stresses that contributed to breakdown and calculating the relevant genetic, personality and environmental factors pertinent to the illness.
H. A treatment plan (modalities recommended, medication, inpatient or outpatient, type and frequency of psychotherapy, and target symptoms to be given priority).

The formulation of an integrated report from diverse and sometimes conflicting data requires an intimate knowledge of the typical signs and symptoms of both organic and functional mental disorders. Assessment of the prognosis of the specific patient and consideration of all the pertinent variables are important psychiatric skills.

Classification is a technique wherein the complexity of phenomena is simplified by categorizing them according to some established criteria. The rationale of a standardized classification of the mental disorders is to facilitate more specific communication about such complex phenomena. The ideal classification would be an aetiological one leading to the control of these dysfunctions by allowing the selection of more specific treatments. Unfortunately, this ideal cannot yet be realized in psychiatry as the aetiology of most psychiatric illnesses is poorly understood. For this reason, most classification is based on the syndromal approach (that is, the consistent association of certain clusters of symptoms and signs). The American Psychiatric Association's *Diagnostic and Statistical Manual of Mental Disorders* (DSM-III) (1980) is an example of a comprehensive classificatory system.

DSM-III is proving to be a useful tool. Its classification system generally makes few assumptions concerning aetiology except for certain specific dysfunctions in which the aetiology and pathogenesis have been definitely established, such as the organic mental disorders. Where aetiology is unknown or uncertain, it relies upon a descriptive syndromal approach, providing comprehensive illustrations of clinical features. Specific diagnostic criteria are given for each mental disorder.

DSM-III is a multi-axial system for evaluation. Axes I and II represent mental disorders and conditions not attributed to a mental disorder that are the object of concern. Axis III allows the psychiatrist to note any current physical diseases, outside of the mental disorders section of *International Classification of Diseases,* ninth edition, Clinical Modification, that contribute to an understanding, and hence improved management, of the patient. Axis IV provides a seven point rating scale for coding the severity of psychosocial stressors that may be influencing a patient's current disorder. Axis V allows the psychiatrist to estimate the highest level of adaptive functioning exhibited by a patient during the past year on a seven point scale. Kaplan, *et al.* (1981) provide encyclopaedic references showing how the multitude of mental disorders may be integrated within the DSM-III system. Clinical neuropsychologists can benefit greatly by familiarizing themselves with this pragmatic approach.

What characterizes the professional training of psychiatrists is a specialized knowledge of the plethora of mental disorders, both functional and organic, and expertise in their diagnosis and treatment. This training develops the capacity to judge the need for intervention in the areas of intrapsychic conflict, psychosocial environment or somatic diseases after an initial interview. Consequently, psychiatry remains an important source of referral in the comprehensive management of individuals with potential or established organic brain disease.

The work of psychiatrists ranges across the whole field of disturbance of human behaviour and sometimes overlaps with the activities of clinical psychologists. As many patients have concomitant psychiatric and physical illnesses (for example, a patient with a brain tumour presenting with a psychosis) there are several instances in which referral to a psychiatrist is obligatory (Strub and Black, 1979). Psychiatrists should be consulted with respect to: (i) all patients with pre-existing psychiatric disturbances, regardless of the type of concomitant neurological and/or medical condition; (ii) previously emotionally stable persons who develop significant emotional disturbance and management problems due to neurological conditions (for example, depression after aphasia); (iii) patients in whom there is uncertainty regarding the differential diagnosis of dementia from depression and other potentially pseudoneurological conditions; and (iv) some patients initially seen by neurologists, such as those with hysterical conversion reactions, whose disturbances are emotional rather than organic. Of course, some psychiatrists specialize in areas such as forensic assessment, in which there is opportunity for integrating psychiatric data with information obtained from neurological examination and neuropsychological assessment.

THE RELATION OF CLINICAL NEUROPSYCHOLOGY TO PSYCHIATRY

The most obvious difference between psychiatry and clinical neuropsychology is the comprehensive scope of the former. This contrasts with more exclusive concern of clinical neuropsychology with brain related determinants of human behaviour and the use of associated technology for monitoring cerebral functioning. Consequently, the multifaceted interests of psychiatrists include neuropsychology (though not the use of its technical tools). These biological concerns are integrated with the contributions of the psychological and sociocultural sciences.

In contrast, the psychosocial determinants of behaviour are of a peripheral interest to clinical neuropsychologists. The extent of specialization within psychology is demonstrated by the fact that in 1982 the American Psychological Association listed 42 well defined divisions, of which clinical neuropsychology is a recent addition (namely, division 40). However, it is acknowledged that despite the divisions of responsibility generated by the nature of professional training, the personality, interests and abilities of individuals causes a considerable blurring of roles. For example, although Freud was trained as a physician and neurologist he functioned primarily as a psychologically oriented clinician, as reflected by the contents of his psychoanalytic publications.

Many neuropsychologists work within psychiatric settings. Their most frequent referrals are requests to help determine whether disturbed behaviour is functional or organic in aetiology. Ostensibly, this is an appropriate appeal since neuropsychological tests have the reputation for being sensitive to cerebral dysfunction. However, most of the tests were validated in neurological environments where behavioural dysfunctions were directly related to organic brain disease. In contrast, the majority of psychiatric patients exhibit behavioural disorders that are usually thought to have a functional aetiology.

Differentiating between functional and organic disorder on the basis of neuropsychological test results is complicated by the effects of complex emotional factors. A characteristic of brain damaged persons is reduced information processing capacity (Visser, 1980). However, such disruption of cognitive functioning may also occur in psychiatric patients with allegedly purely functional illnesses, and even temporarily in normal subjects under conditions of stress. The danger exists that neuropsychological assessment may be invalidated within the psychiatric environment because emotional disturbance disrupts maximal performance on cognitive tests. Heaton and Crowley (1981) comprehensively reviewed the effects of psychiatric disturbance and their somatic treatments on neuropsychological test results. Their conclusions are summarized below.

During the past 20 years, there have been more than 130 studies in which attempts have been made to differentiate between organic and functional psychiatric patients using neuropsychological tests (Heaton and Crowley, 1981). The diagnostic accuracy was extremely poor when chronic or process schizophrenics were used to represent the functional groups. Accuracy rates paralleled the excellent results obtained in differentiating between organic and non-psychiatric control subjects when other psychiatric groups were used to represent patients with functional disorders. These results suggest that neuropsychological assessment can validly differentiate between organic and emotional disorders within the psychiatric environment except where schizophrenia is concerned.

Crockett, *et al.* (1981) review the evidence that research contrasting patients grossly defined as either organic or functional may be of limited usefulness. The issue may not be that of differentiating organic from functional aetiology *per se,* but rather that lateralized or localized brain lesions may facilitate a higher probability of developing specific psychiatric disturbances. Rutter (1981) has noted this potential effect in his findings of the psychological sequelae of brain damage in children.

Thus what is of greater significance than "organic" and "functional" comparisons is the assessment of specific psychiatric populations in order to form differential neuropsychological profiles. This atheoretical descriptive approach parallels DSM-III methodology and may contribute to a better understanding of the nature of such psychiatric disorders.

Boll (1978) suggests that the seemingly reasonable referral request from a psychiatrist to differentiate between brain damage and schizophrenia on the basis of neuropsychological test results may be based upon the following potentially untenable assumptions: (i) schizophrenia is not itself a neurological disease; (ii) a schizophrenic patient will not independently acquire brain damage; and (iii) brain damaged individuals cannot become schizophrenics.

The causes of neuropsychological deficits among schizophrenic patients have not been unequivocally documented. However, there are many data suggesting that such traditionally accepted "functional" mental disorders as schizophrenia and the affective psychoses may be a consequence of as yet poorly understood abnormalities of brain chemistry (Heaton and Crowley, 1981). Although specific organic factors have not been adequately documented for schizophrenia (relegating it to a functional category by definition) this does not rule out the possibility of definitively implicating such organic factors with further advances in the neurosciences.

Compared to other psychiatric populations, schizophrenic patients show a higher rate of cerebral abnormalities on diagnostic neurological laboratory tests (electroencephalography, computerized tomography, etc.) and autopsy findings. These neurological abnormalities, as defined by laboratory tests, have been correlated with the extent of impaired neuropsychological profiles in schizophrenics (Heaton and Crowley, 1981). The most recent research in this area used computerized tomography to identify abnormalities in schizophrenic patients. The results were supportive of the hypothesis that there are primary structural deficits in some (but not all) schizophrenic patients in the vicinity of the left (dominant) hemisphere (Golden, *et al.,* 1981a; Golden, *et al.,* 1983).

Consequently, some schizophrenic patients may appear to have cerebral dysfunction on neuropsychological tests because their schizophrenia is indeed organic (Pincus and Tucker, 1978). It is unlikely that schizophrenia is a single, discrete disorder. Rather, it is probably a multifactorial phenomenon, with potentially varying degrees of cerebral deficit and psychopathological disturbance interactions, experienced with greater or lesser severity by individual patients. Schizophrenic patients seem to be more incapacitated than patients with affective disorders on many neuropsychological measures. However, on measures of non-dominant hemisphere functioning, both groups of patients are equally impaired (Golden, *et al.,* 1983).

Other illnesses thought to be "functional" may also have an organic substrate. For example, infantile autism is associated with structural brain abnormalities and has many features in common with less severe paediatric language disturbances (Denckla, 1979).

Neuropsychological evaluation of psychiatric patients receiving somatic treatments occurs with enough frequency to make these physical treatments (electroconvulsive therapy, drugs, etc.) important factors to be taken into account when interpreting test results. A review by Heaton and Crowley (1981) suggests that different somatic treatments with different doses and durations have varying neuropsychological effects upon specific psychiatric subgroups.

Increases in dosage of neuroleptic drugs are associated with sedative, anticholinergic, or extrapyramidal motor side effects which may initially impair performance of neuropsychological tests. The patient's condition usually stabilizes within a few weeks. Long-term treatment of schizophrenic patients with neuroleptic drugs may even enhance performance on neuropsychological tests which require alertness.

Lithium, which is used in the treatment of affective disorders, may mildly disrupt neuropsychological assessment. Tricyclic antidepressants do not appear to significantly influence test results. Sedative, hypnotic, and antianxiety drugs may mildly affect performance levels, but these effects occur only during the few hours following ingestion.

A review of memory and learning difficulties occurring after electroconvulsive therapy (ECT) suggests that this treatment is unlikely to produce permanent brain damage (Templer and Veleber, 1982). The memory deficits noticeable shortly after ECT tend to remit over a period of two weeks. However, vast individual differences are possible and a small minority of patients appears to exhibit irreversible cognitive deficits, even when differences before ECT are allowed for. Reports of spontaneous seizures occurring long after ECT suggest permanent cerebral changes.

In summary, although somatic treatments of psychiatric patients may mildly disrupt neuropsychological test performance, the sophisticated examiner can easily compensate for such factors. Awareness of the general condition of the patient, including the physical treatment being administered, allows for testing to be scheduled at optimal times and also for adjustments to be made correctly when interpreting quantitative test scores.

Psychiatry in the mid-19th century was characterized by the dominance of the "somatic" school, which is epitomized in Griesinger's (1845) famous dictum that all mental disease could be explained on the basis of physical changes in the nervous system. However, the great advances in neuroanatomy and neuropathology later in the century were not reflected in clinical practice. Clinical neurologists like Charcot and Freud had to invent explanatory systems for their clinical formulations. Freud's developments from Charcot's ideas on hypnosis culminated in the elaboration of the libido theory of psychoanalysis—a mechanistic construct aspiring to physiological status.

Paradoxically, the influence of the psychoanalytical school led to an almost exclusive emphasis on psychosocial rather than organic determinants of behavioural disturbance, as well as laying some emphasis on the importance of psychogenic factors in general medicine.

As late as 1978, Lishman lamented in the preface to his text on *Organic Psychiatry* that despite the inherent relationship between psychiatry and neurology there has been a paucity of publications integrating these overlapping disciplines. Neurology deals directly with the structure underlying mind, yet insufficient attention has been paid to mental disorder itself. In contrast, psychiatry deals with mental disorder, but has neglected the cerebral structures upon which mind depends. Consequently, the patient with organic mental disease can be overlooked by both disciplines.

Such criticisms are becoming less pertinent with recent advances in the neurosciences and their clinical applications. The trend for psychiatry to return to its medical roots is exemplified by the resurgence of neuropsychiatry. During 1981, four major works were published in this field (Strub and Black; Taylor; Freeman; Jefferson and Marshall).

This interface between medicine and psychology has swung the pendulum back to the ideals of the neuropsychiatrists who practised in the 19th century, but now these ideals are backed by the technological tools of the 20th century.

The swing of the pendulum makes modern psychiatry more sceptical of purely psychogenic diagnoses. This caution is an admirable corrective, as the statistics of Jefferson and Marshall (1981) show. These authors reviewed a variety of studies to show that from 5 per cent to 80 per cent of patients admitted to psychiatric units have undiagnosed and significant medical diseases (depending on the population and facility). One study of 2090 psychiatric patients revealed that 43 per cent (902) had at least one major medical disorder. Almost 50 per cent of these patients had been undiagnosed by the referral source. Of these 902 patients, the psychiatric condition was judged to be caused by the medical illness in 18 per cent, aggravated by the disease in 51 per cent and coexisting independently in 31 per cent. Apparently, overtly physical problems are likely to be neglected in psychiatric patients.

Advances in the neurosciences have made clinical neuropsychology the fastest growing speciality in psychology. This same progress in the biological sciences is also responsible in the resurgence of interest in organic psychiatry. Since both neuropsychology and neuropsychiatry have overlapping interests in brain–behaviour relationships, this reinforces the development of closer relationships between these disciplines. That is, both clinical neuropsychologists and psychiatrists share an interface between medicine and the behavioural sciences.

DEMENTIA AND PSEUDODEMENTIA

Discrimination of organic mental disorders from functional mental disorders does not negate the holistic approach. Nor does such differentiation imply that the so-called "functional" mental disorders are independent of brain mechanisms. Rather, it is generally accepted that all psychological functions, both normal and pathological, depend upon the brain. The brain is acknowledged to be the basis of cognition, including memory, affect and decision making processes. Without brain there is no consciousness, and no personality. And without a psychosocial environment the brain cannot function.

Classification of illnesses as organic or functional is clinically convenient. It allows priorities to be set in the search for pathological cause–effect relationships. This can be a challenging enterprise as shown by the differential diagnosis of dementia from pseudodementia. The frequency of this type of difficult referral to neuropsychologists working in psychiatric settings warrants separate discussion.

In medicine, dementia refers to a clinical syndrome that results from impairment of brain function due to diffuse organic disease. The pathology of the dementia depends upon the underlying disease. Symptom severity has been "directly related to the mass of tissue loss, the density of senile plaques and neurofibrillary tangles found in diseased brains, and the mass of ischemic softening in affected brains" (Wells and Duncan, 1980:83).

Neuropsychologically, dementia is characterized as a gross loss of intellectual function. It is an acquired loss as opposed to that of congenital mental retardation. The concept that dementia is a syndrome with various causes illustrates a basic rule about the reaction of the brain to disease. Whatever the cause of the disease, symptoms tend to be a function of the locus rather than the type of disorder. Thus atrophy or tumour affecting the frontal lobes may result in similar symptoms. Consequently, it is often useful diagnostically to classify dementias according to localization as symptoms are dependent on this rather than aetiology (Joint and Shoulson, 1979).

In pseudodementia, patients with functional disorders exhibit symptoms that mimic those of true dementia. The neurological examination and computerized tomography results are normal in pseudodementia, but this may also be true of dementing patients. Consequently, neuropsychological assessment, including personality testing, and the taking of a detailed history can make a most useful contribution to the diagnosis.

An acute organic brain syndrome is usually responsible for an abrupt onset of cognitive disturbance, usually of short duration. However, such symptoms may also be due to pseudodementia. While dementia may proceed in a step like manner from one or more cerebrovascular accidents, it is usually characterized by an insidious onset of long duration (Wells and Duncan, 1980).

In pseudodementia, the major characteristic of the neuropsychological profile is marked variability in performance between tests and even within subtests of similar degree of difficulty. This scattered profile tends not to fit any known organic brain syndrome. Retesting a patient with pseudodementia will often yield discrepant results from previous testing. In contrast, brain damaged patients tend to exhibit consistently inadequate performance on tasks of similar difficulty. Retesting will not reveal signs of abrupt restoration of cognitive function over short periods of time. In pseudodementia, both recent and remote memory tend to be equally disrupted. Attention and concentration are usually intact. Dementia shows a greater deterioration in recent memory relative to remote and there is often an impairment of concentration.

Patients with pseudodementia commonly have a previous history of psychiatric disturbance. Affective changes are often pervasive. The onset of behavioural disturbance in an achieving elderly adult with previously intact functioning is usually associated with true cerebral dysfunction. A psychiatric history is not common in dementia. Affect in dementia is often labile and shallow.

Patients with pseudodementia have a qualitatively different test response style to that of those with dementia. Pseudodementia patients often make detailed, but distressed, complaints about intellectual deterioration. They tend to be unmotivated during testing and to dramatize their failures, yet they are also able to demonstrate intact islands of performance at variance with their complaints of profound deterioration. Those with dementia tend to be relatively unconcerned about cognitive deterioration. Upon direct questioning their complaints are vague and imprecise. Often, there is an attempt to conceal their disabilities. There is a tendency to give maximal effort during testing and to be elated by even minor successes. General behaviour is usually consistent with the degree of intellectual deterioration.

Documentation of the underlying psychiatric disorder is of prime significance as this is the basis of coherent treatment. Some psychiatrists will only accept an unequivocal diagnosis of pseudodementia after treatment has cured or significantly controlled the symptoms involved. Most researchers implicate depression as the major cause of pseudodementia, but it is not limited to the affective disorders (Wells and Duncan, 1980). Golden, *et al.* (1983) suggest the following guidelines for assessment of geriatric patients: brief testing to control fatigue; the use of simple subtests to maximize performance; and comprehensive testing to counteract problems in evaluating patients with peripheral sensory-motor deficits.

CONCLUSION

It must be reiterated that interdisciplinary co-operation needs to be developed and followed. Too often, there has been inadequate co-operation between psychiatrists and psychologists, sometimes to the detriment of patient care. A common complaint by psychiatrists is undue delay in obtaining test results. For example, Freeman (1981) undiplomatically states that "psychiatrists often rely on formal neuropsychological testing, waiting days or even weeks for the final report, when a few minutes of bedside evaluation might give an immediate and direct diagnosis". Such comments should not be interpreted to mean that psychiatrists should irrevocably "go it alone".

Another controversial issue concerns who should make the final diagnosis. Ethically, this is the prerogative of the psychiatrist who has the legal responsibility for overall management of the patient. When psychiatrists have referred their own patients to a neuropsychologist for assessment, they usually view the latter's role as that of a consultant. They do not expect the neuropsychologist to take over the primary responsibility for case management. Consequently, the neuropsychologist's major duty under such circumstances is to provide a set of observations which will be helpful to psychiatrists considering a definitive diagnosis. Lishman (1978) points to the importance of corrective mutual collaboration by noting that neuropsychologists tend to overdiagnose brain damage while psychiatrists tend to underdiagnose brain damage.

Let the young know they will never find a more interesting, more instructive book than the patient himself.

Samuel Johnson

10
Sample Case Reports

IN THIS chapter, some recent clinical reports will be examined to illustrate how patients referred for neuropsychological assessment may be approached. These vignettes were selected as being characteristic of cases commonly referred to psychologists working in a large general hospital anywhere in the world.

A selected variety of problems in patients at differing developmental stages (age, premorbid functioning, and cultural background), and sometimes presenting difficulties in clinical interpretation, is included. The problems are: (i) educational difficulty in an adolescent; (ii) lateralized brain injury in a mature adult; (iii) mildly diffuse cognitive deterioration due to alcoholism in an elderly, yet high achieving, professional adult; (iv) marked cognitive deterioration due to surgical complication; (v) cerebrovascular accident; (vi) complications of the medico-legal process; and (vii) the spurious neuropsychological profile.

The seven case reports included here are entirely fictitious and any resemblance to actual persons is entirely coincidental. The reports are included only for teaching purposes.

The extent of background information contained in the history approximates the data available to the psychologist at the time of writing the report. Historical data are generally of variable amount and quality, and generally subjective, mostly being obtained from the patient during interview. Consequently, these cases are not models which are based on ideal circumstances. Rather, they exemplify the battery's typical performance under routine clinical conditions (lack of patient co-operation or incapacity, shortage of time for testing, paucity of objectively verifiable background data, vague referrals, etc.). Also, the type of referral, and the stated urgency, determined the style and content of each report. They are of variable quality as they are drafted under different conditions and not always by the same person. However, the use of a standardized report format, upon which test scores are coded and interpreted, accounts for much of the similarity in phrasing.

For teaching purposes only, some cases were written up virtually "blind" without the incorporation of diagnostic neurological investigation results. To give a semblance of reality, appropriate results were appended to the report. This teaching technique demonstrates the validation of psychological test interpretation in terms of neurological criteria. It also allows different perspectives between these disciplines to be compared and suggests how functionally and structurally oriented levels of analysis normally complement each other.

The case reports were written up at an elementary level of expertise. That is, it seems as if a standard form of the battery was administered without special efforts to obtain further clinical data to that obtained from other intensive and more specialized approaches.

Test interpretations were based upon quantitative analyses of levels and patterns of performance together with comparisons of performance on one side of the body relative to the other. No real attempt was made to test the limits or engage in a qualitative search for the reasons for specific error patterns, and hence to elucidate the nature of a particular deficit. Although more intensive approaches are a matter of routine for experienced clinicians, they are beyond the scope of generalists and students. This basic approach is in harmony with our goal of leading the way towards acceptable cognitive evaluation by means of the easiest available path, even at the risk of over simplification and undue structuring.

Each report contains raw and standardized data concerning test performance in the form of appendices which make possible a reinterpretation of such test results. More experienced clinicians may find it interesting to go beyond the elementary conclusions and to formulate their own more sophisticated hypotheses taking into account the additional neurological data appended to these reports. Illustrations of the results of personality inventories in the form of graphs (for example, MMPI profiles, etc.) were not included in the appendices in order to conserve space. Such findings were summarized under "personality organization" within the report. The need for rehabilitation was noted, but detailed rehabilitation programmes were not included in these reports.

As stated previously, these reports emphasize basic normative interpretations of quantitative data at the expense of analysis of qualitative patterns of performance. In some instances they provide more detail than would normally be encountered in clinical practice as commentaries were included for teaching purposes.

The figures appended to the case reports are not intended to be a comprehensive or detailed summary of the functional categories assessed. Rather, they have been included as clinically useful visual aids and should therefore be interpreted in this context. They form a profile of neuropsychological strengths and deficits of benefit for the referral sources. The major variables included in the battery may be plotted on a graph as follows: the verbal IQ, performance IQ and full scale IQ are entered in the form of percentile ranks; the reading, spelling and arithmetic subtest scores from the wide range achievement test are also entered as percentile ranks; expressive language ability may be represented by the controlled word association test percentile score; and the comprehension subtest score from the Wechsler intelligence scale is transformed into a percentile rank and can be plotted to represent receptive language ability. Memory processes, visuo-spatial abilities and sensory-motor skills are functional categories and the results of subtests which measure them do not easily transform into percentile ranks. However, an average of levels of performance may be used to convey whether the sub-test scores tend to be above average, average or below average. The 75th percentile can function as the cut-off point for above average performance. The 25th percentile serves as a cut-off point for below average performance. An inadequate score on one side of the body during sensory-motor tests is obviously clinically significant despite superior scores on the intact side of the body. For example, if poor grip strength is noted only on the dominant side, a below average score for grip strength should be plotted (below the 25th percentile) on the graph.

CASE 1: REPORT OF NEUROPSYCHOLOGICAL ASSESSMENT

Name: Ronald Glass *Age:* 13 years
Purpose of evaluation: Assessment of potential learning difficulties
Referred by: Psychiatrist *Date:* August 14th, 1983

Evaluation based upon the following

MOTOR FUNCTIONING
Laterality preference schedule
Grooved pegboard
Finger tapping test
Hand dynamometer

AUDITORY PERCEPTUAL FUNCTIONING
Speech–sounds perception test
Seashore rhythm test

TACTILE PERCEPTUAL FUNCTIONING
Face hand test
Finger agnosia
Graphaesthesia
Tactile form recognition test

VISUO-SPATIAL FUNCTIONING
Trail making test (Part B)
Benton visual retention test
Rey–Osterrieth complex figure test (copy)

LANGUAGE ABILITY
Aphasia language performance scales
Controlled word association test

MEMORY PROCESSES
Modified Wechsler memory scale
Rey–Osterrieth complex figure test (recall)
Walton–Black modified new word learning test

HIGHER COGNITIVE PROCESSES
Wechsler intelligence scale for children—revised (WISC–R)
Wide range achievement test
Progressive achievement tests (reading comprehension)
Stroop colour–word test

PERSONALITY ORGANIZATIONS
Neuroticism scale questionnaire
Neuropsychological structured interview

History

Ronald Glass is a 13-year-old, eighth grade school boy attending a private school with a high academic reputation. He had been in psychotherapy for the whole of the previous year without progress in school adjustment. His parents recently changed to a new psychiatrist who promptly referred him for a neuropsychological assessment to explore potential learning difficulties. At school he was described as a lonely and isolated child who was often a victim of teasing and violence.

Ronald is the elder of two children. There is a brother, aged five. Father (aged 50) is an architect and mother (aged 38) works as his secretary and at home. Ronald was a wanted child, born following a miscarriage. The pregnancy was difficult but labour appears to have been normal. His milestones were adequate although he began to speak a little late (2.5–three years of age). He was described as a shy, nice boy who "never did anything wrong". His problems apparently began when he started school and he had been seen for weekly psychotherapy for about a year because he had problems with other children at school. He seems to have become jealous of his brother two years ago and there has been some competition between them ever since. School performance is above average in maths, but below average in English, history and science. Ronald's major interest appears to be football.

Behavioural Observations

When seen for testing the patient was alert and well oriented. He was accompanied by his parents who supplied most of the history. Test taking attitude was excellent. The patient presented as a likeable boy who appeared to be slightly younger than his stated age, but articulate and appropriate. He seemed to feel high expectations placed on him. He wants to become an accountant and he said that he liked his present school.

Intellectual Functioning

The patient's intellectual function was assessed using the Weschler intelligence scale for children–revised diagnostic and remedial education diskettes compatible with an Apple II computer. The results were computer scored and interpreted with software programmed by Trifiletti, *et al.* (1982). These results served as useful hypotheses to be interpreted within the context of the rest of the neuropsychological data base.

The patient achieved a verbal IQ score of 109 (73rd percentile), a performance IQ score of 78 (7th percentile) and a full scale IQ score of 93 (32nd percentile). This shows a highly significant difference between verbal and performance IQ scores (95 per cent confidence level). Whereas verbal IQ approaches the bright–normal range the performance IQ approaches the borderline mentally retarded range.

Marked intellectual impairments were noted on profile analysis when significant differences in subtest scores from the patient's own mean became obvious. Visuo-spatial skills were particularly impaired (poor planning ability, slow psychomotor speed, poor visual organization, and poor spatial abilities).

Significant cognitive strengths were also noted on this patient's profoundly scattered and uneven profile. Some above average subtest scores reflected better than average attention span, concentration and mental alertness. There is also evidence of freedom from distractibility and good attention to auditory stimuli.

Educational Achievement

Reading fluency (word recognition) is at the 8.7 grade level (81st percentile); reading comprehension is at the 6.0 grade level (25th percentile); spelling is at the 8.9 grade level (82nd percentile); and maths is at the 7.6 grade level (50th percentile). There is a discrepancy of almost three years between reading fluency and reading comprehension.

Motor Functioning

The patient demonstrated consistent right hand dominance. Most individuals with right hand dominance have verbal functions represented in the left hemisphere with visuo-spatial skills in the right. The patient's gross motor speed in the upper limbs was intact. Fine motor co-ordination was adequate. Power was normal in the arms.

Auditory Perceptual Functioning

Auditory perceptual functioning was excellent. The patient had no difficulty in discriminating between pairs of rhythms or different consonant sounds.

Tactile Perceptual Functioning

Tactile perceptual functioning was relatively intact. No errors of extinction or displacement occurred. There were no errors for finger agnosia, graphaesthesia and stereognosis.

Visuo-spatial Functioning

The hypothesis of particularly impaired visuo-spatial skills was confirmed by the results of other neuropsychological tests. Visuomotor speed was below average. Visual organization and planning was poor, with a lack of alertness for fine graphic detail. Spatial abilities were also inadequate.

Language Ability

Language ability was generally intact except for reading comprehension. There was no evidence of dysarthria as articulation was adequate and expressive speech was fluent. Vocabulary level fell within the average range (63rd percentile). Listening and auditory comprehension and number comprehension scores were above average. Writing and spelling scores were above average. Reading fluency (word recognition) and word finding fluency scores were also above average.

Memory Processes

The patient obtained a general memory quotient of 106 (66th percentile) which fell within the average range. This was relatively consistent with verbal intelligence. Immediate memory was intact. Recent memory, including the ability to learn both new verbal and visual information, was adequate. Remote memory was satisfactory.

Freedom from distractibility quotient was 108 (78th percentile). This fell into the average range. Thus, there was no evidence of a typical attention deficit disorder.

Personality Organization

Due to the patient's reading comprehension deficits, the neuroticism scale questionnaire, a brief, easily administered inventory, was administered orally by the examiner and the patient's responses were marked accordingly by the clinician. The personality profile (Fig. 1) elicited was relatively unremarkable. There was no evidence of a general trend towards neuroticism, nor did the patient appear to be clinically anxious or depressed. It appeared that any anxiety present is specifically associated with school.

Comments

In summary, the patient showed significant discrepancies on his neuropsychological profile with an extreme scatter of strengths and deficits. He is specifically deficient in reading comprehension, together with severe deficits in the visuo-spatial modality (poor visuomotor speed, visual organization and planning, and below average spatial ability).

Significant cognitive strengths were also noted as follows: intact memory processes (immediate, recent and remote) with freedom from an attention deficit disorder; and generally adequate language skills (average vocabulary with which he is articulate, superior reading fluency and word finding fluency, superior spelling, and adequate auditory comprehension and number comprehension).

The most significant functional deficit is reading comprehension. His linguistic–lexigraphic coding skills are excellent (for example, adequate oral, reading and writing codes) such as the ability to write to dictation, spell, and recognize words which facilitate fluent reading. However, a specific semantic factor disrupts his educational potential.

Reading functions are extremely complex with the interaction of many independent and some dependent factors. He is not dyslexic as this syndrome is characterized by coding deficits rather than by defects of comprehension.

It is important to differentiate between coding skills and semantics. Linguistics is concerned with the principles of verbal coding whereas semantics deals with the principles of thought formation. Thinking and reading are neuropsychologically independent functions. For example, this patient is an excellent reader (and hence a superior coder), but he does not comprehend what he is reading about, perhaps because of some central processing disorder. Reading is basically a vehicle of thought but it is not a meaningful communication in itself. That is, the code carries the contents of the communication but it is not thought itself.

The patient appears to have a neurodevelopmental anomaly characterized by an extreme discrepancy between superior coding skills and inferior semantic ability. This semantic disability is specific to reading comprehension as other aspects of comprehension (for example, oral and number comprehension) are intact.

There is no evidence of family pathology. The patient lives in a supportive, emotionally secure home without socioeconomic deprivation. Ronald does not have a primary emotional disturbance and most of his behavioural problems appear to be secondary to his learning disability. Consequently, psychotherapy may be discontinued in favour of remedial education.

Management should be mainly in the school milieu. There can be an emphasis upon compensating for reading comprehension deficits by making full use of alternative intact educational skills while upgrading such deficits at the same time. It is acknowledged that the school curriculum relies specifically upon reading comprehension and this difficult challenge cannot be permanently avoided. Valett's (1980) neuropsychologically based lesson plans cross-indexed to specific problems have been recommended to the remediation teacher concerned wih Ronald's progress. Vocational counselling, perhaps with a view to capitalizing upon his adequate numerical comprehension (for example, accountancy) will need to be scheduled in the future. A change to a school with less emphasis upon academic achievement may be considered although such a change would have risks because of the need for readjustment, finding new friends and so on.

Neurological Investigations

Because of the extreme discrepancy between verbal and performance IQ scores, which was suggestive of a structural lesion to the psychiatrist referring this patient, computerized tomography and electroencephalography were scheduled. The results were: CT brain scan without contrast ("The ventricles appear normal in shape, size and distribution and no density abnormality or evidence of structural congenital or post traumatic lesion is seen"); and EEG report ("9-10 Hz alpha is symmetrical and responsive; hyperventilation and photic stimulation had no significant effect; no focal or epileptic activity seen; conclusion: within normal limits for age").

Commentary

Learning disorders without primary emotional aetiology imply the existence of a central processing disorder of organic origin. Brain dysfunction is inferred, but, as in this case, has not yet been satisfactorily demonstrated. Approximately 10 to 15 per cent of children are estimated to have central processing disorders that disrupt learning. However, the results of neurological diagnostic investigations generally prove to be "normal". Perhaps our tools are not yet refined enough to physically document such developmental deficits. Promising neurological analogies, such as the concept of neurodevelopmental lag, are useful theoretical contributions guiding research.

Finally, it must be emphasized that there are no general characteristics of children with learning disabilities. For example, similar levels of deficient neuropsychological performance in certain children can be the result of radically different patterns of brain-related strengths and deficits.

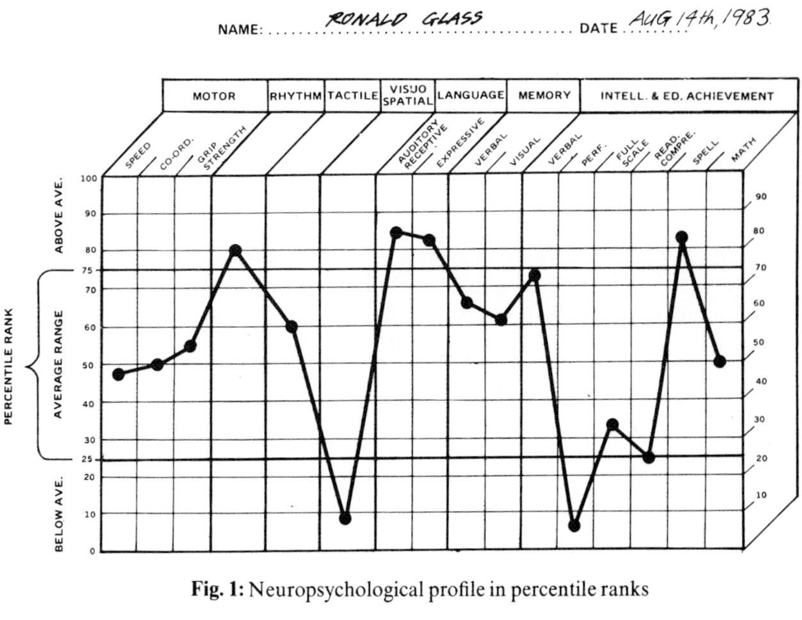

Fig. 1: Neuropsychological profile in percentile ranks

Appendix to Case 1 (test score record form) (August 14th, 1983)

Laterality preference schedule: Consistent right hand dominance.
Grooved Pegboard:
Dominant Hand = Normal Non-Dominant Hand = Normal
Finger Tapping Test:
Dominant Hand = Normal Non-Dominant Hand = Normal
Hand Dynamometer:
Dominant Hand = Normal Non-Dominant Hand = Normal
Speech–sounds perception test: Within normal limits.
Seashore rhythm test: Above average score.
Tactile perceptual functioning: Within normal limits.
Trail making test: Outside normal limits.
Benton visual retention test: Within normal limits.
Aphasia language performance scales:
Listening and auditory comprehension is intact, number comprehension intact.
Reading fluency (word recognition) above average.
Talking within normal limits.
Writing within normal limits.
Controlled word association test: 99th percentile.
Wechsler memory scale:
Memory quotient = 106 (66th percentile)
Verbal short-term memory = within normal limits
Verbal long-term memory = within normal limits
Semantic % retained = within normal limits
Visual short-term, memory = within normal limits
Visual long-term memory = within normal limits
Visual % retained = within normal limits
Complex figure: Outside normal limits.
Walton–Black: Within normal limits.
Wechsler intelligence scale for children (in percentile ranks):

Information	75th percentile	Coding	16th percentile*
Comprehension	75th percentile	Picture completion	16th percentile*
Arithmetic	84th percentile	Block design	63rd percentile*
Similarities	50th percentile	Picture arrangement	25th percentile*
Digit span	91st percentile	Object assembly	1st percentile*
Vocabulary	63rd percentile	Performance IQ = 78	(7th percentile)*
Verbal IQ = 109	(73rd percentile)	Full scale IQ = 93	(32nd percentile)*

Stroop: Within normal limits.

*Indicates score in impaired range.

Wide range achievement test:
Reading fluency 8.7 grade (81st percentile)
Spelling 8.9 grade (82nd percentile)
Maths 7.6 grade (50th percentile)
Progressive achievement tests: Reading comprehension: 6.0 grade (25th percentile)*

CASE 2: REPORT OF NEUROPSYCHOLOGICAL ASSESSMENT

Name: Judy Rosenberry *Age:* 18 years
Purpose of evaluation: Vocational rehabilitation and placement
Referred by: Rehabilitation physician *Date:* October 21st, 1982

Evaluation based upon the following

MOTOR FUNCTIONING
Laterality preference schedule
Grooved pegboard
Finger tapping test
Hand dynamometer

AUDITORY PERCEPTUAL FUNCTIONING
Speech-sounds perception test
Seashore rhythm test

TACTILE PERCEPTUAL FUNCTIONING
Face hand test
Finger agnosia
Graphaesthesia
Tactile form recognition test

VISUO-SPATIAL FUNCTIONING
Trail making test (Part B)
Benton visual retention test
Rey–Osterrieth complex figure test (copy)

LANGUAGE ABILITY
Aphasia language performance scales
Controlled word association test

MEMORY PROCESSES
Modified Wechsler memory scale
Rey–Osterrieth complex figure test (recall)
Walton–Black modified new word learning test

HIGHER COGNITIVE PROCESSES
Wechsler adult intelligence scale–revised
Wide range achievement test
Stroop colour-word test

PERSONALITY ORGANIZATION
Neuroticism scale questionnaire
Neuropsychological structured interview

History

Judy Rosenberry is an 18-year-old single, Australian female who was referred for a neuropsychological evaluation to determine possible vocational rehabilitation and placement plans. She was involved in a motor vehicle accident on September 25th, 1980, and sustained a severe head injury.

On admission to hospital, she was noted to be deeply unconscious, responding only in a decerebrate fashion to pain with reactive pupils and bilateral papilloedema. Computerized tomography scans showed diffuse cerebral oedema with a small, right subdural collection of blood and some right to left midline shift. A right frontotemporal craniotomy was performed on September 25th, 1980, and the subdural collection of blood was drained. Further exploration on September 27th, 1980, revealed necrotic brain tissue in the right temporal and posterior right frontal lobes. After prolonged unconsciousness and convalescence, a cranioplasty was performed on November 18th, 1980. Judy was then transferred to a rehabilitation unit.

The patient left school after completing eighth grade and was unemployed at the time of the accident. There were no previous or subsequent head injuries or psychiatric problems. Since the accident, she has made significant improvement in most areas of functioning. Miss Rosenberry is now able to walk without assistance and can carry out most activities of daily living including feeding, dressing and toileting. She shows little personal initiative in speech or action, according to her mother.

Behavioural Observations

When seen for testing the patient was alert and well oriented. She was accompanied by her sister who supplied most of the history. Test taking attitude was relatively satisfactory, although an impairment of concentration was noted throughout the testing.

Symptomatology

The patient and her sister listed the following problems since the accident:

1. Loss of use of the left arm.
2. Random headaches.
3. Impairment of memory and concentration.
4. Personality change (low frustration tolerance, moody, overtalkative, and apathetic without constructive future plans).
5. Disrupted social life (unable to go out on her own, and self-conscious concerning dysfunctional left arm).

Intellectual Functioning

The patient achieved a verbal IQ score of 90, a performance IQ score of 68 and a full scale IQ score of 78. The verbal–performance discrepancy is dramatic. Marked intellectual impairments were noted on the subtests of the Wechsler adult intelligence scale. There was strong evidence of subtest scatter in the form of extreme scale score deviations. Performance subtests, which tend to monitor visuo-spatial functioning, were indicative of predominantly right hemisphere dysfunction.

Full scale IQ scores suggest that current general intellectual functioning falls within the borderline mentally retarded range (7th percentile). Premorbid intelligence was estimated to fall within the low average range (using Mahan's converted residual technique and demographic data statistical formulae). Thus, there was evidence of significant intellectual deterioration. Her premorbid full scale IQ score most probably approached her current verbal IQ score of 90, and possibly even surpassed it.

Educational Achievement

Reading skills are at 6.8 grade level (19th percentile); spelling is at 4.5 grade level (5th percentile); and maths is at 5.6 grade level (14th percentile). It was also noted that her general fund of information (1st percentile) and vocabulary level (9th percentile) were very deficient.

Reading, spelling, general knowledge and vocabulary are skills that tend to be extremely resistant to brain damage. This fact, within the context of restricted 8th grade education and inadequate vocational performance before the accident, is suggestive of learning disability which is unrelated to her motor vehicle accident. This is especially so as her brain damage is predominately lateralized to the right hemisphere whereas her left hemisphere (upon which language skills such as reading and spelling depend) is relatively more intact.

She also admits to never having liked school primarily because of spelling inability. This is suggestive of specific learning disability of developmental origin in an individual of estimated low average premorbid intelligence. This handicap was the primary reason for early termination of schooling.

Motor Functioning

The patient demonstrated consistent right hand dominance. Most individuals with right hand dominance have verbal functions represented in the left hemisphere with visuo-spatial skills in the right. The patient's gross motor speed, fine motor co-ordination and grip strength were all profoundly impaired in the left arm. However, the right arm was relatively intact. This is indicative of brain damage lateralized to the right hemisphere (in the absence of damage to peripheral limb structures).

Auditory Perceptual Functioning

Auditory perceptual functioning was intact. The patient had no difficulty in differentiating between pairs of rhythms of different consonant sounds.

Tactile Perceptual Functioning

Tactile perceptual functioning was relatively impaired. There was loss of normal sensation in the left hand and confusing results were obtained for the tactile perceptual tests. This should be further followed up by a neurologist.

Visuo-spatial Functioning

Visuo-spatial functioning appeared to be impaired. There was evidence of constructional dyspraxia. Visuomotor speed was impaired. Visual memory was also impaired. Signs of visual neglect were also evident on scanning tasks.

Language Ability

Language ability was relatively unaffected by her motor vehicle accident but, as noted previously, she has below average abilities in this area. This is most probably of developmental origin.

Comprehension is relatively intact. She listens well and responds adequately to questions. Reading ability is also consistent with her low average premorbid intelligence and restricted degree of education. There is no evidence of disturbance in articulation. She expresses herself well and in fact is overtalkative (which may be suggestive of a disinhibition syndrome). Word finding fluency was above average (75th percentile). Writing was slow but adequate. As suggested previously, she may have a specific learning disability of developmental aetiology in the area of spelling.

Memory Processes

The patient obtained a general memory quotient of 89 (23rd percentile) which fell within the low-average range. This was relatively consistent with estimated low-average premorbid intelligence. Immediate memory was intact. However, it was noted that visual memory was impaired whereas verbal memory was more adequate. This is further evidence of lateralized right hemisphere cerebral dysfunction.

Personality Organization

The patient's impairment of concentration and her deteriorated condition precluded valid administration of the Minnesota multiphasic personality inventory. Consequently, the much shorter neuroticism scale questionnaire was substituted, and she was able to complete this. Profile configuration (Fig. 2) was relatively unremarkable except for the presence of mild oversensitivity and anxiety (perhaps related to self-consciousness regarding her left arm and disrupted social life).

Of more significance than results of personality inventories was the disturbing theme of lack of personal initiative in speech and action after the accident, together with overtalkativeness. She is apathetic about long-term plans for her life and is deficient in planning and organizing daily activities. This personality change is probably organic in origin and highly suggestive of frontal lobe involvement.

Diagnostic Impression

A traumatically induced severe right hemisphere dysfunction accompanied by frontal lobe involvement in an individual with a developmental specific learning disability (spelling).

Comments

In summary, Judy Rosenberry is an individual of estimated low average, premorbid intelligence, with a learning disability of developmental origin (unrelated to her motor vehicle accident). However, there is unequivocal evidence of severe brain damage directly related to this accident. Neuropsychological tests clearly lateralize cerebral dysfunction to predominant right hemisphere involvement. This explains her poor performance on visuospatial tasks within the context of relatively more adequate verbal performance. There is also behavioural evidence of frontal lobe dysfunction. Prognosis is poor for any significant change in her condition, although a definitive prognostic statement should be delayed for another year.

Despite the patient's severe residual deficits there are some significant areas of intact functioning. She is young and remains alert, her comprehension is intact and she follows directions well. She expresses herself adequately upon questioning. Miss Rosenberry is also ambulatory and able to perform skills necessary for independent living. However, she is incapable of returning to gainful employment on the open labour market. Consequently, the most realistic vocational plan is placement in a sheltered workshop. Specific cognitive rehabilitation efforts may focus upon compensating for her visuo-spatial deficits whilst capitalizing upon skills correlated with the relatively more intact left hemisphere. A structured environment with close supervision may also compensate for some of her apathy and lack of initiative.

Neurological Investigation

Shortly after the completion of neuropsychological testing, a follow-up neurological examination was completed. Extracts from the report are as follows: "There was still evidence of bilateral corticospinal damage with a marked left sided hemiparesis and left sided parietal signs of neglect and sensory extinction. Her memory remains impaired and there are signs of marked right hemisphere damage as well as frontal lobe damage. Although the patient has been making mild to moderate motor sensory recovery from head injury she will be left with severe deficiencies of intellectual and cognitive functioning".

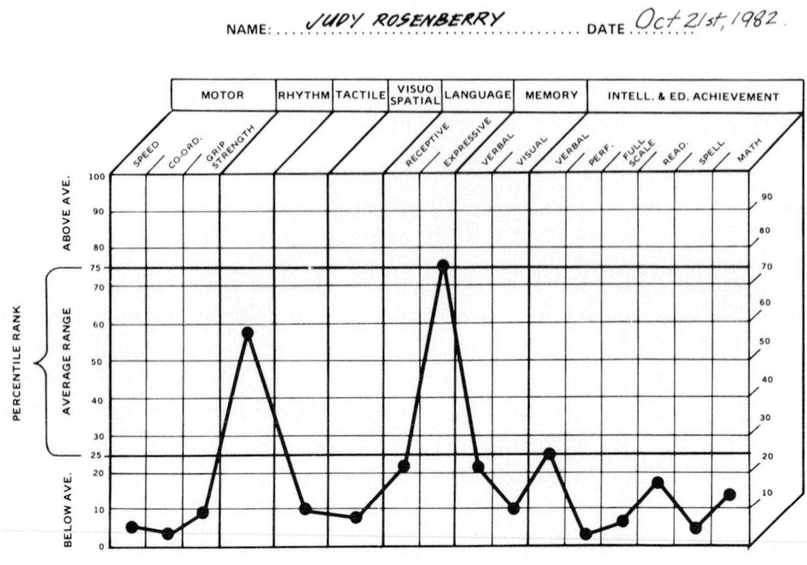

Fig. 2: Neuropsychological profile in percentile ranks

Appendix to Case 2 (test score record form) (October 21st, 1982)

Laterality preference schedule: Consistent right hand dominance.
Grooved pegboard: Dominant Hand = 93 secs
Non-Dominant Hand = Unable to do*
Finger tapping test: Dominant Hand = 51 taps
Non-Dominant Hand = 16 taps*
Hand dynamometer: Dominant Hand = Normal
Non-Dominant Hand = Abnormal*
Speech–sounds perception test: Within normal limits.
Seashore rhythm test: Rank score of 3 (within normal limits).
Tactile perceptual functioning: Loss of sensation in the left hand.*
Trail making test: 151 secs (5th percentile).*
Benton visual retention test: Outside normal limits.*
Aphasia language performance scales:
Listening within normal limits.
Reading within normal limits.
Talking within normal limits.
Writing within normal limits.
Controlled word association test: 75th percentile.
Wechsler memory scale:
Memory quotient = 89 (23rd percentile)
Verbal short-term memory = borderline score*
Verbal long-term memory = borderline score*
Semantic % retained = borderline score*
Visual short-term memory = outside normal limits*
Visual long-term memory = outside normal limits*
Visual % retained = outside normal limits*
Complex figure: Outside normal limits.*
Walton–Black: Outside normal limits.*
Wechsler adult intelligence scale (in percentile ranks):

Information	1st percentile	Digit symbol	1st percentile*
Comprehension	16th percentile	Picture completion	5th percentile*
Arithmetic	9th percentile	Block design	9th percentile*
Similarities	50th percentile	Picture arrangement	9th percentile*
Digit span	84th percentile	Object assembly	2nd percentile*
Vocabulary	9th percentile*	Performance IQ = 68	(2nd percentile)*
Verbal IQ = 90	(25th percentile)	Full scale IQ = 78	(7th percentile)*

Stroop: 61 seconds (outside normal limits)
Wide range achievement test:
Reading 6.8 grade level (19th percentile)
Spelling 4.5 grade level (5th percentile)
Maths 5.6 grade level (14th percentile)

* Indicates score in impaired range.

CASE 3: REPORT OF NEUROPSYCHOLOGICAL ASSESSMENT

Name: George Beston *Age:* 64 years
Purpose of evaluation: Presence/absence of cognitive impairment
Referred by: Patient's family physician *Date:* January 11th, 1984

Evaluation based upon the following

MOTOR FUNCTIONING
Laterality preference schedule
Grooved pegboard
Finger tapping test
Hand dynamometer

AUDITORY PERCEPTUAL FUNCTIONING
Speech-sounds perception test
Seashore rhythm test

TACTILE PERCEPTUAL FUNCTIONING
Face hand test
Finger agnosia
Graphaesthesia
Tactile form recognition test

VISUO-SPATIAL FUNCTIONING
Trail making test (Part B)
Benton visual retention test
Rey–Osterrieth complex figure test (copy)

LANGUAGE ABILITY
Aphasia language performance scales
Controlled word association test

MEMORY PROCESSES
Modified Wechsler memory scale
Rey–Osterrieth complex figure test (recall)
Walton–Black modified new word learning test

HIGHER COGNITIVE PROCESSES
Wechsler adult intelligence scale
Wide range achievement test
Stroop colour–word test

PERSONALITY ORGANIZATION
Minnesota multiphasic personality inventory
Neuropsychological structured interview

History

George Beston is a medium built, 64-year-old Australian married male who was referred for a neuropsychological evaluation when he recently complained of increasing difficulties with his work, a tendency to be unsteady on his feet and persistent headaches.

Both his wife and physician classify him as a heavy sporadic "binge" drinker of many years' standing. He has some momentary blackouts, but no true episodes of severe loss of consciousness. He has had one bout of severe acute pancreatitis together with a major coronary attack. As yet, he has not been neurologically investigated. There was no previous history of head injuries or psychiatric problems.

Premorbid intellectual functioning appears to have been superior. He is a lawyer, with a successful private practice, whose main recreational interest is reading in the social sciences.

Behavioural Observations

When seen for testing the patient was fully alert and well oriented. However, he appeared to be mildly depressed. His interpersonal skills were excellent and he was co-operative and highly motivated during testing, thus increasing the probability of obtaining a valid data base. However, he became relatively guarded when discussing his drinking problem.

Some potential signs of organicity were elicited during the interview. He was garrulous, had mild dysarthria and his gait was mildly ataxic. The patient was accompanied by his wife who appeared to be highly supportive.

Symptomatology

The patient's following complaints were recorded verbatim:

1. Recently, I've been getting frequent headaches.
2. I lack co-ordination when I'm walking and have a tendency to lose my balance and fall forward.
3. I get lost more easily when I'm driving and tend to take more wrong turns.
4. My left arm gets partially numb.
5. I get split-second blackouts.
6. My memory has been progressively getting worse. I can't recall legal references in my work as I used to.
7. My spelling and arithmetic are not what they used to be.

8. I can't cope with an 8-hour day and have had to shorten my working time because of fatigue.
9. My wife complains that I'm moody and harder to get along with.

Intellectual Functioning

The patient achieved a verbal IQ score of 131, a performance IQ score of 114 and a full scale IQ score of 125. These scores suggest that current general intellectual functioning falls within the superior range (95th percentile). Marked intellectual impairments were not noted on the subtests of the Wechsler adult intelligence scale except for a mild to moderate scatter of discrepant scores. Normally, there are high correlations between subtests, but an analysis of the weighted scores revealed clinically significant inconsistencies in abilities. For example, vocabulary level was within the very superior range (as was estimated premorbid functioning) in contrast to some below average subtest scores (for example, digit span, digit symbol, and object assembly).

Higher cognitive functions (comprehension, abstract thinking and problem solving) appeared to be generally intact. However, the patient had some difficulty in maintaining a uniform course of action independent of intruding stimuli.

Educational Achievement

Reading skills are at 10.9 grade level (86th percentile); spelling is also at 10.9 grade level (90th percentile); and maths is at 6.6 grade level (68th percentile). These achievement scores are relatively consistent with the patient's superior premorbid intelligence, level of scholastic attainment and current vocational performance except for his mediocre arithmetic skills. He explained that maths has always been his weakest subject. However, there is also the possibility of an impairment of concentration compounding difficulties in calculating ability. There is no evidence of a specific learning disability.

Motor Functioning

The patient demonstrated consistent right hand dominance. Most individuals with right hand dominance have verbal functions represented in the left hemisphere with visuo-spatial skills in the right. The patient's motor speed in the upper limbs was moderately slow bilaterally. He also showed mild impairment of fine motor co-ordination in the upper limbs. Power was normal in the arms, however.

Auditory Perceptual Functioning

The patient showed no evidence of objective sensory loss. Auditory perceptual functioning was within normal limits. He could adequately differentiate pairs of rhythms and differing consonant sounds.

Tactile Perceptual Functioning

Tactile perceptual functioning was also satisfactory. No errors of extinction or displacement occurred. Also, there were no errors for finger agnosia, graphaesthesia and stereognosis.

Visuo-spatial Functioning

Visuo-spatial functioning appeared to be mildly to moderately impaired. There was no specific evidence of pure constructional dyspraxia as the patient was able to process visual information and reconstruct it by means of perceptual motor act. However, performance within the spatial perceptual modality was inadequate because of visuomotor slowing, borderline attentive functions and impaired visual memory. The copying of complex figures was significantly superior to that of visual recall.

Language Ability

The clinical impression of mild language disturbance (dysarthria and garrulousness) was confirmed during testing. Some errors of articulation were evident. Besides slurring of speech the patient's below average word finding fluency was discrepant with his superior premorbid intelligence. This may be suggestive of a central expressive disorder. However, there were no difficulties with listening, comprehension, and reading, thus ruling out receptive aphasia. Dysgraphia was also excluded in the absence of an aphasic writing impairment.

Memory Processes

The patient obtained a general memory quotient of 108 (70th percentile) which fell within the upper level of the average range. This was relatively discrepant from estimated superior premorbid intelligence. Immediate memory fell within the borderline to adequate range.

Recent memory, including the ability to learn both new verbal and visual information, was moderately impaired. However, remote memory was intact.

Personality Organization

The profile configuration of the Minnesota multiphasic personality inventory was relatively unremarkable. There was no evidence of clinically significant psychological disturbance. Depression was merely mild. This mild emotional disorder may be a reaction to the patient's appropriate concern over his declining work capacity.

Since the patient was rather guarded and tended to give socially appropriate responses it was difficult to discover the dynamics responsible for his drinking behaviour. This defensive attitude appeared to be more related to shame concerning his drinking rather than to outright denial. His wife reported that incidents of personality change are directly related to alcohol. Normally, he is a placid, rather studious individual who only became moody and aggressive during episodes of "binge" drinking. In view of his productive work record, excellent interpersonal skills, and absence of gross antisocial behaviour it is possible that he is a neurotic type of drinker wherein drinking bouts are stress-related rather than the more typical case of "alcoholic personality disorder".

Diagnostic Impression

Mild to moderate diffuse impairment of cognitive function associated with alcoholism.

Comments

In summary, George Beston is an individual of superior premorbid intelligence who displayed a mild to moderate generalized pattern of cognitive deterioration on the results of tests. It is estimated that 50 per cent of alcoholics over the age of forty who have been drinking heavily for 20 years develop cerebral atrophy. However, it has not been established whether his "binge" drinking can be classified as a clear cut case of chronic alcoholism.

The patient's gait was ataxic and there was also an impairment of motor co-ordination in the upper limbs. This may be suggestive of cerebellar involvement.

Test performance deficits showed no lateralizing signs. Rather, they were compatible with the involvement of both hemispheres. For example, recent memory, including the ability to learn both new verbal and visual information, was moderately impaired. Impairment of new learning is often a result of damage to the hippocampi or the mamillary bodies/medial thalamic nuclei. Mild dysarthria and the possible presence of a central expressive disorder were also noted.

Since the patient merely deteriorated from the superior to mediocre level in certain areas of functioning he may not be considered to be markedly handicapped. Some difficulties may arise in new situations, but he should be able to cope with the more routine aspects of his vocational environment.

Despite his documented deficits, the patient also has obvious strengths which can form the basis of rehabilitation efforts (Fig. 3). Higher cognitive functions are generally intact and general intelligence currently remains within the superior range. He is a high achieving individual with a lifelong history of generally superior premorbid functioning–intellectually, socially and vocationally–despite episodic drinking. He has insight into his condition, is appropriately disturbed by his symptoms and appears to be highly motivated to change. The marital relationship is stable and there is the presence of a supportive family structure. Consequently, prognosis is encouraging.

Because the aetiology of his problems is directly related to alcohol there is room for some improvement in his condition if he stops drinking. He should also be counselled to reduce his work load. A behaviour modification programme has been formulated for him.

Reassessment has been scheduled for six months after the patient abstains from alcohol, if this is achievable, followed by further regular follow-ups in order to determine whether his memory disorder is a reversible phenomenon. In the meantime, the results of the neuropsychological testing are of enough significance to warrant neurological investigation.

Neurological Investigations

Two weeks after neuropsychological testing, the patient was evaluated by a consultant neurologist and underwent computerized tomography. Extracts from these reports are quoted below.

The neurologist's report: "Clinically, I felt no doubt that he had evidence of a cerebral and cerebellar degenerative process, most likely secondary to alcohol. I have also received a copy of the psychologist's report which confirms the fact the patient has evidence of intellectual impairment. The CT scan shows evidence of a moderate degree of cerebral and cerebellar atrophy confirming our diagnosis".

The computerized tomography report: "There is some symmetrical dilation of the ventricles and Sylvian fissures cisterns with prominent cortical cerebral sulci".

Follow-Up

At follow-up two years later, the patient showed an unusual degree of improvement. He reports that he has totally abstained from alcohol during the past 18 months and believes that he has regained his general health. The symptomatology that he complained of is absent and no longer disruptive to his functioning.

The patient has returned to full time work and this high achieving individual has even expanded his legal practice and is currently pursuing new business ventures. He claims he is not unduly fatigued by this escalation of activity, which is suggestive of more than adequate stamina in a man of 68 years of age. Mr Beston remains mentally alert and has returned to his premorbid habit of indulging in approximately three hours per day of recreational reading.

The patient's wife confirms his total abstinence from alcohol and the subsequent unusual amount of progress. She also stated that their marital relationship has improved with the cessation of his drinking.

Reassessment results were consistent with the improvements reported above. There was no evidence of depression, and the patient appeared to be generally symptom free. However, improvement in recent memory appeared to be merely mild to moderate but this possibly residual deficit appeared to be well compensated for by the marked restitution of his general condition.

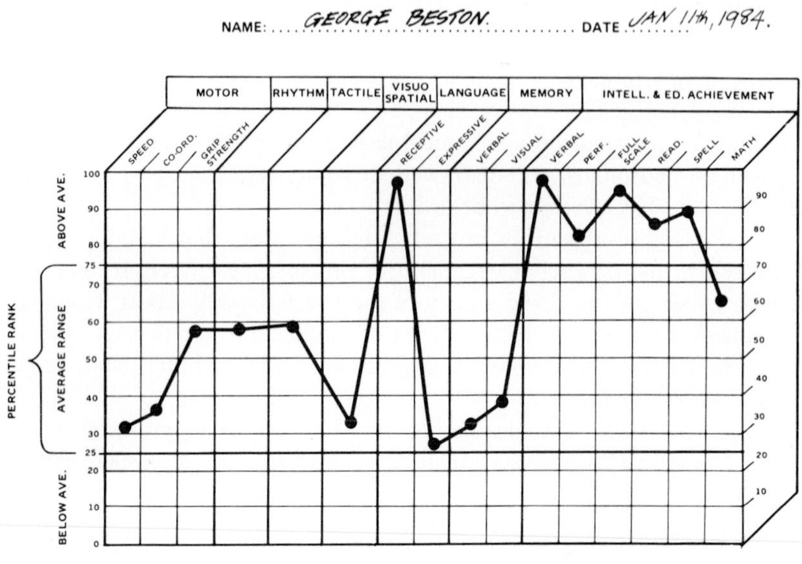

Fig. 3: Neuropsychological profile in percentile ranks

Appendix to Case 3 (test score record form) (January 11th, 1984)

Laterality preference schedule: Consistent right hand dominance.
Grooved pegboard: Dominant Hand = 105 secs*
Non-Dominant Hand = 107 secs*
Finger tapping test: Dominant Hand = 35 taps*
Non-Dominant Hand = 32 taps*
Hand dynamometer: Dominant Hand = 36 kilos
Non-Dominant Hand = 34 kilos
Speech–sound perception test: Within normal limits.
Seashore rhythm test: Rank score of 3 (within normal limits).
Tactile perceptual functioning: Within normal limits.
Trail making test: 174 secs (24th percentile)*
Benton visual retention test: 9 errors above expected score*
Aphasia language performance scales:
Listening within normal limits.
Reading within normal limits.
Talking mildly disturbed.*
Writing within normal limits.
Controlled word association test: 25th percentile (borderline score).*
Wechsler memory scale:
Memory quotient = 108 (70th percentile); below expected score*
Verbal short-term memory = outside normal limits*
Verbal long-term memory = outside normal limits*
Semantic % retained = 49%*
Visual short-term memory = within normal limits
Visual long-term memory = outside normal limits*
Visual % retained = 47%*
Complex figure: Borderline score.*
Walton–Black: Learned five new words in seven trials (borderline response).*
Wechsler adult intelligence scale (in percentile ranks):

Information	98th percentile	Digit symbol	37th percentile*
Comprehension	99th percentile	Picture completion	99th percentile
Arithmetic	63rd percentile	Block design	63rd percentile
Similarities	99th percentile	Picture arrangement	75th percentile
Digit span	37th percentile*	Object assembly	25th percentile*
Vocabulary	99th percentile	Performance IQ = 114	(81st percentile)
Verbal IQ = 131	(98th percentile)	Full scale IQ = 125	(95th percentile)

Stroop: 56 secs*
Wide range achievment test:
Reading 10.9 grade level (86th percentile)
Spelling 10.9 grade level (90th percentile)
Maths 6.6 grade level (68th percentile)*

*Indicates score in impaired range.

CASE 4: REPORT OF NEUROPSYCHOLOGICAL ASSESSMENT

Name: Elvina Bugeja *Age:* 38 years
Purpose of evaluation: Routine neuropsychological evaluation
Referred by: Hospital staff physician *Date:* March 27th, 1984

Evaluation based upon the following

MOTOR FUNCTIONING
Laterality preference schedule
Grooved pegboard
Finger tapping test
Hand dynamometer

AUDITORY PERCEPTUAL FUNCTIONING
Speech-sounds perception test
Seashore rhythm test

TACTILE PERCEPTUAL FUNCTIONING
Face hand test
Finger agnosia
Graphaesthesia
Tactile form recognition test

VISUO-SPATIAL FUNCTIONING
Trail making test (Part B)
Benton visual retention test
Rey–Osterrieth complex figure test (copy)

LANGUAGE ABILITY
Aphasia language performance scales
Controlled word association test

MEMORY PROCESSES
Modified Wechsler memory scale
Rey–Osterrieth complex figure test (recall)
Walton–Black modified new word learning test

HIGHER COGNITIVE PROCESSES
Wechsler adult intelligence scale
Wide range achievement test
Stroop colour–word test

PERSONALITY ORGANIZATION
Neuroticism scale questionnaire
Neuropsychological structured interview

History

Elvina Bugeja is a 38-year-old divorced Ukrainian female who was referred for a routine neuropsychological evaluation as part of a comprehensive assessment of her blindness.

The patient has suffered an episode of cerebral anoxia during Caesarean section causing generalized spasticity and blindness due to occipital lobe damage. In April, 1982, she delivered a premature child after 8 months' gestation, and had central placenta praevia (placentaccreta). The child was delivered by Caesarean section and, because of two severe episodes of post partum haemorrhage where the patient had lost 7500 mL of blood and developed severe shock, a subtotal hysterectomy was performed. The patient suffered a cardiac arrest during this. She also developed a deep venous thrombosis of her left leg, a pelvic abscess and septicaemia. The patient remained comatose for two months and when she regained consciousness had difficulty with speech and sight and diminished motor power, all of which indicated residual cerebral deficit.

Behavioural Observations

Because of the patient's level of incapacitation a house call was made. It was noted that she used a wheelchair and walking frame. When seen for testing the patient was co-operative but obviously limited in the number of tests that she could complete. For example, she was unable to cope with visuo-spatial items because of her cortical blindness. Other members of the family were available to contribute to the history.

The patient and her family stated that she was in good health before her operation and had no previous head injuries or psychiatric problems. She lived a normal life, worked in factories and held a driver's licence. When examined, she led a vegetative existence confined to her wheelchair. The patient was particularly regretful that she has lost custody of her children because of her disabilities. Her former husband refers to her as a "robot", and has abandoned her. She lives with her parents and other relatives in an extended family system.

Intellectual Functioning

Superficially, the patient gives an impression of generally normal intelligence because of her adequate comprehension and vocabulary level, which remains within the average range. However, significant brain damage always has functional cognitive consequences.

Premorbid intellectual functioning was estimated to be within the average range on the basis of adequate comprehension and vocabulary level at the time of examination, and 10th grade level of education. The patient's verbal IQ score is currently 95 (37th percentile) which falls within the lower level of the average range. However, performance and full scale IQ scores cannot be calculated because of the patient's visual and other limitations. Whatever intellectual resources remain cannot be given full functional expression because of such limitations together with an impairment of memory and concentration. For example, the patient is no longer able to read and write.

Educational Achievement

Educational achievement could not be validly assessed because the patient was unable to complete the standardized tests. She is unable to read, or write down mathematical calculations, because of her cortical blindness. Spelling also could not be meaningfully assessed as she is an immigrant and English is her second language. The patient was reputedly an average student in her native country.

Sensory-Motor Functioning

The patient was apparently right handed before her operation. Power was relatively adequate in her arms, but this had little functional advantage because of the extent of spasticity and the lack of co-ordination in all her limbs. Gross motor speed and fine motor co-ordination were profoundly disturbed in the upper limbs. There was also evidence of borderline sensory loss. Auditory perceptual functioning was below average as the patient had difficulty in differentiating between pairs of rhythms and differing consonant sounds. Tactile perceptual functioning was borderline as the patient was vaguely confused on some of the items involving bilateral stimulation of the body. However, there were no marked errors for finger agnosia, graphaesthesia and stereognosis.

Visuo-spatial Functioning

Visuo-spatial functioning was inherently and profoundly impaired. The patient was unable to complete any visuo-spatial tests. At most, she is able to see colours and forms at close contact.

Language Ability

Language ability was impaired. Speech was slow, monotonous and slurred, but remained understandable. Such a pattern of articulation is not uncommonly associated with brain stem type injuries. Word finding fluency was severely impaired (4th percentile) and thus suggestive of a central expressive disorder. As mentioned previously, the patient was unable to read and write. However, comprehension and listening skills were relatively adequate.

Memory Processes

The patient obtained a general memory quotient of 64 (1st percentile) which fell within the mentally retarded range. Immediate and recent memory were impaired, but remote memory remained relatively intact. The ability to learn new information was severely impaired.

Personality Organization

As the patient cannot read, she was unable to attempt the Minnesota multiphasic personality inventory. Consequently, the shorter number of items in the neuroticism scale questionnaire were read to the patient and her responses appropriately noted by the examiner. The resultant profile was suggestive of the presence of marked anxiety. However, she did not appear to be clinically depressed despite the magnitude of her losses, both physical and emotional.

From the functional viewpoint, the patient is no longer the same person she was before the operation. Her lifestyle has altered profoundly from that of a normal, active married female to that of an invalid, confined to a wheelchair and leading a vegetative existence. Fortunately, she feels reasonably adjusted and secure within the confines of the extended family system in which she lives.

Diagnostic Impression

Severely diffuse impairment of cognitive function associated with cerebral anoxia.

Comments

In summary, Elvina Bugeja is an individual of estimated average premorbid intelligence who displayed a severely generalized pattern of cognitive deterioration (Fig. 4). There were no clear lateralizing signs on the tests, this pattern being compatible with the involvement of both hemispheres. She was found to have profound intellectual, motor, visuo-spatial, language and memory disabilities. Her medical history suggests that these are most probably a direct result of the severe brain damage that she sustained after her operation.

This unfortunate individual appears to be totally and permanently disabled for gainful employment and obviously there are limitations on her enjoyment of normal social activities.

Mrs Bugeja's major strength is the extremely supportive extended family system in which she lives. Without such support, she would require institutional care as her capacity for independent living is non-existent.

The prognosis is poor and the incapacitation appears to be permanent. Further speech therapy and some physiotherapy may be beneficial as the patient does not appear to have given these modalities a sufficiently fair trial. The patient now spends most of the day sitting at home listening to television. It may be appropriate to reinforce a wider range of stimulating activities, both inside and outside her home.

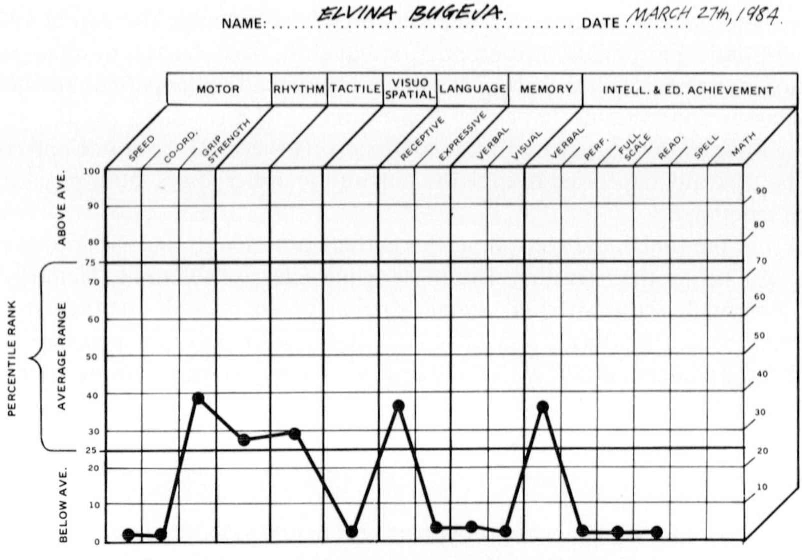

Fig. 4: Neuropsychological profile in percentile ranks

Appendix to Case 4 (Test Score Record Form) (March 27th, 1984)

Laterality preference schedule: Premorbid history of consistent right hand dominance.

Grooved pegboard: Dominant Hand = Unable to do*
Non-Dominant Hand = Unable to do*

*Indicates score in impaired range.

Finger tapping test: Dominant Hand = Unable to do*
Non-Dominant Hand = Unable to do*

Hand dynamometer: Dominant Hand = Normal
Non-Dominant Hand = Normal

Speech–sounds perception test: Borderline score*
Seashore rhythm test: Rank of 10 (moderately impaired)*
Tactile perceptual functioning: Borderline scores*
Trail making test: Unable to complete*
Benton visual retention test: Unable to complete*
Aphasia language performance scales:
Listening within normal limits
Reading unable to read functionally (blind)*
Talking outside normal limits*
Writing unable to write functionally (blind)*
Controlled word association test: 4th percentile*
Wechsler memory scale:
Memory quotient = 64 (1st percentile)*
Verbal short-term memory = outside normal limits*
Verbal long-term memory = outside normal limits*
Semantic % retained = outside normal limits*
Visual short-term memory = unable to complete*
Visual long-term memory = unable to complete*
Visual % retained = unable to complete*
Complex figure: Unable to complete*
Walton–Black: Learned three new words in five trials (outside normal limits)*
Wechsler adult intelligence scale (in percentile ranks):

Information	50th percentile	Digit symbol	Unable to complete*
Comprehension	50th percentile	Picture completion	Unable to complete*
Arithmetic	16th percentile*	Block design	Unable to complete*
Similarities	63rd percentile	Picture arrangement	Unable to complete*
Digit span	16th percentile	Object assembly	Unable to complete*
Vocabulary	50th percentile	Performance IQ =	Could not be calculated*
Verbal IQ = 95 (37th percentile)		Full scale IQ =	Could not be calculated*

Stroop: Unable to complete.*
Wide range achievement test:
Reading unable to complete.*
Spelling unable to complete.*
Maths unable to complete.*

CASE 5: REPORT OF NEUROPSYCHOLOGICAL EXAMINATION

Name: Dr Peter Smith *Age:* 51 years
Purpose of evaluation: Neuropsychological examination including assessment of memory, attention and judgement as well as competency to continue veterinary practice
Referred by: Physician *Date:* October 1, 1982

Evaluation based upon the following

LATERAL DOMINANCE
Hand/feet dominance survey

MOTOR FUNCTIONING
Grooved pegboard
Finger tapping test
Hand dynanometer

AUDITORY PERCEPTUAL FUNCTIONING
Seashore rhythm test

TACTILE PERCEPTUAL FUNCTIONING
Stereognosis survey
Finger agnosia
Graphaesthesia

VISUO-SPATIAL FUNCTIONING
Trail making test (Part B)
Benton visual retention test
Rey–Osterrieth complex figure test (copy)

LANGUAGE ABILITY
Controlled word association test
Modified token test

INTELLECTUAL FUNCTIONING
Wechsler adult intelligence scale
Stroop colour–word test

MEMORY PROCESSES
Wechsler memory scale (modified)
Rey–Osterrieth complex figure test (recall)

EDUCATIONAL ACHIEVEMENT
Wide range achievement test

PERSONALITY ORGANIZATION

Neuropsychological structured interview

History and Behavioural Observations

Dr Peter Smith is a 51-year-old divorced veterinary surgeon who was referred for a neuropsychological examination after a severe cerebrovascular accident in February, 1982. Repeated computerized tomography on August 14, 1982, revealed a large infarction involving the right middle cerebral artery territory with associated loss of cerebral tissue on the right side. The results of electroencephalography performed on the same day were normal.

When seen for evaluation, Dr Smith was alert and well orientated, but his affect was somewhat blunted. He was understandably quite anxious and concerned about his performance on the various tests and whether the outcome of the examination would affect his future career. Dr Smith had recently consulted a cardiologist complaining of chest pain. This may have been related to his anxiety concerning the assessment.

Dr Smith has only been working for three hours per day over the past few months. He complained of a general loss of interest as well as difficulties with fine motor co-ordination. He reported having experienced difficulties at work whilst performing certain surgical procedures.

Dr Smith has discontinued his hobby—illustrating children's books—because of his loss of interest and problems with fine motor co-ordination.

He completed all the tasks assigned to him during the assessment.

Intellectual Functioning

Dr Smith obtained a verbal IQ score of 131 (98th percentile), a performance IQ score of 112 (79th percentile) and a full scale IQ score of 124 (94th percentile). He is currently functioning intellectually within the superior range of intelligence. Premorbid intelligence was estimated to fall within the superior range of intelligence using Mahan's converted residual technique and demographic statistical formulae. There was no statistically significant evidence of a marked global deterioration in his intellectual functioning. However, there was evidence of subtest scatter on the Wechsler adult intelligence scale with a significant scale score deviation on the picture arrangement subtest. This subtest provides the evaluation of several major skills including visual perception of individual pictures, organization of a series of pictures, awareness of social sequences, planning skills, ability to form and test hypotheses, flexibility and a general ability to sequence material in a logical order.

Educational Achievement

Dr Smith's profile on the wide range achievement test was discrepant with his estimated premorbid intelligence, level of scholastic attainment and current vocational performance. His spelling was at the 47th percentile and his mathematical ability at the 32nd percentile. Dr Smith reported that his spelling had always been poor and attributed this to inadequate tuition at school during World War II. His poor performance on a test of mathematical ability probably reflects impaired concentration and difficulties with spatial reasoning. Examples of errors made include: $6\frac{1}{4} + 1\frac{5}{8} + 4\frac{1}{2} = 6\frac{1}{2}$; and $809 \times 47 = 33\,023$.

Neuropsychological Functioning

Dr Smith demonstrated consistent right hand dominance. Most individuals with right hand dominance have verbal functions represented in the left hemisphere with visuo-spatial skills in the right. His gross motor speed in the upper limbs was intact. Fine motor co-ordination was impaired in the left hand. Power was normal in the arms.

Auditory perceptual functioning was intact. Dr Smith had no difficulty in differentiating pairs of rhythms.

Tactile perceptual functioning was relatively intact. He was unable to distinguish one number out of four written on the palm of his left hand. There were no errors for finger agnosia and stereognosis.

Visuo-spatial functioning was within normal limits. There was no evidence of constructional dyspraxia. Visual memory was intact.

Language ability was generally adequate. There was no evidence of dysarthria or dysphasia. His vocabulary level fell within the very superior range. Motor aspects of speech were intact and there was no evidence of disturbance in articulation and repetition. Comprehension of speech was adequate and there was no evidence to suggest a receptive aphasia. Dr Smith experienced word finding difficulties, but these appeared to be related to his high level of anxiety during the assessment rather than to an expressive aphasia.

Dr Smith obtained a general memory quotient of 116 which fell within the bright normal range (85th percentile). This was relatively consistent with his estimated premorbid intelligence.

Immediate memory was intact. However, recent memory, including the ability to learn new verbal information, was impaired.

The freedom from distractibility quotient was 113 (80th percentile) and fell within the bright normal range. There was no evidence of a marked impairment of concentration, residual attentional deficits or other deficiencies in low level processing functions.

Comments

Dr Smith is currently functioning intellectually within the superior range of intelligence which is consistent with his estimated premorbid intellectual capabilities. There was no evidence to suggest a clinically significant deterioration in his global intellectual abilities. However, a number of specific deficits were apparent, including difficulties with planning and judgement, mathematical calculations, short term memory difficulties, and a reduced ability to acquire new verbal information. These impairments are consistent with the structural damage that has occurred (Fig. 5). It is the neuropsychologist's opinion that these mild deficits may adversely affect his clinical judgement in tasks requiring complex decision making. However, he may cope quite adequately with less complicated, well learned routine procedures. At present, it would appear to be in his best interest not to carry a heavy case-load or to assume a large degree of responsibility in the practice.

Improvements in neuropsychological functioning occur up to three years after trauma. It is suggested that Dr Smith's condition be reassessed in 12 months' time.

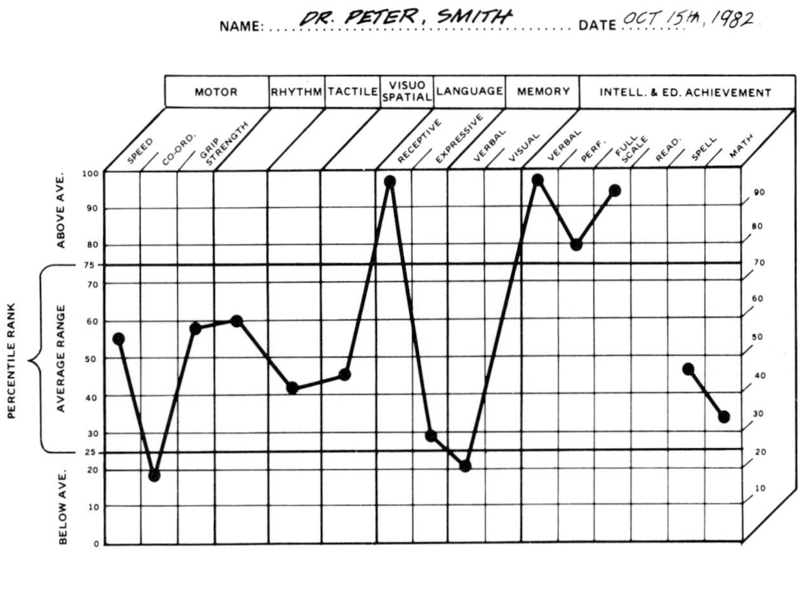

Fig. 5: Neuropsychological profile in percentile ranks

Appendix to Case 5 (test score record form) (October 1st, 1982)

Laterality preference schedule: Consistent right hand dominance.
Grooved pegboard: Dominant Hand = 65 secs
Non-Dominant Hand = 91 secs*
Finger tapping test: Dominant Hand = 64 taps
Non-Dominant Hand = 55 taps
Hand dynamometer: Dominant Hand = normal
Non-Dominant Hand = normal
Seashore rhythm test: Within normal limits
Tactile perceptual functioning: One error (within normal limits).
Trail making test: 23rd percentile*
Benton visual retention test: Within normal limits.
Token test: Within normal limits.
Controlled word association test: 29th percentile.
Wechsler memory scale:
Memory quotient = 116 (85th percentile)
Verbal short-term memory = within normal limits*
Verbal long-term memory = outside normal limits*
Semantic % retained = 33%*
Visual short-term memory = within normal limits
Visual long-term memory = within normal limits*
Visual % retained = 100%*
Complex figure: Copying = normal; recall = borderline*
Wechsler adult intelligence scale (in percentile ranks):

Information	98th percentile	Digit symbol	63rd percentile
Comprehension	98th percentile	Picture completion	95th percentile
Arithmetic	75th percentile	Block design	63rd percentile
Similarities	91st percentile	Picture arrangement	16th percentile
Digit span	91st percentile	Object assembly	84th percentile
Vocabulary	98th percentile	Performance IQ = 112	(79th percentile)
Verbal IQ = 131	(98th percentile)	Full scale IQ = 124	(94th percentile)

Stroop: Within normal limits.

Wide range achievement test:
Reading not administered.
Spelling 47th percentile.
Maths 32nd percentile*.

*Indicates score in impaired range.

CASE 6: REPORT OF NEUROPSYCHOLOGICAL ASSESSMENT

Name: Verity Stark *Age:* 24 years
Purpose of evaluation: Medico-legal report
Referred by: Plaintiff's lawyer *Date:* March 28th, 1984; April 2nd, 1984

Evaluation based upon the following

MOTOR FUNCTIONING
Laterality preference schedule
Grooved pegboard
Finger tapping test
Hand dynamometer

AUDITORY PERCEPTUAL FUNCTIONING
Speech–sounds perception test
Seashore rhythm test

TACTILE PERCEPTUAL FUNCTIONING
Face hand test
Finger agnosia
Graphaesthesia
Tactile form recognition test

VISUO-SPATIAL FUNCTIONING
Trail making test (Part B)
Benton visual retention test
Rey–Osterrieth complex figure test (copy)

LANGUAGE ABILITY
Aphasia language performance scales
Controlled word association test

MEMORY PROCESSES
Modified Wechsler memory scale
Rey–Osterrieth complex figure test (recall)
Walton–Black modified new word learning test

HIGHER COGNITIVE PROCESSES
Wechsler adult intelligence scale–revised
Wide range achievement test
Stroop colour–word test

PERSONALITY ORGANIZATION
Minnesota multiphasic personality inventory
Neuropsychological structured interview

History

Verity Stark is a 24-year-old Australian female who was referred for a neuropsychological evaluation by her lawyer after a motor vehicle accident on September 11th, 1981. Available medical reports show that she sustained a severe head injury.

She was admitted to the local hospital in a conscious state, but cerebral function was clearly impaired. A diagnosis was made of brain contusion to both frontal lobes. The patient remained drowsy, confused and disoriented for two weeks when she was transferred to a major metropolitan hospital for further investigation. Computerized tomography demonstrated that the ventricles were marginally enlarged, but did not show ventricular displacement, cerebral contusion or intracranial haematoma. Electroencephalography showed a 10 Hz alpha rhythm and a moderate excess of slow wave activity, mostly marked over the frontal and temporal poles. Electroencephalography six weeks later showed normal results, however. The duration of amnesia after trauma was estimated to be between two to three weeks. The hospital discharge summary concluded as follows: "Neurologically, there were no focal signs. The patient was quite alert and oriented and co-operative. Her recent memory did not appear to be markedly impaired. The clinical findings seemed to be consistent with a recent head injury with only some mild mental changes which appeared to be improving. Her prognosis remains good for continued recovery".

It was noted that the patient had been repeatedly investigated for medico-legal purposes. A count through encyclopaedic medical files revealed involvement with 51 doctors during the past three years. The patient's life consisted of attending medical appointments. This not unusual litigation process generated a voluminous and sometimes conflicting data base. Consequently, two neuropsychological assessments were scheduled three weeks apart in order to give time to integrate this massive data base, and to allow a more detailed evaluation of the patient.* The rationale of these cross-checking procedures is discussed by Boyar (1981).

The patient is a horsewoman and had had three riding accidents in early childhood. These resulted in concussion and limb fractures. She had a history of irregular menstruation. She had always been an above average student until her final year of high school. Throughout elementary school she was top of the class. In high school, the level of achievement progressively de-

*Note that this report provides only the quantitative data base for the second report dated April 2nd, 1984.

creased and the patient obtained a mediocre pass in her final year. There was a history of chronic family conflict. Her parents finally divorced after the patient's high school graduation. Her parents still do not speak to each other. After the completion of high school, the patient enrolled in a nursing course at a large metropolitan hospital, but failed her second year examination and was asked to leave. She returned to her home in the country and enrolled in the local nursing school. The patient passed her second year examinations and was in her third year of training at the time of the accident (September 11th, 1981). She had been involved in another motor vehicle accident on December 31st, 1980, but no objective details were available. After the accident the patient had indulged in a six-month period of promiscuity which she stated she now regretted. There was also one uncharacteristic episode of aggressive behaviour in 1983. She returned to nursing in 1982, but resigned voluntarily after one month.

Behavioural Observations

When seen for testing Miss Stark proved to be a well groomed young woman. She was alert and well oriented. Her test taking attitude was satisfactory. Her behaviour was generally appropriate, although there were signs suggestive of disinhibition in the form of a mildly overfamiliar and relaxed manner. It was not known whether this could be attributed to the fact that she had seen so many doctors and consequently had become desensitized to medico-legal examination. However, there was one clear incident of social inappropriateness when the patient complained that it was hot and that her bra was too tight and she loosened the strap of her bra in the presence of the examiner.

Symptomatology

Miss Stark described her problems in a rather apathetic manner, listing them as follows:

1. Impairment of memory and concentration.
2. Random headaches.
3. Personality change (moody, irritable, depressed, unable to maintain long term friendships, and lack of confidence).
4. Frequent dizzy spells.
5. Orthopaedic restrictions (for example, a stiff left knee).
6. Unable to return to nursing because of the above problems.

The patient explained that her memory has been improving over time. A major problem was loss of confidence. She had a particular fear of falling and hitting her head. This fear had generalized to the extent that she feared trying new things. She was depressed by the fact that she was unemployed. The patient also admitted that she resented the continual medical investigations arranged by her own lawyers and the insurance company, that she was forced to undergo.

Intellectual Functioning

The patient achieved a verbal IQ score of 120, a performance IQ score of 115 and a full scale IQ score of 121 during first testing. Further testing resulted in essentially similar scores (verbal IQ score of 119, performance IQ score of 115 and a full scale IQ score of 120). These scores suggested that her intellectual functioning remained generally within the superior range (approximately 90th percentile). Premorbid intelligence was estimated to fall within a similar range on the basis of her early educational performance. Intellectual deficits were not apparent with the results of subtests of the Wechsler adult intelligence scale and there were isolated, but marked, discrepancies on the digit span and digit symbol subtests during both testing and retesting. The same pattern of discrepancies was noted in other psychological reports. This may be indicative of residual deficits in immediate memory or of an impairment of concentration or may be a general indicator of the presence of cerebral dysfunction.

Higher cognitive functions (comprehension, and abstract thinking) appeared to be adequate. However, the patient failed the complex figure test. A clinically significant discrepancy between copying and memory scores was noted. However, this was not due to a primary disorder of memory, as the patient's visual memory remains superior. Rather, there was a disruption in planning functions (piecemeal approach) according to Visser's (1980) criteria for evaluating the drawing sequence. The patient's difficulties were suggestive of frontal lobe involvement.

Educational Achievement

Reading skills were at 11.0 grade level (86th percentile); spelling at 11.2 grade level (82nd percentile); and maths at 10.3 grade level. These standardized achievement scores are relatively consistent with premorbid intelligence and level of scholastic attainment. There is no evidence of specific learning disability.

Motor Functioning

The patient demonstrated consistent right hand dominance. Her gross motor speed and fine motor co-ordination was adequate in the upper limbs. Power was also normal in the arms.

Auditory Perceptual Functioning

There was no evidence of objective sensory loss. Auditory perceptual functioning was intact as the patient could adequately differentiate between pairs of rhythms. Also, there were no difficulties in discriminating between different consonant sounds.

Tactile Perceptual Functioning

Tactile perceptual functioning was also satisfactory. No errors of extinction or displacement occurred. There were no errors for finger agnosia, graphaesthesia or stereognosis.

Visuo-spatial Functioning

Visuo-spatial functioning appeared to be generally adequate. There was no evidence of constructional dyspraxia. There was no evidence of marked visuomotor slowing (except for one isolated discrepancy on digit symbol). Visual memory was also intact.

Language Ability

Language ability remains intact. There was no evidence of dysarthria or dysphasia. The patient was able to express herself clearly and articulately. Word finding fluency was above average (approximately 70th percentile), thus ruling out central expressive disorder. Comprehension, listening skills and reading ability were also intact, thus ruling out receptive aphasia. Dysgraphia was also excluded in the absence of an aphasic writing impairment.

Memory Processes

The patient obtained a general memory quotient of 134 (99th percentile) which fell within the very superior range. Scores for subtests of the Wechsler memory scale, together with the scores for more specific tests, document that recent memory, the ability to learn both new verbal and visual information and remote memory are all intact. This was a surprisingly good performance and evidence of "better than expected" performance after serious head injury. However, there was evidence of an impairment of immediate memory and associated impairment of concentration.

Personality Organization

The profile configuration of the Minnesota multiphasic personality inventory (MMPI) (computer administered, scored and interpreted) was clinically unremarkable. A valid profile was elicited, but no markedly useful hypotheses were generated. However, there were suggestions of a mildly neurotic trend (mild depression and anxiety).

A "normal" MMPI profile does not necessarily rule out organic personality change. The diagnostic use of the MMPI in organic brain dysfunction (despite the use of promising regression formula strategies) has not yet been established.

The possibility of an underlying accident-related behavioural change is difficult to evaluate in the absence of objective premorbid baselines. Some degree of personality disturbance before the accident may be reasonably postulated (school and vocational underachievement, history of irregular periods, and the family conflict and divorce). Collaborating data from objective observers (for example, nursing supervisors) who knew the patient before the accident are vital in this case. If it can be proved that there has been personality change after the accident, the change is most probably directly related to brain trauma.

There is sufficient evidence to suggest frontal lobe involvement. Diagnostic neurological investigations, behavioural observations of disinhibition reported by a number of doctors, and disturbance in planning functions on neuropsychological tests provide consistently complementary data to make this the most plausible explanation for the patient's condition.

As patients with frontal lobe syndromes tend not to display cognitive deficits during the structured confines of quantitative testing, the generally superior neuropsychological profile elicited from Miss Stark (Fig. 6) does not necessarily exclude such a diagnosis (Damasio, 1979).

Diagnostic Impression

Personality change due to traumatically induced frontal lobe dysfunction (mild/moderate), complicated by the litigation process, in a previously underachieving individual of superior intelligence.

Comments

In summary, Verity Stark is an individual of estimated superior premorbid intelligence with a history of educational and vocational underachievement who has sustained medically documented evidence of severe head injury.

There is also evidence of better than expected recovery of cognitive function within the context of such a severe head injury. A number of psychological reports suggest a reassuring progressive improvement over the past three years. Of course, the documentation of such a recovery process is also additional evidence that cerebral dysfunction originally occurred as a direct result of the patient's motor vehicle accident on September 11th, 1981.

The patient's generally superior neuropsychological profile (expressed in quantitive terms in the appendix to this case and Fig. 6) is not significantly discrepant from estimated premorbid intellectual status. However, some residual cognitive deficits are evident (impairment of immediate memory and concentration together with disruption in planning functions).

The patient's major handicap appears to be personality change due to traumatically induced frontal lobe dysfunction. Frontal lobe damage is known to produce disinhibition, apathy, lack of drive and lability of mood. This symptomatology has obviously deleterious implications for the maintenance of long-term interpersonal relationships and the pursuit of vocational advancement.

Through no fault of the patient, rehabilitation has been complicated by the litigation process. Continual and time consuming medical appointments alone have disrupted the prospects for continuing employment. It must be concluded that the patient has many potential strengths (she is young, in relatively good physical health, with superior intelligence and comprehension, intact educational skills, adequate visuo-spatial functioning, above average language ability and generally adequate memory processes). To what extent these assets can be capitalized upon during rehabilitation is uncertain, since the frontal lobe syndrome impairs executive functions which give coherent direction to such capabilities. Fortunately, behavioural evidence suggests that Miss Stark's personality change appears to be mild to moderate rather than profound.

Theoretically, the patient could attempt to return to nursing, a profession in which there are certain duties which can be performed within a highly structural environment and under direct medical supervision. Indeed, the patient did return to nursing for one month after the accident, leaving of her own volition rather than through any dissatisfaction on the part of her supervisors concerning the quality of her work. However, it is unlikely that the patient will return to nursing, or has the self-confidence to attempt to do so. It is more likely that the patient will eventually find employment requiring a lesser degree of skill.

In the interests of rehabilitation, a speedy resolution of litigation is highly recommended. The recognition of the psychological effects of the medicolegal process upon this patient is often unwittingly outlined in her voluminous file. For example, her own rehabilitation physician asserts that "she may well need more help in finding work and I would be quite happy to see her again about this or get her involved again in the rehabilitation service, but perhaps it might be more relevant to wait till after her court case". This revealing quote concedes that the litigation process is playing a significant part in her symptomatology and implies that once medico-legal issues are resolved then the more important tasks of rehabilitation can again take precedence.

Further information in Case 6

It may be of interest to provide an "insider's" perspective on what actually happens to medico-legal reports. The following scenario exemplifies how the adversary system must inherently involve friction between doctors, lawyers and judges in order to operate successfully. The winners are the lawyers and, to a lesser extent, the doctors, for these professionals are guaranteed payment for their efforts. Unfortunately, the plaintiff–patient has no such guarantee of adequate financial compensation, but can only be certain of their symptoms (which tend to remain despite the resolution of litigation).

The Doctors

The vast number of clinicians who may be involved in a large third party claim minimizes the significance of any neuropsychological report. For example, as many as 50 doctors could have been involved in the Verity Stark case and the neuropsychological report would make up less than two per cent of the medical data base. This voluminous information is elicited from a single patient. The very process of doing such intensive examinations over a number of years psychologically alters the person being studied and, hence, the very nature of the data base. Consequently, the quality of such an extensive data base tends to be variable, and contains inevitable inconsistencies. Too many cooks do indeed spoil the "clinical" broth.

The Lawyers

The duties of lawyers and behavioural scientists are not necessarily synonymous and may often be in conflict. Effective lawyers are not concerned with facts *per se* but with the expedient use of them to serve the financial interests of their client, be it an individual or an insurance company. The underlying legal concern is that the amount awarded to the plaintiff for future economic loss is most meagre and it is in respect to this component that the defendant's lawyers are most desirous of mitigating loss. In this they succeeded. The other components were not unqualified successes but their main objective was attained, so on the whole they cannot grumble.

Thus, it is not within the interest of lawyers to present available clinical reports in a balanced or representative manner. Rather, clinical data is selectively chosen to help win a case. It is not unusual for lawyers to subtly pressure clinicians to add or to change the emphasis of data to facilitate victory in forensic struggle. In fact, the basis of cross-examination is to recreate the facts in the way the lawyer would like them to be, if possible. Such influences are inherent within the adversary system and at odds with the ideals of clinical objectivity.

The Judge

The judge has the unenviable task of refereeing confrontations between the legal adversaries whilst integrating the potentially contradictory opinions of expert witnesses in a balanced manner.

The judge is faced with complex technical data, some of which he or she does not have the background to understand. Thus it is an advantage not to emphasize technical terms when writing medico-legal reports as their worth will be assessed by laypersons.

The whole facts are not of interest to the judge since his or her decisions are based purely upon the content and mode of presentation of legally admissible evidence within the confines of the courtroom. Consequently, the style of presentation can be as important as the facts themselves. How well an expert witness can defend their findings under cross-examinations contributes enormously to the weight of such evidence.

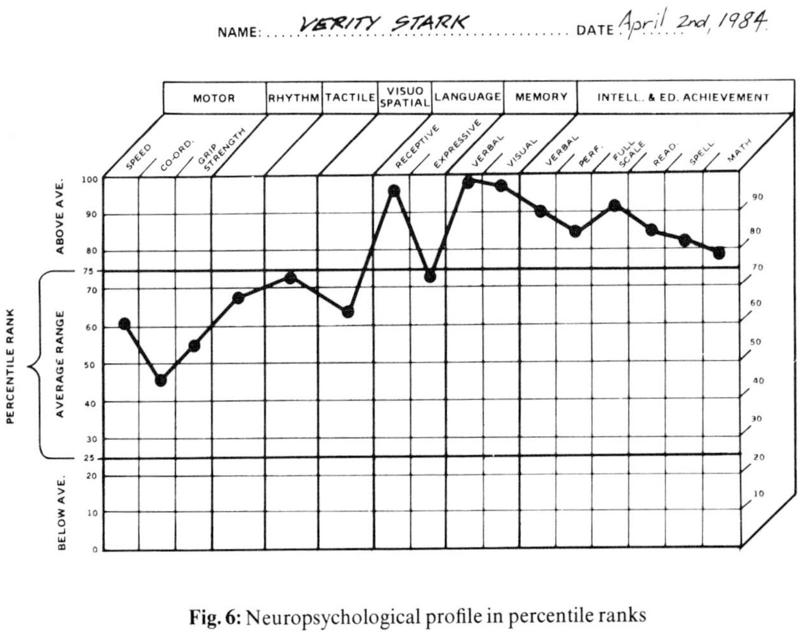

Fig. 6: Neuropsychological profile in percentile ranks

Appendix to Case 6 (test score record form)

Laterality preference schedule: Consistent right hand dominance.
Grooved pegboard: Dominant Hand = 62 secs
Non-Dominant Hand = 65 secs*
Finger tapping test: Dominant Hand = 54 taps
Non-Dominant Hand = 49 taps
Hand dynamometer: Dominant Hand = Normal
Non-Dominant Hand = Normal
Speech sounds perception test: Within normal limits.
Seashore rhythm test: Rank score of 2 (within normal limits).
Tactile perceptual functioning: Within normal limits.
Trail making test: 70 secs (50th percentile)
Benton visual retention test: Within normal limits.
Aphasia language performance scales:
Listening within normal limits.
Reading within normal limits.
Talking within normal limits.
Writing within normal limits.
Controlled word association test: 72nd percentile
Wechsler memory scale:
Memory quotient = 134 (99th percentile)
Verbal short-term memory = Within normal limits
Verbal long-term memory = Within normal limits
Semantic % retained = 97%*
Visual short-term memory = Within normal limits
Visual long-term memory = Within normal limits
Visual % retained = 95%*
Complex figure: Copying (normal); recall (outside normal limits).*
Walton–Black: Within normal limits.
Wechsler adult intelligence scale (in percentile ranks):

Information	91st percentile	Digit symbol	9th percentile*
Comprehension	98th percentile	Picture completion	91st percentile
Arithmetic	75th percentile	Block design	91st percentile
Similarities	95th percentile	Picture arrangement	95th percentile
Digit span	1st percentile	Object assembly	75th percentile
Vocabulary	95th percentile	Performance IQ = 115	(84th percentile)*
Verbal IQ = 119	(90th percentile)	Full scale IQ = 120	(91st percentile)

Stroop: 40 secs (within normal limits).

*Indicates score in impaired range.

Wide range achievment test:
Reading 11.0 grade level (86th percentile)
Spelling 11.2 grade level (82nd percentile)
Maths 10.3 grade level (79th percentile)

CASE 7: REPORT OF NEUROPSYCHOLOGICAL ASSESSMENT

Name: Lorna Jordan *Age:* 19 years
Purpose of evaluation: Routine assessment of cognitive defects
Referred by: Rehabilitation physician *Date:* November 26th, 1984

Evaluation based upon the following

MOTOR FUNCTIONING
Laterality preference schedule
Grooved pegboard
Finger tapping test
Hand dynamometer

AUDITORY PERCEPTUAL FUNCTIONING
Speech–sounds perception test
Seashore rhythm test

TACTILE PERCEPTUAL FUNCTIONING
Face hand test
Finger agnosia
Graphaesthesia
Tactile form recognition test

VISUO-SPATIAL FUNCTIONING
Trail making test (Part B)
Benton visual retention test
Rey–Osterrieth complex figure test (copy)

LANGUAGE ABILITY
Aphasia language performance scales
Controlled word association test

MEMORY PROCESSES
Modified Wechsler memory scale
Rey–Osterrieth complex figure test (recall)
Walton–Black modified new word learning test

HIGHER COGNITIVE PROCESSES
Wechsler adult intelligence scale–revised
Wide range achievement test
Stroop colour–word test

PERSONALITY ORGANIZATION
Minnesota multiphasic personality inventory
Neuropsychological structured interview

History

Lorna Jordan is a single, 19-year-old Australian female who was referred by her rehabilitation physician for a routine evaluation of her cognitive strengths and deficits. She had been involved in an industrial accident on February 2nd, 1984, when she fell from a ladder whilst stocking produce at the supermarket where she worked. She stated that she lost consciousness, but could give very few further specific details. Apparently, she was sent home from the hospital after some hours of neurological observation. Consequently, it is unlikely that she was diagnosed as having a severe head injury.

The patient left school at the age of 16 years, when she had reached the 10th grade. She has worked mostly as a waitress and at the check-out counter of supermarkets. She denied any previous or subsequent head injuries or psychiatric problems.

Behavioural Observations

When seen for testing, the patient was relatively alert and well orientated but apathetic. She proved to be an extremely vague historian. Thus there was a paucity of information on which to formulate hypotheses. She seemed to know little of the current activities of her immediate family and appeared to be estranged from them, though she still lived in the same house.

Her test taking attitude was relatively inadequate. She appeared to be demoralized and so not motivated to produce maximal performance on the tasks. The patient appeared to lose concentration at times and often asked to have instructions repeated to her.

Symptomatology

The patient listed the following problems since the accident:

1. Impairment of memory and concentration.
2. Insomnia.

3. Persistent severe headaches accompanied by double vision which stop her from driving a motor vehicle.
4. Episodes of dizziness.
5. Personality change (anxious and depressed, socially isolated, and loss of libido).
6. Inability to work because of the above symptoms.

She stated that there had been no improvement in her condition, and that she spent most days resting because of severe headaches.

Intellectual Function

The patient achieved a verbal IQ score of 93 (32nd percentile), a performance IQ score of 69 (2nd percentile) and a full scale IQ score of 80 (9th percentile). This shows a significant difference between verbal and performance IQ scores. Premorbid intelligence was estimated to be within the low average range, approximating the patient's verbal IQ score.

Marked intellectual impairments were noted with the results of the subtests of the Wechsler adult intelligence scale. There was evidence of subtest scatter in the form of clinically significant scale score deviations, especially for visuo-spatial items. However, higher cognitive functions (comprehension, abstract thinking, and problem solving) appeared to be generally intact.

Educational Achievement

Reading skills were at 7.8 grade level (37th percentile); spelling at 5.2 grade level (7th percentile); and maths at 8.8 grade level (61st percentile). These standardized achievement scores are relatively consistent with the patient's severe spelling deficiency. There is some evidence of specific learning disability in this area. There is also evidence of lack of interest in the academic area. It is probable that she has been a school underachiever, and that this has compounded her spelling disability.

Motor Functioning

The patient demonstrated ambidexterity with mixed cerebral dominance. Gross motor speed in both upper limbs was impaired. Fine motor coordination was also inadequate. Power was well below average in the arms.

Auditory Perceptual Functioning

Auditory perceptual functioning was impaired. The patient made a large number of errors in differentiating between pairs of rhythms. Inadequate performance was also noted when the patient was attempting to discriminate between different consonant sounds.

Tactile Perceptual Functioning

Tactile perceptual functioning was relatively intact. No errors of extinction or displacement occurred. There were no errors for finger agnosia, graphaesthesia or stereognosis.

Visuo-spatial Functioning

Visuo-spatial functioning appeared to be impaired. Visuomotor speed was impaired. Visual memory was also inadequate. However, there was no evidence of constructional dyspraxia.

Language Ability

Language ability was relatively intact. There was no evidence of dysarthria or dysphasia. Vocabulary level fell within the average range (50th percentile). Motor aspects of speech were intact as there was no evidence of disturbance in articulation or repetition. Speech comprehension was adequate. Word finding fluency was intact (35th percentile). There was no evidence of a reading disability. Writing ability was adequate. However, a specific learning disability was noted for spelling.

Memory Processes

The patient obtained a general memory quotient of 69 (2nd percentile) which fell within the mentally retarded range. This was relatively discrepant from estimated low-average premorbid intelligence. Immediate memory was impaired. Recent memory, including the ability to learn both new verbal and visual information, was also impaired. However, remote memory was satisfactory.

Personality Organization

The patient's performance on the personality inventories was unsatisfactory. A valid profile on the Minnesota multiphasic personality inventory could not be elicited because the validity scales were violated (that is, the patient endorsed an unusually high number of severe psychiatric symptoms).

Comments

Lorna Jordan is an individual of estimated low average premorbid intelligence with a specific learning disability for spelling that has been present throughout her life. There is some evidence that she has been a school underachiever.

Unfortunately, it is not possible to give a satisfactory account of Miss Jordan's actual cognitive status as the neuropsychological profile elicited (see Fig. 7) is meaningless within the context of the history obtained and the clinical presentation. She has sustained a minor head injury yet presented with a scattered profile of dramatic deficits which does not readily fit any plausible pattern for the known organic brain syndromes. We have hypothesized that she is a demoralized, depressed individual showing the vague symptoms of the post-traumatic syndrome and is thus unable to produce maximal performance on the tests.

Her actual test scores cannot be accepted at face value. For example, the memory deficits she displays can only occur in severely deteriorated individuals with documented profound brain damage. She is obviously exaggerating her deficits and perhaps even blatantly malingering. Rather than attempt to make sense of such data it was decided to schedule her for further testing in four weeks' time.

Commentary

As too rarely happens in such cases, information arrived from reliable sources that made further testing of this patient unnecessary. Her rehabilitation physician had ascertained from hospital records that her "head injury" was indeed trivial without loss of consciousness or any significant neurological signs. More disturbingly, police records showed that the family business consisted predominantly of car stealing and freighting such contraband across state borders. The patient herself had convictions for drug offences and larceny. She had no history of continuous employment and had only been working at the supermarket where the accident took place for three weeks.

Rehabilitation unit records reveal that her participation in rehabilitation was perfunctory and that she had been eventually asked to leave because of lack of effort. Apparently, her obvious motivations for attending were to maintain a sickness benefits pension and to facilitate her worker's compensation claim.

Finally, this rather blatant attempt at fraud was not lost upon the insurance company contesting her case. Their private investigators were able to produce films of the patient working part-time in a friend's hairdresser's shop after having been discharged from the rehabilitation unit. Also, films were available showing the patient driving a motor vehicle and carrying heavy pieces of equipment which belied the motor weakness exhibited during formal testing.

The patient's history, obtained from objective sources following the completion of testing, is suggestive of an anti-social personality disorder. However, it must be borne in mind that malingering may be seen in apparently well adjusted individuals without criminal records as well. Malingering is an act, rather than a mental status.

The profile described in Fig. 7, if typical of anything, illustrates the common tendency of individuals exaggerating their deficits to do poorly on sensory-motor tests. Visuo-spatial items are also concrete areas in which to display incompetence. More abstract tasks such as vocabulary level tend to elicit caution in malingerers. Unusually disturbed profiles on the Minnesota multiphasic personality inventory, associated with less than maximal performance on sensory-motor tests, are highly indicative of validity problems. It is preferable to believe such cases are rarely encountered in routine practice. However, neuropsychological deficits are relatively easy to fake as the results, unlike those in diagnostic neurology, are almost totally dependent on the patient's co-operation.

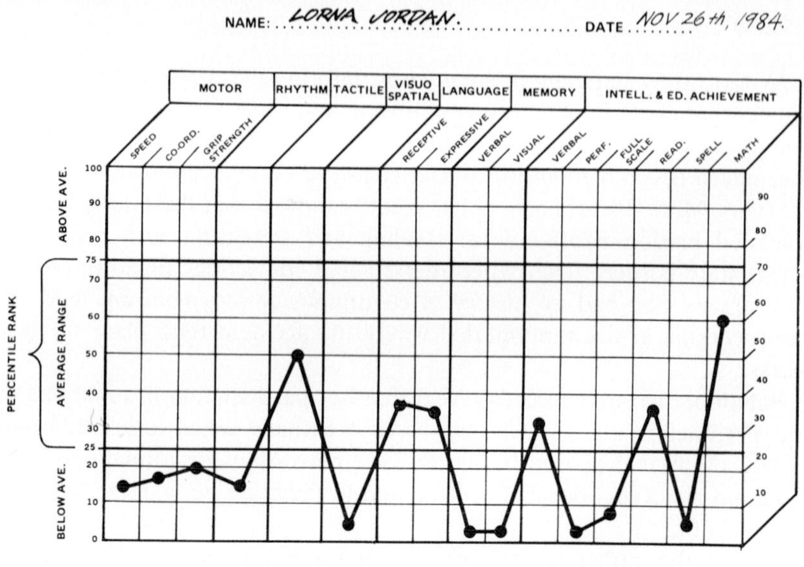

Fig. 7: Neuropsychological profile in percentile ranks

Appendix to Case 7 (test score record form) (November 26th, 1984)

Laterality preference schedule: Mixed dominance.
Grooved pegboard: Dominant Hand = 89 secs*
Non-Dominant Hand = 91 secs*
Finger tapping test: Dominant Hand = 32 taps*
Non-Dominant Hand = 33 taps*
Hand dynamometer: Dominant Hand = Abnormal*
Non-Dominant Hand = Abnormal*
Speech–sounds perception test: Outside normal limits.*
Seashore rhythm test: Outside normal limits.*
Tactile perceptual functioning: Within normal limits.
Trail making test: 172 secs (4th percentile)*
Benton visual retention test: Nine errors above expected score.*
Aphasia language performance scales:
Listening within normal limits.
Reading within normal limits.
Talking within normal limits.
Writing within normal limits.
Controlled word association test: 35th percentile
Wechsler memory scale:
Memory quotient = 69 (2nd percentile)*
Verbal short-term memory = Outside normal limits
Verbal long-term memory = Outside normal limits
Semantic % retained = Outside normal limits
Visual short-term memory = Outside normal limits
Visual long-term memory = Outside normal limits
Visual % retained = Outside normal limits
Complex figure: Outside normal limits.*
Walton–Black: Learned one new word in five trials.
Wechsler adult intelligence scales (in percentile ranks):

Information	50th percentile	Digit symbol	1st percentile*
Comprehension	37th percentile	Picture completion	2nd percentile*
Arithmetic	16th percentile	Block design	37th percentile
Similarities	37th percentile	Picture arrangement	5th percentile*
Digit span	1st percentile*	Object assembly	2nd percentile*
Vocabulary	50th percentile	Performance IQ = 69	(2nd Percentile)*
Verbal IQ = 93	(32nd percentile)	Full scale IQ = 80	(9th percentile)*

Stroop: Outside normal limits.*

*Indicates score in impaired range.

Wide range achievement test:
Reading 7.8 grade level (37th percentile)
Spelling 5.2 grade level (7th percentile)*
Maths 8.8 grade level (61st percentile)

Appendices*

*If required, these Appendices may be reproduced for educational or practical purposes provided that such reproduction complies with the copyright notice located on the reverse of the title page.

APPENDIX I, Part 1

Report of Adult Neuropsychological Assessment

Name: ______________________________ *Age:* __________
Purpose of evaluation: ______________________________
Referred by: ______________________________ *Date:* __________

Evaluation based upon the following

MOTOR FUNCTIONING
Laterality preference schedule
Grooved pegboard
Finger tapping test
Hand dynamometer

AUDITORY PERCEPTUAL FUNCTIONING
Speech–sound perception test
Seashore rhythm test

TACTILE PERCEPTUAL FUNCTIONING
Face hand test
Finger agnosia
Graphaesthesia
Tactile form recognition test

VISUO-SPATIAL FUNCTIONING
Trail making test (Part B)
Benton visual retention test
Rey–Osterrieth complex figure test (copy)

LANGUAGE ABILITY
Aphasia language performance scales
Controlled word association test

MEMORY PROCESSES
Modified Wechsler memory scale
Rey–Osterrieth complex figure test (Recall)
Walton–Black modified new word learning test

HIGHER COGNITIVE PROCESSES
Wechsler adult intelligence scale—revised
Wide range achievement test
Stroop colour–word test

PERSONALITY ORGANIZATION
Minnesota multiphasic personality inventory
Neuropsychological structured interview

Copyright © 1984 by Grune & Stratton Australia
Reproduced from *Handbook of Neuropsychological Assessment*.

APPENDIX I, Part 2

Report of Adolescent Neuropsychological Assessment

Name: ____________________________ *Age:* __________
Purpose of evaluation: ____________________________
Referred by: ____________________________ *Date:* __________

Evaluation based upon the following

MOTOR FUNCTIONING
Laterality preference schedule
Grooved pegboard
Finger tapping test
Hand dynamometer

AUDITORY PERCEPTUAL FUNCTIONING
Speech–sound perception test
Seashore rhythm test

TACTILE PERCEPTUAL FUNCTIONING
Face hand test
Finger agnosia
Graphaesthesia
Tactile form recognition test

VISUO-SPATIAL FUNCTIONING
Trail making test (Part B—children)
Benton visual retention test
Rey–Osterrieth complex figure test (copy)

LANGUAGE ABILITY
Aphasia language performance scales
Controlled word association test

MEMORY PROCESSES
Modified Wechsler memory scale
Rey–Osterrieth complex figure test (recall)
Walton–Black modified new word learning test

HIGHER COGNITIVE PROCESSES
Wechsler intelligence scale for children—revised
Wide range achievement test
Stroop colour–word test

PERSONALITY ORGANIZATION
Child behaviour checklist
Neuropsychological structured interview

Copyright © 1984 by Grune & Stratton Australia
Reproduced from *Handbook of Neuropsychological Assessment*.

APPENDIX I, Part 3

Neuropsychological Report

INSTRUCTIONS: Insert applicable test descriptors in the spaces provided, and strike out inapplicable phrases.

HISTORY

________________________________ is a ____ year old single/married male/female who was referred for a neuropsychological evaluation after a ____________________ on ______________________________
____
____
____
____

The patient left school at ______ years of age after completing ________ ________________________ and has worked mostly at ____________ ____________________. His/her current position is that of __________ ______________________. There were/were no previous or subsequent head injuries, neuropathological conditions or psychiatric problems. ______
____

BEHAVIOURAL OBSERVATIONS/PATHOGNOMONIC SIGNS

When seen for testing the patient was/was not alert and well oriented.
____

The following pathognomonic signs were noted: ____________________
____
____

SYMPTOMATOLOGY

The patient had noticed the following problems since [insert date of accident or onset of symptoms] ____________________________________

1. ____
2. ____
3. ____
4. ____
5. ____
6. ____
7. ____

These problems appear to be improving/getting worse/static.

Copyright © 1984 by Academic Press Australia.
Reproduced from *Handbook of Neuropsychological Assessment.*

INTELLECTUAL FUNCTIONING

The patient achieved a verbal IQ score of ______, a performance IQ score of ______, and a full scale IQ score of ______. These scores suggest that current intellectual functioning falls within the ______ range (______ percentile). Premorbid intelligence was estimated to fall within the ______ range (using Mahan's converted residual technique and demographic data statistical formulae). Thus, there was/was no statistically significant evidence of general IQ loss (loss of approximately ______ IQ points).
Marked intellectual impairments were/were not noted on the subtests of the WAIS/WISC. There was/was no evidence of subtest scatter in the form of clinically significant scale score deviations (for example, ______ ______).
Higher cognitive functions (comprehension, abstract thinking, problem solving) appeared to be generally intact/impaired. ______ ______

EDUCATIONAL ACHIEVEMENT

Reading skills are at ______ grade level (______ percentile); spelling at ______ grade level (______ percentile); and arithmetic at ______ grade level (______ percentile). These standardized achievement scores are relatively consistent/discrepant with the patient's estimated premorbid intelligence, level of scholastic attainment and current vocational performance. There is/is no evidence of specific learning disability: ______ ______

MOTOR FUNCTIONING

The patient demonstrated consistent right/left hand dominance. Most individuals with such dominance have verbal functions represented in the left/right hemisphere with visuo-spatial skills in the right/left. The patient's gross motor speed in the upper limbs was intact/impaired. Fine motor coordination was adequate/impaired. Power was normal/impaired in the arms. Additional comments: ______ ______

AUDITORY PERCEPTUAL FUNTIONING

Auditory perceptual functioning was intact/impaired. The patient had no/had difficulty in differentiating between pairs of words. The ability to differentiate between pairs of rhythms was also intact/impaired. Additional comments: ______

TACTILE PERCEPTUAL FUNCTIONING

Tactile perceptual functioning was relatively intact/impaired. No/some errors of extinction or displacement occurred. There were no/some errors for finger agnosia, graphaesthesia and stereognosis. Additional comments: ____
____

VISUO-SPATIAL FUNCTIONING

Visuo-spatial functioning appeared to be adequate/impaired. There was no/was evidence of constructional dyspraxia. Visuomotor speed was adequate/impaired. Visual memory was intact/impaired. Additional comments: ____

LANGUAGE ABILITY

Language ability was intact/impaired for reading, writing, listening and talking. There was no/was evidence of dysarthria/dysphasia. Vocabulary level fell within the ______________ range (_______ percentile). Motor aspects of speech were intact/impaired as there was no/was evidence of disturbance in articulation and repetition. Comprehension of speech was adequate/inadequate, and thus not indicative/indicative of a receptive disorder. Word finding fluency was intact/impaired (________ percentile) thus not indicative/indicative of an expressive disorder. There was/was no evidence of a reading disability (dyslexia). Writing ability was adequate/impaired, and thus not indicative/indicative of dysgraphia. Additional comments: __
____

MEMORY PROCESSES

The patient obtained a general memory quotient of _______ (_______ percentile) which fell within the _______ range. This was relatively consistent/discrepant with estimated ______________________ premorbid intelligence. Subtest scores were: ____
____

Immediate memory was intact/impaired. Recent memory, including the ability to learn both new verbal and visual information was adequate/impaired. Remote memory was satisfactory/impaired.
Freedom from distractibility quotient was _______ (_______ percentile). This fell into the ________________ range, thus there was no/was evidence of an impairment of concentration, residual attentional deficits or other deficiencies in low level processing functions. Additional comments: ______
____

PERSONALITY ORGANIZATION

The patient's performance on the Minnesota multiphasic personality inventory/child behaviour checklist was unremarkable/unsatisfactory. This profile is valid/invalid
Current clinical description: ____________________________
____
____
____

COMMENTS

Give other information here: ____________________________
____
____
____
____
____
____

APPENDIX II

Test Score Record Form

[An asterisk (*) placed after a score indicates impaired range.]

1. *Laterality preference schedule:* ____________________
2. *Grooved pegboard:* Dominant Hand ______ secs
   Non-Dominant Hand ______ secs
3. *Finger tapping test:* Dominant Hand ______ taps
   Non-Dominant Hand ______ taps
4. *Hand dynamometer:* Dominant Hand ______ kg
   Non-Dominant Hand ______ kg
5. *Speech–sounds perception test:* ____________________
6. *Seashore rhythm test:* ____________________
7. *Tactile perceptual functioning:*
   Face hand test: ____________________
   Finger agnosia: ____________________
   Graphaesthesia: ____________________
   Tactile form recognition test: ____________________
8. *Trail making test (Part B):* ____________________
9. *Benton visual retention test:* ____________________
10. *Complex figure test (copy and recall):* ____________________
11. *Aphasia language performance scales*
    Listening ____________________
    Reading ____________________
    Talking ____________________
    Writing ____________________
12. *Controlled word association test:*
13. *Wechsler memory scale*
    Memory quotient = ____________________
    Verbal short-term memory = ____________________
    Verbal long-term memory = ____________________
    Semantic % retained = ____________________
    Visual short-term memory = ____________________
    Visual long-term memory = ____________________
    Visual % retained = ____________________
14. *Walton–Black:* ____________________
15. *Weschler adult intelligence scale/Wechsler intelligence scale for children (in percentile ranks):*
    Information ______________ Picture completion ______________
    Digit span ______________ Picture arrangement ______________

Copyright © 1984 by Grune & Stratton Australia
Reproduced from *Handbook of Neuropsychological Assessment*.

Vocabulary________	Block design ________
Arithmetic ________	Object assembly ________
Comprehension ________	Digit symbol (Coding) ________
Similarities ________	Performance IQ ________
Verbal IQ ________	Full scale IQ ________

16. *Wide range achievement test*
    Reading = ________ grade level (______ percentile)
    Spelling = ________ grade level (______ percentile)
    Arithmetic = ________ grade level (______ percentile)
17. *Stroop:* ________________

APPENDIX III Neuropsychological Profile in Percentile Ranks

NAME: DATE:

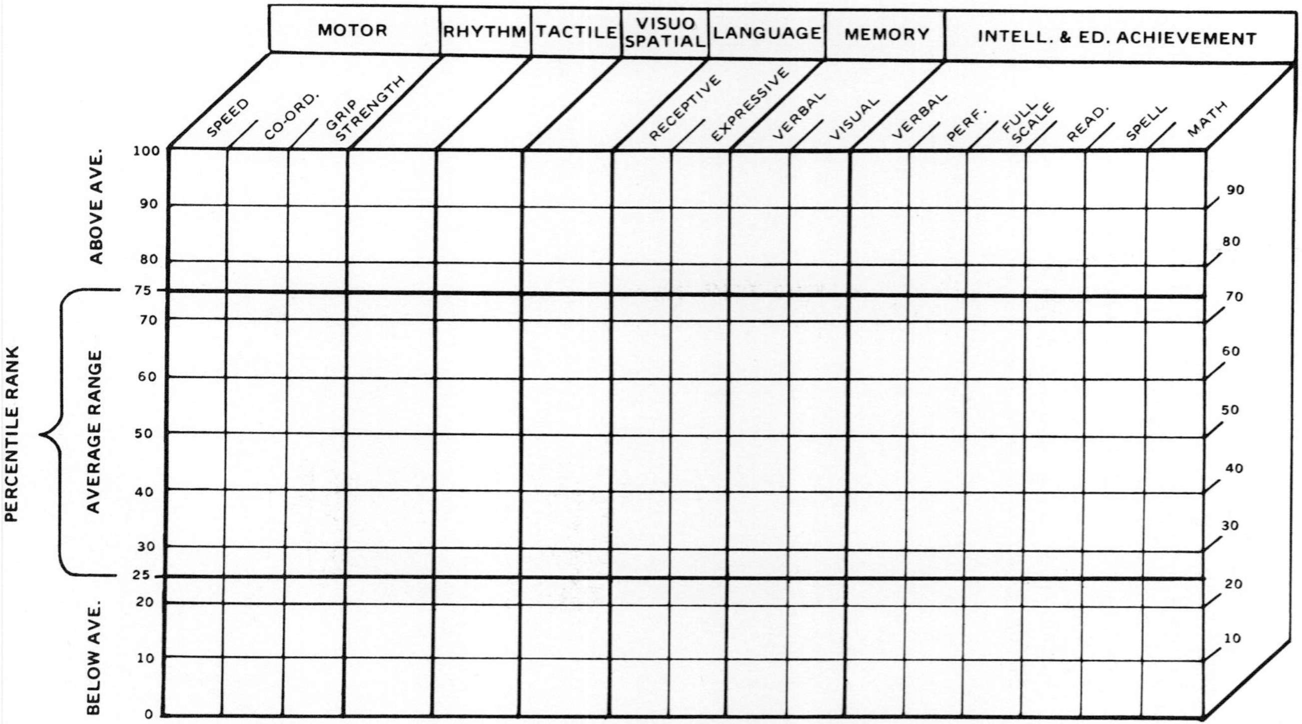

Copyright © 1984 by Grune & Stratton Australia

APPENDIX IV

Structured Neuropsychological Interview

NAME ______________________ DATE TESTED ______________________
ADDRESS ______________________ EXAMINER ______________________
NATIONALITY ______________________ REFERRED BY ______________________
DATE OF BIRTH ______________________
MARITAL STATUS ______________________

REFERRAL QUESTIONS

____

____

PHYSICAL APPEARANCE (height, weight, mannerisms, physical deformities)

____

CURRENT MEDICAL/PSYCHIATRIC STATUS
Description of present illness (onset, duration, behavioural changes) ______

____

Provisional diagnosis ______________________
Treatments ______________________
Medication/dosages ______________________
EEG ______________________
Skull X-ray ______________________
CT scan ______________________
Other investigations ______________________

MEDICAL HISTORY (conditions that may have led to cerebral dysfunction with a focus on the frequency, intensity and recency of symptomatology)
1. Family history of neurological illness ______________________

____

Copyright © 1984 by Grune & Stratton Australia
Reproduced from *Handbook of Neuropsychological Assessment*.

2. Prenatal, perinatal or postnatal problems (for example, inquire whether there were problems at birth, etc.) ______________________________

3. Serious accidents, illnesses, and surgery (traumatic, febrile, infectious, vascular, metabolic, neoplastic, or neuropsychiatric).

Age	Description	Sequelae

4. Episodes of loss of consciousness (for example, head injury; seizures; fainting; alcohol or drug related).

Age	Description	Sequelae (duration and behaviour changes)*

5. Persistent headaches; dizziness; insomnia; change in weight; or altered states of consciousness (for example, changes in taste or smell, or hallucinations) ______________________________

PREMORBID FUNCTIONING

Educational level (special education; grades repeated; reading, writing or maths problems) ______________________________

Occupational history ______________________________

*Estimate duration of retrograde and post-traumatic amnesia.

Contact with any chemicals at work (pesticides, heavy metals, gases) ______

Reading and recreational interests ______

Interpersonal relationships ______
Alcohol consumption ______
Drug use (narcotic, barbiturates, psychedelics) ______
Living situation (for example, own home, institutionalized) ______
Socioeconomic status ______

STATE OF CONSCIOUSNESS (during history taking)
Orientation (person, place and time) ______
Attention/concentration/distractibility/confusion ______

Patient's subjective complaints (current problems in their own words) ______

CURRENT NEUROPSYCHOLOGICAL FUNCTIONING[†]

1. *Motor Functioning*

A. Evidence of paralysis, muscle weakness or lack of co-ordination? Patient may give examples (for example, difficulty in driving, fatigue, loss of bowel or bladder control, or right–left disorientation) ______

B. Presence of tremors in the limbs? ______

C. Difficulties with gait or posture (for example, stiffness, restricted range of movement)? ______

D. Evidence of psychomotor retardation or hyperactivity? ______

2. *Auditory Functioning*

A. Any hearing loss? ______

B. Disturbed by high pitched sounds/ringing in the head? ______

[†]Attempt to integrate specific questions and clinical observations with referral requests.

C. Difficulties perceiving simple pitch relationships (for example, tone deaf) or inability to reproduce basic rhythms (for example, cannot tap out time)?

___

3. *Tactile Functioning*

A. Any complaints of loss of sensation (for example, numbness, pins and needles; sense of touch not as discriminating; less sensitive to pain or change in temperatures)? ___

___

4. *Visuo-spatial Functioning*

A. Any visual problems (for example, double vision) ___

B. Any difficulties in spatial orientation (for example, gets lost easily)? ___

___

C. Any experiences of distortions of body image (for example, change in size of the hands) or other visual hallucinations (for example, distortion of shape and distance of furniture)?___

___

5. *Language Ability*

A. Any problems in comprehending speech and responding to directions?

___

B. Any difficulties in verbal fluency (for example, inability to find the right word; garrulous speech; slurring of words)?___

___

6. *Memory Processes*

A. Has the patient noticed a general deterioration in memory or only specific problems for certain materials (for example, able to recognize faces but cannot remember names)? ___

B. Adequacy of short-term memory (for example, ability to retain a new telephone number while phoning)? ___

C. Adequacy of recent memory (for example, can remember day to day events; able to learn new information)?___

D. Adequacy of remote memory (for example, can remember historical facts and recollect childhood incidents)?___

7. *Higher Cognitive Processes*

A. Any deterioration in general intellectual functioning (for example, working at a lower level to premorbid capacity)? ___

B. Has there been a decline in reading, writing, spelling and calculating abilities? ___

C. Is it more difficult to cope at work (for example, deterioration in thinking, drawing or constructional abilities)? ______

D. Is there any loss of efficiency of planning, organizing, and problem-solving? ______

8. *Personality Organization*[‡]

A. Has the patient, relatives or friends noticed any personality change/ deterioration? ______

i thinking disorder ______

ii mood disorder (depression; elation; anxiety; frustration tolerance ______

iii behaviour (bizarre; agitated) ______

B. Self-concept (how do the patients feel about themselves and their problems)? ______

______

C. Any changes in sexual behaviour (for example, loss of libido)? ______

______

D. How does the patient function in unstructured situations (for example, what do they do in their free time? Is there loss of initiative?) ______

______

ADDITIONAL INFORMATION

______

______

______

SUMMARY OF CLINICAL IMPRESSIONS[§]

1. Validity of the data base

A. Patient's competence as a historian (for example, understands instructions, uses denial, confabulates) ______

______

B. Test attitude (for example, degree of co-operation, performing maximally, malingering) ______

C. Degree of motivation for rehabilitation ______

[‡]Note any disorders of thinking, mood and behaviour during interviewing and testing; and also assess capacities available to compensate for neuropsychological deficits. Any potential psychiatric disorders should be coded within the multi-axial classification recommended by the American Psychiatric Association's *Diagnostic and Statistical Manual of Mental Disorders* (DSM-III) whenever possible.

[§]Clinical impressions from interview are used to generate hypotheses which are further assessed during psychological testing.

2. Major areas of neuropsychological impairment ______________________

____

____

3. Tentative lateralization of lesion ______________________________

____

4. Tentative localization of lesion _______________________________

____

5. Provisional diagnostic impression _____________________________

____

APPENDIX V

Suppliers of Tests and Computer Equipment

Australia

Australian Council for Education Research Ltd,
P.O. Box 210,
Hawthorn, Vic. 3122,
Australia

United Kingdom

NSER–Nelson Publishing Company,
Darville House,
2 Oxford Road East,
Windsor, Berkshire SL4 1DS,
United Kingdom

United States

Codebook Inc.,
110 Main Street,
Suite 111,
Evanston, Wyoming 82930, USA

Compu-Psych Inc.,
119 West Kansas Street,
Liberty, Missouri 64068, USA

Integrated Professional Systems,
5211 Mahoning Avenue, Suite 340,
Youngstown, Ohio 44515, USA

Interpretive Scoring Systems,
P.O. Box 1416B,
Minneapolis, Minnesota 55440, USA

Precision People Inc.,
P.O. Box 17400,
Jacksonville, Florida 32216, USA

Psychological Software Specialists,
c/- Bruce Duthie PhD,
1776 Fowler,
Richland, Washington 99352, USA

Psychsystems,
600 Reisterstown Road,
Baltimore, Maryland 21208, USA

Western Psychological Services,
12031 Wilshire Boulevard,
Los Angeles, California 90025, USA

Copyright © 1984 by Grune & Stratton Australia
Reproduced from *Handbook of Neuropsychological Assessment*.

References

Achenbach, T. M., & Edelbrock, C. S. The child behaviour profile: II. Boys aged 12-16 and girls aged 6-11 and 12-16. *Journal of Consulting and Clinical Psychology,* 1979, *47:* 223.

Adams, K. M. In search of Luria's battery: A false start. *Journal of Consulting and Clinical Psychology,* 1980a, *48:* 511.

Adams, K. M. An end of innocence for behavioural neurology? Adams replies. *Journal of Consulting and Clinical Psychology,* 1980b, *48:* 522.

Adams, K. M., Rennick, P. M., & Rosenbaum, G. Automated clinical interpretation of the neuropsychology battery: An ability based approach. Presented at the Annual Meeting of the International Neuropsychology Society, Tampa, February 6, 1975.

Adams, R. D. Approach to the patient with neurologic disease. In K. J. Isselbacher, R. D. Adams, E. Braunwald, R. G. Petersdorf & J. D. Wilson (Eds). *Harrison's principles of internal medicine,* 9th edition. New York: McGraw-Hill, 1980: 1904.

Adams, R. D., Fisher, C. H., Hakim, S., Ojemann, R. G., & Sweet, W. H. Symptomatic occult hydrocephalus with normal cerebrospinal fluid pressure. *New England Journal of Medicine,* 1965, *273:* 117.

Administration on Aging Document. *Statistical notes* (from The National Clearing House on Aging), 1978 (2): 1.

Ajuriaguerra, J. de & Tissot, R. The apraxias. In P. J. Vinken & G. W. Bruyn (Eds). *Handbook of clinical neurology.* Volume 4. Amsterdam: North Holland Press, 1969.

Altman, H., Angle, H. V., Brown, M. L., & Sletten, I. W. Prediction of length of hospital stay. *Comprehensive Psychiatry,* 1972, *13:* 471.

Altman, H., Evenson, R. C., Sletten, I. W., & Cho, D. W. Computer predictions of psychotropic drug assignment in state mental facilities: Effects of eliminating alcoholics from the study sample. *Diseases of the Nervous System,* 1974, *35:* 505.

American Psychiatric Association. *Diagnostic and statistic manual of mental disorders* (DSM-III). 3rd edition. Washington: American Psychiatric Association, 1980.

Anastasi, A. *Psychological testing.* New York: MacMillan, 1976.

Australian Medical Association. *Submission to the Senate Standing Committee inquiring into compensation and rehabilitation in Australia.* Sydney: 1981.

Bak, J., & Greene, R. Changes in neuropsychological functioning in an aging population. *Journal of Consulting and Clinical Psychology,* 1980, *48:* 395.

Bash, I., & Alpert, M. The detection of malingering. In F. Wright & C. Rieber (Eds). *Forensic psychology and psychiatry.* New York: The New York Academy of Sciences, 1980.

Bender, M. Extinction and other patterns of sensory interaction. In E. Weinstein & R. Friedland (Eds). *Hemi-inattention and hemisphere specialization.* New York: Raven Press, 1977: 107.

Benson, D. Foreword. In R. L. Strub & F. W. Black, *Organic brain syndromes: An introduction to neurobehavioural disorders.* Philadelphia: F. A. Davis, 1981.

Benton, A. L., Meyer, R., & Polder, G. C. Some aspects of handedness. *Psychiatry and Neurology* (Basel), 1962, *144:* 321.

Benton, A. L. Differential behavioural effects in frontal lobe disease. *Neuropsychologia,* 1968, *6:* 53.

Benton, A. L. The measurement of aphasic disorders. In A. Cáceres Velasquez (Ed.). *Aspectos patólogicos del lengage.* Lima: Centro Neuropsicologico, 1973.

Benton, A. L. *Benton revised visual retention test.* New York: Psychological Corporation, 1974.

Benton, A. L. Some conclusions about dyslexia. In A. L. Benton & D. Pearl (Eds). *Dyslexia: An appraisal of current knowledge.* New York: Oxford University Press, 1979.

Benton, A. L. Psychological testing for brain damage. In H. I. Kaplan, A. M. Freedman & B. J. Sadock (Eds). *Comprehensive textbook of psychiatry/III.* 3rd edition. Baltimore: Williams & Wilkins, 1981: 966.

Benton, A. L., & Joynt, R. J. Reaction time in unilateral cerebral disease. *Confinia Neurologica,* 1959, *19:* 247.

Beumont, P. J. V. The endocrinology of psychiatry. In K. Granville-Grossman (Ed.). *Recent advances in clinical psychiatry 3.* London: Churchill Livingstone, 1979: 185.

Bingley, T. Mental symptoms in temporal lobe epilepsy and temporal lobe gliomas. *Acta Psychiatrica et Neurologica,* 1958, *33* (supplement 120).

Boll, T. J. Diagnosing brain impairment. In B. B. Wolman (Ed.). *Clinical diagnoses of mental disorders: A handbook.* New York: Plenum, 1978.

Boll, T. J. The Halstead–Reitan neuropsychological battery. In S. B. Filskov & T. J. Boll (Eds). *Handbook of clinical neuropsychology.* New York: Wiley, 1981 (Chapter 18).

Boll, T. J., Berent, S., & Richards, H. Tactile-perceptual functioning as a factor in general psychological abilities. *Perceptual and Motor Skills,* 1977, *44:* 535.

Boll, T. J., & Reitan, R. M. Motor and tactile-perceptual deficits in brain-damaged children. *Perceptual and Motor Skills,* 1972, *34:* 343.

Boll, T., & Reitan, R. M. Effects of age on performance on the trail making test. *Perceptual and Motor Skills,* 1973, *36:* 691.

Boyar, J. Coping with non-organic factors on neuropsychological examination: Utility of repeated neuropsychological measures. *Clinical Neuropsychology,* 1981, *3:* 15.

Brain, W. R. *Diseases of the nervous system.* 5th edition London: Oxford University Press, 1955.

Branch, C., Milner, B., & Rasmussen, T. Intracarotid sodium amytal for the lateralization of cerebral speech dominance. *Journal of Neurosurgery,* 1964, *21:* 399.

Broe, G. A. The nature and effects of brain damage following severe head injuries in young subjects. In *Proceedings of the Australian Neurological Foundation's conference on head injuries, April 26-28, 1979.* Sydney: Australian Neurological Foundation.

Buros, O. K. *The eighth mental measurements yearbook.* Highland Park, N.J.: Gryphon Press, 1978.

Catanzarite, V. A., Greenburg, A. G., & Bremermann, H. J. Computer assisted diagnosis and computer consultation in neurology: Preliminary testing of diagnostic accuracy for the NEUROLOGIST system. *International Journal of Neuroscience,* 1981, *3:* 43.

Caveness, W. F., & Walker, A. E. *Head injury.* Philadelphia: Lippincott, 1966.

Christensen, A. L. *Luria's neuropsychological investigation.* 2nd edition. Copenhagen: Munksgaard, 1979.

Christie, J., Mori, H., Go, R., Cornel, S., & Schapiro, R. Computed tomography and radionuclide studies in the diagnosis of intracranial disease. *American Journal of Roentgenology,* 1976, *127:* 171.

Colby, K. M., Watt, J. B., & Gilbert, J. P. A computer method of psychotherapy: Preliminary communication. *Journal of Nervous and Mental Disease,* 1966, *142:* 148.

Cole, E. B., Johnson, J. H., & Williams, T. A. When psychiatric patients interact with computer terminals: Problems and solutions. *Behaviour Research Methods and Instrumentation,* 1976, *8:* 92.

Comalli, J. R. P., Wapner, S., & Werner, H. Interference effects of the Stroop colour-word test in childhood, adulthood, and aging. *Journal of Genetic Psychology,* 1962, *100:* 47.

Cooke, G. (Ed.). *The role of the forensic psychologist.* Springfield, Ill.: Charles C. Thomas, 1980.

Couch, R. Computer diagnosis: Review and comment. *Pathology Annual,* 1976, *11:* 141.

Critchley, M. *The parietal lobes.* London: Edward Arnold, 1953.

Crockett, D., Clark, C., & Klonoff, H. An overview of neuropsychology. In S. B. Filskov & T. J. Boll (Eds). *Handbook of clinical neuropsychology.* New York: Wiley, 1981 (Chapter 1).

Croft, D. Is computerised diagnosis possible? *Computers in Biomedical Research,* 1972, *5:* 351.

Cronbach, L. J. *Essentials of psychological testing.* 3rd edition. New York: Harper & Row, 1970.

Crosson, B., & Warren, R. L. Use of the Luria-Nebraska neuropsychological battery in aphasia: A conceptual critique. *Journal of Consulting and Clinical Psychology,* 1982, *50:* 22.

Damasio, A. R. The frontal lobes. In K. M. Heilman & E. Valenstein (Eds). *Clinical neuropsychology.* New York: Oxford University Press, 1979: 360.

Davies, A. D. Measures of mental deterioration in aging and brain damage. In S. S. Chown & K. F. Reigel (Eds). *Interdisciplinary topics in gerontology.* Volume 1. Basel and New York: S. Karger, 1968.

Davis, K., Taveras, J., Roberson, G., & Ackerman, R. Some limitations of computed tomography in the diagnosis of neurological diseases. *Americal Journal of Roentgenology,* 1976, *127:* 111.

Dawdy, S. C. Pediatric neuropsychology: Forging the discipline. *Clinical Neuropsychology,* 1980, *2:* 86.

Dean, R. S. Personality and lateral preference patterns in children. *Clinical Neuropsychology,* 1981, *3:* 22.

Dean, R. S. Assessing patterns of lateral preference. *Clinical Neuropsychology,* 1982, *4:* 124.

Dee, H. L., & Van Allen, M. W. Speed of decision-making process in patients with unilateral cerebral disease. *Archives of Neurology,* 1973, *28:* 163.

Delis, D., & Kaplan, E. Assessment of aphasia with the Luria-Nebraska neuropsychological battery: A case critique. *Journal of Consulting and Clinical Psychology,* 1982, *50:* 32.

De Myer, W. *Techniques of the neurological examination.* New York: McGraw-Hill, 1974.

Denckla, M. Childhood learning disabilities. In K. M. Heilman & E. Valenstein (Eds). *Clinical neuropsychology.* New York: Oxford University Press, 1979 (Chapter 17).

Diament, J. Similarities and differences in the approach of R. M. Reitan and A. R. Luria. *Acta Psychiatrica Scandinavica,* 1981, *63:* 431.

Dimond, S. J. *Neuropsychology.* London: Butterworths, 1980.

Dodrill, C. B. The hand dynamometer as a neuropsychological measure. *Journal of Consulting and Clinical Psychology,* 1978, *46:* 1432.

Doerr, H. O., & Storrie, M. C. Neuropsychological testing in the People's Republic of China: The Halstead-Reitan Seattle/Chan Sha project. *Clinical Neuropsychology,* 1982, *4:* 49.

Edelbrock, C., & Achenbach, T. M. A typology of child behaviour profile patterns: Distribution and correlates for disturbed children aged 6-16. *Journal of Abnormal Child Psychology,* 1980, *8:* 441.

Ellard, J. Psychological reactions to compensatable injury. *Medical Journal of Australia,* 1970, *2:* 349.

Engel, G. L., & Romano, J. Delirium, a syndrome of cerebral insufficiency. *Journal of Chronic Diseases,* 1959, *9:* 260.

Falconer, M. A. Mesial temporal (Ammon's horn) sclerosis as a common cause of epilepsy. *Lancet,* 1974, *2:* 767.

Feuerstein, R. *The dynamic assessment of retarded performers: The learning potential assessment device, theory, instruments and techniques.* Baltimore: University Park Press, 1979.

Feuerstein, R. *Instrumental enrichment: An intervention program for cognitive modifiability.* Baltimore: University Park Press, 1980.

Fields, F. R., & Fullerton, J. R. Influence of heroin addiction on neuropsychological functioning. *Journal of Consulting and Clinical Psychology,* 1975, *43:* 114.

Filskov, S. B., & Boll, T. J. (Eds). *Handbook of clinical neuropsychology.* New York: Wiley, 1981.

Filskov, S. B., & Goldstein, S. Diagnostic validity of the Halstead–Reitan neuropsychological battery. *Journal of Consulting and Clinical Psychology,* 1974, *42:* 382.

Filskov, S. B., & Leli, D. A. Assessment of the individual in neuropsychological practice. In S. B. Filskov and T. J. Boll (Eds). *Handbook of clinical neuropsychology.* New York: Wiley, 1981 (Chapter 17).

Finlayson, M. A. J., Johnson, K. A., & Reitan, R. M. Relationship of level of education to neuropsychological measures in brain-damaged and non-brain-damaged adults. *Journal of Consulting and Clinical Psychology,* 1977, *45:* 536.

Fowler, R. D. Computer interpretation of personality tests: The automated psychologist. *Comprehensive Psychiatry,* 1967, *8:* 455.

Frederiks, J. A. M. Disorders of the body schema. In P. J. Vinken & G. W. Bruyn (Eds). *Handbook of clinical neurology.* Volume 4. Amsterdam: North Holland Press, 1969.

Freeman, F. R. *Organic mental disease.* New York: SP Medical & Scientific Books, 1981.

Frisch, G. R. & Handler, L. A. A neuropsychological investigation of "functional disorders of speech articulation". *Journal of Speech and Hearing Research,* 1974, *17:* 432.

Gazzaniga, M. S. (Ed.) *Handbook of behavioural neurobiology.* Volume 2. New York: Plenum Press, 1978.

Geschwind, N. Foreword. In R. L. Strub & F. W. Black. *The mental status examination in neurology.* Philadelphia: F. A. Davis, 1979: vi.

Giannetti, R. A., Johnson, J. H., Williams, T. A., & McCusker, C. F. Development of an on-line problem oriented system for the evaluation of mental health treatment services. *Research Methods and Instrumentation,* 1977, *9:* 133.

Giannetti, R. A., Klingler, D. E., Johnson, J. H., & Williams, T. A. The potential for dynamic assessment systems using on line computer technology. *Behaviour Research Methods and Instrumentation,* 1976, *8:* 101.

Gilandas, A. J. The problem-oriented record in a psychiatric hospital. *Hospital and Community Psychiatry,* 1972, *23:* 336.

Gilandas, A. J. Implications of the problem oriented record for utilization review and continuing education. *Hospital and Community Psychiatry,* 1974, *25:* 22.

Gilandas, A. J., & Touyz, S. A cost-efficient battery for the assessment of brain damage. Presented at the annual meeting of the Australian Psychological Society, Sydney, August 23, 1981.

Glueck, B. C. Computers at the institute of living. In J. L. Crawford, D. A. Morgan & D. T. Gianturco (Eds). *Progress in mental health information systems computer applications.* Cambridge, Mass.: Ballinger, 1974.

Golden, C. J. Identification of brain disorders by the Stroop color and word test. *Journal of Clinical Psychology,* 1976a, *32:* 654.

Golden, C. J. The identification of brain damage by an abbreviated form of the Halstead–Reitan neuropsychological battery. *Journal of Clinical Psychology,* 1976b, *32:* 821.

Golden, C. J. Validity of the Halstead–Reitan neuropsychological battery in mixed psychotic and brain-impaired populations. *Journal of Consulting and Clinical Psychology,* 1977, *45:* 1043.

Golden, C. J. *Diagnosis and rehabilitation in clinical neuropsychology.* Springfield, Ill.: Charles C. Thomas, 1978.

Golden, C. J. *Clinical interpretation of objective psychological tests.* New York: Grune & Stratton, 1979.

Golden, C. J. A standardized version of Luria's neuropsychological tests: A quantitative and qualitative approach to neuropsychological examination. In S. B. Filskov & T. J. Boll (Eds.). *Handbook of clinical neuropsychology.* New York: Wiley, 1981a (Chapter 19).

Golden, C. J. The Luria–Nebraska children's battery: Theory and formulations. In G. W. Hynd & J. E. Obrzut (Eds). *Neuropsychological assessment and the school age child.* New York: Grune & Stratton, 1981b: 294.

Golden, C. J., Ariel, R. N., McKay, S. E., Wilkening, G. N., Wolf, B. A., and MacInnes, W. D. The Luria–Nebraska neuropsychological battery: Theoretical orientation and comment. *Journal of Consulting and Clinical Psychology,* 1982, *50:* 291.

Golden, C. J., Graber, B., Coffman, J., Berg, R., Newlin, D. B., & Bloch, S. Structural brain deficits in schizophrenia. *Archives of General Psychiatry,* 1981, *38:* 1014.

Golden, C. J., Hammeke, T., & Purisch, A. *The Luria–Nebraska neuropsychological battery manual.* Los Angeles: Western Psychological Services, 1980.

Golden, C. J., & Kuperman, S. Graduate training in clinical neuropsychology. *Professional Psychology,* 1980, *11:* 55.

Golden, C. J., Moses, J. A., Coffman, J. A., Miller, W. R., & Strider, F. D. *Clinical neuropsychology: Interface with neurological and psychiatric disorders.* New York: Grune & Stratton, 1983.

Golden, C. J., Osmon, D. C., Moses, J. A., & Berg, R. A. *Interpretation of the Halstead–Reitan neuropsychological test battery.* New York: Grune & Stratton, 1981.

Goldstein, G. The use of clinical neuropsychological methods in the lateralization of brain lesions. In J. Dimond & J. G. Beaumont (Eds). *Hemisphere functions in the brain.* New York: Wiley, 1974.

Goldstein, G., & Neuringer, C. Schizophrenic and organic signs on the trail making test. *Perceptual and Motor Skills,* 1966, *22:* 347.

Goldstein, S., Deysach, R., & Kleinknecht, R. Effects of experience and amount of information on identification of cerebral impairment. *Journal of Consulting and Clinical Psychology,* 1973, *41:* 30.

Goodglass, H., & Kaplan, E. Assessments of cognitive deficit in the brain injured patient. In M. Gazzaniga (Ed.). *Handbook of behavioural neuropsychology.* Volume 2. New York: Plenum Press, 1979: 3.

Goody, W. Introduction in R. Hoops, Y. Lebrun, & E. Buyssens (Eds). *Selected papers on the history of aphasia.* Amsterdam: Swets & Zeitunger, 1977: 10.

Gordon, N. G. Diagnostic efficiency of the trail making test as a function of cut-off score, diagnosis, and age. *Perceptual and Motor Skills,* 1978, *47:* 191.

Gorman, W. F. Defining malingering. *Journal of Forensic Sciences,* 1982, *27:* 401.

Graetz, R. E. The computer: A new tool for psychiatry. *Hospital and Community Psychiatry.* 1966, *17:* 21.

Griesinger, W. Pathology and therapy of mental diseases, published in Germany, 1845. In H. I. Kaplan, A. M. Freedman, & B. J. Sadock (Eds). *Comprehensive textbook of psychiatry/ III.* 3rd edition. Baltimore: Williams & Wilkins, 1981.

Gunn, J. C. The prevalence of epilepsy among prisoners. *Proceedings of the Royal Society of Medicine,* 1969, *62:* 60.

Halstead, W. *Brain and intelligence: A quantitative study of the frontal lobes.* Chicago: University of Chicago Press, 1947.

Hawkes, M. N., & Pusakulich, R. L. Efficacy of neuropsychological evaluations over computerized tomography findings: A case review. *Clinical Neuropsychology,* 1982, *4:* 38.

Hayward, R. W., *Management of acute head injuries.* London: Blackwell Scientific Publications, 1980.

Heaton, R. K., & Crowley, T. J. Effects of psychiatric disorders and their somatic treatments on neuropsychological test results. In S. B. Filskov & T. J. Boll (Eds). *Handbook of clinical neuropsychology.* New York: Wiley, 1981 (Chapter 15).

Heaton, R. K., Smith, H. H., Lehman, R., & Vogt, A. T. Prospects for faking believable deficits on neuropsychological testing. *Journal of Consulting and Clinical Psychology,* 1978, *46:* 892.

Heaton, S. K., & Heaton, R. K. Testing the impaired patient. In S. B. Filskov & T. J. Boll (Eds). *Handbook of clinical neuropsychology.* New York: Wiley, 1981 (Chapter 16).

Hebb, D. O. Man's frontal lobe: A critical review. *Archives of Neurology and Psychiatry,* 1945, *54:* 10.

Hecaen, H., & Alber, M. L. *Human neuropsychology.* New York: Wiley, 1978.

Hedlund, J. L., Sletten, I. W., & Altman, H. Prediction of patients who are dangerous to others. *Journal of Clinical Psychology,* 1973, *29:* 443.

Heilman, K. M., & Valenstein, E. (Eds). *Clinical neuropsychology.* New York: Oxford University Press, 1979.

Hevern, V. Recent validity studies of the Halstead–Reitan approach to clinical neuropsychological assessment. *Clinical Neuropsychology,* 1980, *2:* 49.

Hollis, J. W., & Donn, P. A. *Psychological report writing theory and practice.* Muncie, Ind.: Accelerated Development Inc., 1980.

Horton, A. M. Behavioural neuropsychology: A clinical case study. *Clinical Neuropsychology,* 1979, 1: 44.

Horton, A. M. Some suggestions regarding the clinical interpretation of the trailmaking test. *Clinical Neuropsychology,* 1979, *1:* pages unknown.

Hulicka, I. Age differences in the Wechsler memory scale scores. *Journal of Genetic Psychology,* 1966, *109:* 135.

Husserl, E. *Cartesian meditations: An introduction to a phenomenology.* New York: Heineman, 1973.

Interpretive Scoring Systems. *The Minnesota report.* Minneapolis: Interpretive Scoring Systems, 1983.

Isselbacher, K. J., Adams, R. D., Braunwald, E., Petersdorf, R. G., & Wilson, J.D. (Eds). *Harrison's principles of internal medicine.* 9th Edition. New York: McGraw-Hill, 1980.

Jackson, J. H. On the duality of the brain. *Medical Press,* 1874, 1: 19 (reprinted in J. Taylor (Ed.). *Selected writings of John Hughlings Jackson.* London: Hodder and Stoughton, 1932).

Jackson, J. H. On the anatomical and physiological localisation of movements in the brain (*Lancet,* 1873) (reprinted in J. Taylor (Ed.). *Selected writings of John Hughlings Jackson,* London: Staples Press, 1958: 37).

Jastak, J. F., & Jastak, S. R. *The wide range achievement test: Manual of instructions.* Wilmington, Del.: Guidance Associates, 1978.

Jefferson, J. W., & Marshall, J. R. *Neuropsychiatric features of mental disorders.* New York: Plenum Medical, 1981.

Johnson, J. H., Giannetti, R. A., and Williams, T. A. Realtime psychological assessment and evaluation of psychiatric patients. *Behaviour Research Methods and Instrumentation,* 1975, *7:* 199.

Johnson, J. H., Giannetti, R. A., & Williams, T. A. Computers in mental health care delivery: A review of the evolution toward interventionally relevant on-line processing. *Behaviour Research Methods and Instrumentation,* 1976, *8:* 83.

Johnson, J. H., Giannetti, R. A., & Williams, T. A. A self-contained micro-computer system for psychological testing. *Behaviour Research Methods and Instrumentation,* 1978a, *10:* 579.

Johnson, J. H., Giannetti, R. A., & Williams, T.A. Psychological systems questionnaire: An objective personality test designed for on-line computer presentation, scoring and interpretation. *Behaviour Research Methods and Instrumentation,* 1979, *11:* 257.

Johnson, J. H., and Williams, T. A. The use of on-line computer technology in a mental health admitting system. *American Psychologist,* 1975, *30:* 388.

Johnson, J. H., and Williams, T. A. Using a microcomputer for on-line psychiatric assessment. *Behaviour Research Methods and Instrumentation,* 1978, *10:* 576.

Johnson, J. H., Williams, T. A., Giannetti, R. A., and Klingler, D. E. Clinical testing and assessment: Using a micro-computer for on-line psychiatric assessment. *Behaviour Research Methods and Instrumentation,* 1978b, *10:* 576.

Johnson, J. H., Williams, T. A., Klingler, D. E., and Giannetti, R. A. Interventional relevance and retrofit programming: Concepts for the improvement of computer-generated assessment reports. *Behaviour Research Methods and Instrumentation,* 1977, *9:* 123.

Joint, R. J., & Shoulson, I. Dementia. In K. M. Heilman, & E. Valenstein (Eds). *Clinical neuropsychology.* New York: Oxford University Press, 1979 (Chapter 15).

Joyston-Bechal, M. P. The clinical features and outcome of stupor. *British Journal of Psychiatry,* 1966, *117:* 119.

Kaplan, A. A. A philosophical discussion of normality. *Archives of General Psychiatry,* 1967, *17:* 325.

Kaplan, H. I., Freedman, A. M., & Sadock, B. J. (Eds). *Comprehensive Textbook of psychiatry/III.* 3rd Edition. Baltimore: Williams & Wilkins, 1981.

Kaplan, J. & Smith, W. An evaluation program for a regional mental health centre. In Crawford, J. L., Morgan, D. W., & Gianturco, D. T. (Eds). *Progress in mental health information systems: Computer applications.* Cambridge, Mass.: Ballinger, 1974.

Kaufman, A. S. *Intelligence testing with the WISC-R.* New York: Wiley-Interscience, 1979.

Kay, A. W., Beamish, P., & Roth, M. Old age mental disorders in Newcastle-upon-Tyne. *British Journal of Psychiatry,* 1962, 110: 668.

Kazdin, A. E. *Research design in clinical psychology.* New York: Harper & Row, 1980.

Keenan, J. S. & Brassell, E. G. *Aphasia language performance scales.* Murfreesboro, Tenn.: Pinnacle Press, 1975.

Keith, R. A., Brechenridge, K., & O'Neill, W. A. Rehabilitation hospital characteristics from the hospital utilization project system. *Archives of Physical Medicine and Rehabilitation,* 1977, *58:* 260.

Kiernan, R., & Mathews, C. Impairment index versus T-score averaging in neuropsychological assessment. *Journal of Consulting and Clinical Psychology,* 1976, *44:* 951.

Kiloh, L. G. Pseudo-dementia. *Acta Psychiatrica Scandinavica.* 1961, *37:* 336.

Kimura, D. Functional asymmetry of the brain in dichotic listening. *Cortex,* 1967, *3:* 163.

Kingsbourne, M., & Hiscock, M. Cerebral lateralization and cognitive development: Conceptual and methodological issues. In G. W. Hynd & J. E. Obrzut (Eds). *Neuropsychological assessment and the school-age child. Issues and procedures.* New York: Grune & Stratton, 1981: 125-166.

Klingler, D. E., Johnson, J. H., & Williams, T. A. Strategies in the evaluation of an on-line computer-assisted unit for intake assessment of mental health patients. *Behaviour Research Methods and Instrumentation.* 1976, *8:* 95.

Klingler, D. E., & Miller, D. A. Process evaluation of an on-line computer-associated unit for intake assessment of mental health patients. *Behaviour Research Methods and Instrumentation,* 1977, 9: 110.

Klonoff, H., Fibiger, C. H., & Hutton, G. H. Neuropsychological patterns in chronic schizophrenia. *Journal of Nervous and Mental Diseases,* 1970, *150:* 291.

Klonoff, H., & Low, M. Disordered brain function in young children and early adolescents: Neuropsychological and electroencephalographic correlates. In R. M. Reitan & L. A. Davison (Eds). *Clinical neuropsychology: Current status and applications.* Washington; V. H. Winston & Sons, 1974: 92.

Knights, R. M., & Norwood, J. A. *A neuropsychological test battery for children.* Ottowa: Psychological Consultants, 1979.

Knights, R. M. & Stoddart, C. Profile approaches to neuropsychological diagnosis in children. In G. W. Hynd & J. E. Obrzut (Eds). *Neuropsychological assessment and the school-age child.* New York: Grune & Stratton, 1981: 335.

Kolb, B., & Whishaw, I.Q. *Fundamentals of human neuropsychology.* San Francisco: W. H. Freeman, 1980.

Korchin, S. J. *Modern clinical psychology.* New York: Basic Books, 1976.

Lachar, D. & Gdowski, C. *Actuarial assessment of child and adolescent personality: An interpretive guide for the personality inventory for children profile.* Los Angeles: Western Psychological Services, 1979.

Laska, E. The multi-state information system. In J. L. Crawford, D. W. Morgan and D. T. Gianturco (Eds). *Progress in mental health information systems: Computer applications.* Cambridge, Mass.: Ballinger, 1974:

Laska, E., Logemann, G. W., & Weinstein, A. The multi-state information system for psychiatric patients. *Transactions of the New York Academy of Sciences,* 1971, *33:* 780.

Lazarus, A. A. *Behaviour therapy and beyond.* New York: McGraw-Hill, 1971.

Lazarus, A. A. *The practice of multimodal therapy.* New York: McGraw-Hill, 1981.

Lenneberg, E. *Biological foundations of language.* New York: Wiley, 1967.

Levin, H. S., Benton, A. L., & Grossman, R. G. *Neurobehavioural consequences of closed head injury.* New York: Oxford University Press, 1982.

Lezak, M. D. *Neuropsychological assessment.* New York: Oxford University Press, 1976.

Lipowski, Z. J. A new look at organic brain syndromes. *American Journal of Psychiatry,* 1980, 137: 674.

Lishman, W. A. *Organic psychiatry: The psychological consequences of cerebral disorder.* London: Blackwell Scientific Publishing, 1978.

Lloyd, J. Compensation neurosis. *Australian Family Physician,* 1980, *9:* 84.

Locke, G. Estimating extent of disability. Paper presented at a Seminar of Disability for Medicolegal Purposes. Queen Elizabeth II Rehabilitation Centre, Camperdown, NSW, Australia, August 12, 1981.

Locke, G. Estimation of disability. Presented at the Seminar on Disability for Medicolegal Purposes. Queen Elizabeth II Rehabilitation Centre, Sydney. August 12, 1981.

London, P. *The modes and morals of psychotherapy.* New York: Holt, 1964.

Luria, A. R. Kurt Goldstein and neuropsychology, *Neuropsychologia,* 1966: 311-313.

Luria, A. R. *The working brain.* New York: Basic Books, 1973: 344.

Luria, A. R. Neuropsychology and the study of higher cortical functions. In A. L. Christensen. *Luria's neuropsychological investigation.* 2nd Edition. Copenhagen: Munksgaard, 1979: 17.

Luria, A. R. *Higher cortical functions in man.* 2nd Edition. New York: Basic Books, 1980.

Luria, A. R. & Majovsky, L. Basic approaches used in American and Soviet clinical neuropsychology. *American Psychologist,* 1977, *32:* 959.

McFie, J. *Assessment of organic intellectual impairment,* London: Academic Press, 1975.

McGlone, J., & Kertesz, A. Sex differences in cerebral processing of visuospatial tasks. *Cortex,* 1973, *9:* 313.

McKay, S. E., & Golden, C. J. Empirical derivation of experimental scales for localizing brain lesions using the Luria-Nebraska neuropsychological battery. *Clinical Neuropsychology,* 1979, *4:* 19.

McKay, S. E. & Golden, C. J. The assessment of specific neuropsychological skills using scales derived from factor analysis of the Luria–Nebraska neuropsychological battery. *International Journal of Neuroscience,* 1981, *14:* 189.

McMahon, E. A., & Satz, P. Clinical neuropsychology: Some forensic applications. In S. B. Filskov & T. J. Boll (Eds). *Handbook of clinical neuropsychology.* New York: Wiley, 1981 (Chapter 21).

Mahan, H. C. Measuring intellectual impairment with the WAIS: An improved approach to scoring. *Clinical Neuropsychology,* 1979, 1: 56.

Martin, W. T. *Writing psychological reports.* Springfield, Ill. Charles C. Thomas, 1972.

Mason, S., & Swash, M. *Hutchinson's clinical methods.* 17th Edition. London: Bailliere Tindall, 1980: 340.

Matarazzo, J. D. *Wechsler's measurement and appraisal of adult intelligence.* 5th edition. Baltimore: Williams & Wilkins, 1980.

Matarazzo, J. D., Matarazzo, R. G., Weins, A. N., Gallo, A. E., & Klonoff, H. Retest reliability of the Halstead impairment index in a normal, a schizophrenic, and two samples of organic patients. *Journal of Clinical Psychology,* 1976, *32:* 338.

Mathews, C. G., Shaw, D. J., & Klove, H. Psychological test performances in neurologic and "pseudo-neurologic" subjects. *Cortex,* 1966, *2:* 244.

Mathews, C. G. Neuropsychology practice in a hospital setting. In S. B. Filskov & T. J. Boll (Eds). *Handbook of clinical neuropsychology.* New York: Wiley, 1981 (Chapter 20).

Maultsby, M. C., & Slock, W. V. A computer-based psychiatry history system. *Archives of General Psychiatry,* 1971, *25:* 570.

Meehl, P. E. *Clinical versus statistical prediction.* Minneapolis: University of Minnesota Press, 1954.

Meier, M. J. Education for competency in human neuropsychology: Antecedents, models and directions. In S. B. Filskov & T. J. Boll (Eds). *Handbook of clinical neuropsychology.* New York: Wiley, 1981 (Chapter 24).

Meikle, S., & Gerritse, R. A. A comparison of psychiatric symptom frequency under narrative and checklist conditions. *American Journal of Psychiatry,* 1970, *127:* 155.

Meyer, V., & Falconer, M. A. Defects of learning ability with massive lesions of the temporal lobe. *Journal of Mental Science,* 1960: 472.

Miller, E. The long-term consequences of head injury: A discussion of the evidence with special reference to the preparation of legal reports. *British Journal of Social and Clinical Psychology,* 1979, *18:* 87.

Miller, H. Mental sequelae of head injury. *Proceedings of the Royal Society of Medicine,* 1966, *59:* 257.

Milner, B. Intellectual functions of the temporal lobes. *Psychological Bulletin,* 1954, 51:42.

Milner, B. Laterality effects in audition. In V. B. Mountcastle (Ed.). *Interhemispheric relations and cerebral dominance.* Baltimore: Johns Hopkins University Press, 1962.

Milner, B. Brain mechanisms suggested by studies of temporal lobes. In F. L. Darley (Ed.). *Brain mechanisms underlying speech and language.* New York: Grune & Stratton, 1967.

Milner, B. Memory mechanisms. *Canadian Medical Association Journal,* 1977, *116:* 1374.

Mindham, R. H. S. Psychiatric symptoms of Parkinson's disease. *British Journal of Hospital Medicine,* 1974, *11:* 411.

Mirabile, C. A., Houck, J. H., & Glueck, B. C., Jr. Computer prediction of treatment success. *Comprehensive Psychiatry,* 1971, *12:* 48.

Mohr, J. P., & Adams, R. D. Affections of speech. In K. J. Isselbacher, R. D. Adams, E. Braunwald, R. G. Petersdorf & J. D. Wilson (Eds). *Harrison's principles of internal medicine.* 9th edition. New York: McGraw-Hill, 1980: 139.

Nemiah, J. C. Psychiatry: The inexhaustible science. In H. I. Kaplan, A. M. Freedman & B. J. Sadock (Eds). *Comprehensive textbook of psychiatry/III.* 3rd Edition. Baltimore: Williams & Wilkins, 1981: 1.

Neugarten, B. L. The future and the young-old. *Gerontologist,* 1975, *15:* 4.

Obrzut, J. E. Neuropsychological procedures with school-age children. In G. W. Hynd & J. E. Obrzut (Eds). *Neuropsychological assessment and the school-age child.* New York: Grune & Stratton, 1981: 237.

Orne, M. On the social psychology of the psychological experiment; with particular reference to demand characteristics and their implications. *American Psychologist,* 1962, 17: 776.

Orton, S. T. *Reading, writing and speech problems in children.* New York: W. W. Norton, 1961.

Osborne, D., & Davis, L. J. Standard scores for Wechsler memory scale subtests. *Journal of Clinical Psychology,* 1978, *34:* 115.

Parsons, O. A., & Prigatano, G. P. Methodological considerations in clinical neuropsychological research. *Journal of Consulting and Clinical Psychology,* 1978, *46:* 608.

Parsons, O., & Stewart, K. Effects of supportive versus disinterested interviews on perceptual-motor performance in brain-damaged and neurotic patients. *Journal of Consulting Psychology,* 1966, *30:* 260.

Patterson, K. E. Neuropsychological approaches to the study of reading. *British Journal of Psychology,* 1981, *72:* 151.

Pearson, J. S., Swenson, W. M., Rome, H. P., Matata, P. & Brannick, T. L. Development of a computer system for scoring and interpretation of Minnesota multiphasic personality inventories in a medical clinic. *Annals of the New York Academy of Science,* 1975, *126:* 682.

Piercy, M. The effects of cerebral lesions on intellectual function. *British Journal of Psychiatry,* 1964, *110:* 310.

Pincus, J. H., & Tucker, G. J. *Behavioural neurology.* 2nd Edition. New York: Oxford University Press, 1978.

Piotrowski, Z. A digital-computer interpretation of inkblot test data. *Psychiatric Quarterly,* 1964, *38:* 1.

Pirozzollo, F. J., & Campanella, D. J. The neuropsychology of developmental speech disorders and learning disabilities. In G. W. Hynd & J. E. Obrzut (Eds). *Neuropsychological assessment and the school-age child.* New York: Grune & Stratton, 1981 (Chapter 5).

Prechtl, H. F. R., Bocke, P. E., & Schut, T. The electroencephalogram and performance in epileptic patients. *Neurology* (Minneapolis), 1961, *11:* 296.

Prigatano, G. P. & Parsons, O. A. Relationship of age and education to Halstead test performance in different patient populations. *Journal of Consulting and Clinical Psychology,* 1976, *44:* 527.

Rasmussen, T., & Milner, B. Clinical and surgical studies of the cerebral speech area in man. In K. J. Zulch, O. Creutzfeldt & G. Galbraith (Eds). *Otfrid Foerster symposium on cerebral localization.* Heidelberg: Springer-Verlag, 1975.

Rathbun, J., & Smith, A. Comment on the validity of Boyd's validation study of the Hooper visual organization test. *Journal of Consulting and Clinical Psychology,* 1982, *50;* 281.

Reitan, R. M. Investigation of the validity of Halstead's measures of biological intelligence. *AMA Archives of Neurology and Psychiatry,* 1955, *73;* 28.

Reitan, R. M. Psychological deficits resulting from cerebral lesions in man. In J. M. Warren & K. Akert (Eds.). *The frontal granular cortex and behaviour.* New York: McGraw-Hill, 1964.

Reitan, R. M. Problems and prospects in studying the psychological correlates of brain lesions. *Cortex,* 1966a, *2;* 127.

Reitan, R. M. Diagnostic inferences of brain lesions based on psychological test results. *The Canadian Psychologist,* 1966b, 7a (Inst. Suppl.): 368.

Reitan, R. M. *Manual for administration of neuropsychological test batteries for adults and children.* Indianapolis: R. M. Reitan, 1969.

Reitan, R. M. Neurological and physiological bases of psychopathology. *Annual Review of Psychology,* 1976, *26;* 189.

Reitan, R. M. & Davison, L. A. (Eds). *Clinical neuropsychology: Current status and applications.* New York: Halsted, 1974.

Rie, H. & Rie, E. (Eds). *Handbook of minimal brain dysfunction: A critical view.* New York: Wiley, 1980.

Rosenberg, M., & Glueck, B. C. Automation of behavioural observations on hospitalized psychiatric patients. *Hospital Topics,* 1969, *47:* 27.

Rourke, B. P. Neuropsychological assessment of children with learning difficulties. In S. B. Filskov & T. J. Boll (Eds). *Handbook of clinical neuropsychology.* New York: Wiley, 1981 (Chapter 14).

Rourke, B. P., & Gates, R. D. Neuropsychological research and school psychology. In G. W. Hynd & J. E. Obrzut (Eds). *Neuropsychological assessment and the school-age child.* New York: Grune & Stratton, 1981 (Chapter 1).

Russell, E. W. A multiple scoring method for the assessment of complex memory functions. *Journal of Consulting and Clinical Psychology,* 1975, *43:* 800.

Russell, E. W. Three patterns of brain damage on the WAIS. *Journal of Clinical Psychology,* 1979, *35:* 611.

Russell, E. W., Neuringer, C., & Goldstein, G. *Assessment of brain damage: A neuropsychological key approach.* New York: Wiley-Interscience, 1970.

Russell, R. Neuropsychology in perspective. *Australian Psychologist,* 1981, *16:* 203.

Rustam, H. Evidence for neuromuscular disorder in methyl mercury poisoning. *Archives of Environmental Health,* 1975, *30:* 190.

Rutter, M. The psychological sequelae of brain damage in children. *American Journal of Psychiatry,* 1981, 138: 1533.

Rutter, M. Developmental neuropsychiatry: Concepts, issues and prospects. *Journal of Clinical Neuropsychology,* 1982, *4:* 91.

Ryan, J. J., Larsen, J., & Prifitera, A. Short form of the speech sounds perception test: Further considerations. *Clinical Neuropsychology,* 1982, *4:* 97.

Satz, P., & Fletcher, J. Emergent trends in neuropsychology: An overview. *Journal of Consulting and Clinical Psychology,* 1981, *49:* 851.

Satz, P., Taylor, H. G., Friel, J., & Fletcher, J. M. Some developmental and predictive precursors of reading disabilities: A six year follow-up. In A. L. Benton & D. Pearce (Eds). *Dyslexia: An appraisal of current knowledge.* New York: Oxford University Press, 1978.

Satz, P., and Van Nostrand, G. Developmental dyslexia: An evaluation of a theory. In P. Satz & J. Ross (Eds). *The disabled child: Early detection and intervention.* Rotterdam: Rotterdam University Press, 1973.

Savage, R. D. Intellectual assessment. In P. Mittler (Ed.). *The psychological assessment of mental and physical handicaps.* London: Methuen, 1970.

Scadding, J. C. Diagnosis: The clinician and the computer. *Lancet,* 1967, 2: 877.

Schreiver, D. J., Goldman, H., Kleinman, K. M., Goldfader, P. R., & Snow, M. Y. The relationship between independent neuropsychological and neurological detection and localization of cerebral impairment. *Journal of Nervous and Mental Disease,* 1976, 162: 360.

Selz, M. Halstead-Reitan neuropsychological test batteries for children. In G. W. Hynd & J. E. Obrzut (Eds). *Neuropsychological assessment and the school-age child.* New York: Grune & Stratton, 1981.

Selz, M., & Reitan, R. M. Neuropsychological test performance of normal, learning-disabled and brain-damaged older children. *Journal of Nervous and Mental Disease,* 1979, *167:* 298.

Shankweiler, D. P. A study of developmental dyslexia. *Neuropsychologia,* 1963, *1:* 267.

Shylman, R. Vitamin B12 deficiency and psychiatric illness. *British Journal of Psychiatry,* 1967, *113:* 252.

Slater, E., Beard, A. W., & Clithero, E. The schizophrenia-like psychoses of epilepsy. *British Journal of Psychiatry,* 1963, *109:* 95.

Smith, A. Neuropsychological testing in neurological disorders. In W. J. Friedlander (Ed.). *Advances in Neurology,* Volume 7. New York: Raven Press, 1975.

Smith, A. Practices and principles of clinical neuropsychology. *International Journal of Neuroscience,* 1979: 233.

Smith, A. Principles underlying human brain functions in neuropsychological sequelae of different neuropathological processes. In S. B. Filskov & T. J. Boll (Eds). *Handbook of clinical neuropsychology.* New York: Wiley, 1981: 219.

Smith, A., & Centofani, C. C. *The single and double simultaneous (face–hand) stimulation test.* Los Angeles: Western Psychological Services, 1979.

Spiers, P. A. Have they come to praise Luria or to bury him?: The Luria–Nebraska battery controversy. *Journal of Consulting and Clinical Psychology,* 1981, *49:* 331.

Spiers, P. A. The Luria–Nebraska neuropsychological battery revisited: A theory in practice or just practicing? *Journal of Consulting and Clinical Psychology,* 1982, *50:* 301.

Spitzer, R. L., & Endicott, J. DIAGNO. A computer program for psychiatric diagnosis. *Archives of General Psychiatry,* 1968, *18:* 746.

Spitzer, R. L., & Endicott, J. DIAGNO II. Further developments in a computer program for psychiatric diagnosis. *American Journal of Psychiatry,* 1969 (Supp.), *125:* 12.

Spitzer, R. L., Endicott, J. Can the computers assist clinicians in psychiatric diagnosis? *American Journal of Psychiatry,* 1974, *131:* 523.

Spitzer, R. L., & Endicott, J. Medical and mental disorder: Proposed definition and criteria. In R. L. Spitzer & D. T. Klein (Eds). *Critical issues in judging psychiatric diagnosis.* New York: Raven Press, 1978: 37.

Spreen, O., & Benton, A. L. Comparative studies of some psychological tests for cerebral damage. *Journal of Nervous and Mental Disease,* 1965, *140:* 323.

Spreen, O., & Gaddes, W. H. Developmental norms for 15 neuropsychological tests age 6 to 15. *Cortex,* 1969, *5:* 171.

Stendig-Lindberg, G. Hypomagnesaemia in alcohol encephalopathies. *Acta Psychiatrica Scandinavica,* 1974, *50:* 465.

Sterne, D. M. The Benton, Porteus and WAIS digit span tests with normal and brain-damaged subjects. *Journal of Clinical Psychology,* 1969, *25:* 173.

Stott, D., Moyes, F., & Henderson, S. *Test of motor impairment.* Ontario: Ontario Brooks Educational Publishing Ltd, 1972.

Strub, R. L., & Black, F. W. *The mental status examination in neurology.* Philadelphia: F. A. Davis, 1979.

Strub, R. L. & Black, F. W. *Organic brain syndromes: An introduction to neurobehavioural disorders.* Philadelphia: F. A. Davis, 1981.

Stuss, E. & Trites, R. L. Classification of neurological status, using multiple discriminant function analysis of neuropsychological test scores. *Journal of Consulting and Clinical Psychology,* 1977, *45:* 145.

Surridge, D. An investigation into some psychiatric aspects of multiple sclerosis. *British Journal of Psychiatry,* 1969, *115:* 749.

Swiercinsky, D. P. *Manual for the adult neuropsychological evaluation.* Springfield, Ill.: Charles C. Thomas, 1978.

Swiercinsky, D. P. Factorial pattern description and comparison of functional abilities in neuropsychological assessment. *Perceptual and Motor Skills,* 1979, 47: 231.

Tallent, N. *Psychological report writing.* Englewood Cliffs, N.J.: Prentice-Hall, 1976.

Taylor, M. A. *The neuropsychiatric mental status examination.* New York: SP Medical & Scientific Books, 1981.

Templer, D. I., & Veleber, D. M. Can ECT permanently harm the brain? *Clinical Neuropsychology,* 1982, *4:* 62.

Terry, R. D., & Wisneiwski, H. M. Structural and chemical changes of the aged brain. In S. Gershon & A. Raskin (Eds). *Aging.* Volume 2. New York: Raven Press, 1975.

Teuber, H. L. The riddle of frontal lobe function in man. In J. M. Warren & K. Akert (Eds). *The frontal granular cortex and behaviour.* New York: McGraw-Hill, 1964 (Chapter 20).

Time. The computer moves in. 1983, 1: 5.

Trifiletti, D., Trifiletti, R. H., & Trifiletti, R. J. *A diagnostic program for the Wechsler intelligence scale for children—revised.* Jacksonville, Fla: Precision People Inc., 1982.

Trites, R. L. *Neuropsychological test manual.* Ontario: Lafayette Instrument Co., 1977.

Valett, R. *Dyslexia: A neuropsychological approach to educating children with severe reading disorders.* Belmont, Ca: Fearon Pitman, 1980.

Van Hof, M. W. Development and recovery from brain damage. In K. Connolly & H. F. R. Prechtl (Eds). *Maturation and development: Biological and psychological perspectives. Clinics in developmental medicine Nos 77/78.* London: Heinemann Medical/SIMP, 1981.

Vega, A., & Parsons, O. Cross-validation of the Halstead-Reitan tests for brain damage. *Journal of Consulting Psychology,* 1967, *31:* 619.

Veneklasen, J., & Long, C. J. Comparison of neuropsychological assessment and other diagnostic techniques in detecting brain tumor recurrence. *Clinical Neuropsychology,* 1983, *4:* 48.

Visser, R. S. *Manual of the complex figure test.* 2nd Edition. Amsterdam: Swets & Zeitlinger, 1980.

Walsh, K. W. *Neuropsychology: A clinical approach.* New York: Churchill Livingstone, 1978.

Walton, D., & Black, D. The validity of a psychological test of brain-damage. *British Journal of Medical Psychology,* 1957, *30:* 270.

Wardle, A., & Wardle, L. Computer-aided diagnosis: A review of research. *Methods of Information in Medicine,* 1978, *17:* 15.

Wechsler, D. *Manual for the Wechsler intelligence scale for children—revised.* New York: Psychological Corporation, 1974.

Wechsler, D. *Wechsler adult intelligence scale—revised manual.* New York: Psychological Corporation, 1981.

Wechsler, D., & Stone, C. *Wechsler memory scale manual.* New York: Psychological Corporation, 1973.

Wedding, D. Comparison of statistical and actuarial models for predicting lateralization of brain damage. *Clinical Neuropsychology,* 1983, *4:* 20.

Weitzel, W. D., Morgan, D. W., Guyden, T. E., and Robinson, J. A. Towards a more efficient mental status examination. *Archives of General Psychiatry,* 1972, *28:* 215.

Wells, C., & Duncan, G. *Neurology for psychiatrists.* Philadelphia: F. A. Davis, 1980.

Wheeler, L., Burke, C., & Reitan, R. An application of discriminant functions to the problem of predicting brain damage using behavioural variables. *Perceptual and Motor Skills,* 1963, *16:* 417.

Wheeler, L. & Reitan, R. M. Discriminant functions applied to the problem of predicting cerebral damage from behavioral tests: A cross-validation study. *Perceptual and Motor Skills,* 1963, *16:* 681.

Whitaker, H. A., & Ojemann, G. A. Lateralization of higher cortical functions: A critique. In S. J. Dimond & D. A. Blizard (Eds). *Evaluation and lateralization of the brain.* New York: New York Academy of Sciences, 1977: 459.

Whitlock, F. A. The Ganser syndrome. *British Journal of Psychiatry,* 1967, *113:* 19.

Wiener, F. Computer simulation of the diagnostic process in medicine. *Computers in Biomedical Research,* 1975, *8:* 129.

Williams, A. T., Harding Burns, F., and Morey, S. Prevalence of alcoholism in a Sydney teaching hospital. *Medical Journal of Australia,* 1978, *2:* 608.

Williams, T. A. Computer technology in mental health care: "Toys or tools"? *Behaviour Research Methods and Instrumentation,* 1977, *9:* 108.

Williams, T. A., Johnson, J. H., & Bliss, E. L. A computer-assisted psychiatric assessment unit. *American Journal of Psychiatry,* 1975, *132:* 1074.

Wilson, P. J. E. The surgical treatment of epilepsy. *British Journal of Hospital Medicine,* 1973, February: 161.

Winchendon Group. *Econometric linear forecasting.* The Winchendon Group, P.O. Box 10114, Alexandria, Va, U.S.A., 1982.

Wing, J. K., Cooper, J. E. & Sartorius, N. *The measurement and classification of psychiatric systems: An instruction manual for the PSE and Catego program.* London: Cambridge University Press, 1974.

Winick, C. Emerging field of law and psychology. *Contemporary Psychology: A Journal of Reviews,* 1981, *26:* 353.

Witelson, S. Sex and the single hemisphere: Specialization of the right hemisphere for spatial processing. *Science,* 1976, *193:* 425.

World Safety Organization. Road Accident Statistics. *Proceedings of the 1981 convention, Singapore.* Singapore: World Safety Organization.

Yeudall, L., Fedora, O., Fedora, S., & Wardell, W. Neurosocial perspective on the assessment and etiology of persistent criminality. *Australian Journal of Forensic Sciences,* 1981, *13:* 131.

Zimmerman, I. L., & Woo-Sam, J. M. *Clinical interpretation of the Wechsler adult intelligence scale.* New York: Grune & Stratton, 1973.

Ziskin, J. *Coping with psychiatric and psychological testimony.* 3rd edition. Marina Del Rey, Ca: Law & Psychology Press, 1981.

Author Index

THIS index give the page numbers on which works listed in the References are cited. For full bibliographical details consult the References section. Works with more than one author are listed in chronological order under the name of the first author. The index also includes references to authors and researchers mentioned in the text without citations to individual works.

The author index, subject index and test index have been compiled by Alan Walker, member, The Australian Society of Indexers.

Test Index

THIS index gives the page numbers on which individual tests and test batteries are mentioned. It also includes names of computer software. Scoring and suppliers are given in the *description and administration* section for individual tests.

Subject Index

E

F

G

H

4 5 6 7 8 9 0 1 2 3
A B C D E F G H I J

0394898 I 27/3/85.